Praise for Seyward Darby's

Sisters in Hate

"For those who have never encountered it firsthand, the world of right-wing extremism may seem like an alien planet. As this blockbuster exposé reveals, however, we exist in closer proximity to proud white supremacists than we may have ever suspected."

—Keely Weiss, *Harper's Bazaar*

"Skillfully combined with history and analysis, Darby's subjects' stories provide a better picture of the forces driving white backlash than several of the bestsellers that attempted to do so in the wake of Trump's election." —Susan Neiman, *New York Times Book Review*

"Seyward Darby's eye-opening and unforgettable book sheds light on the often-hidden movers of America's growing white-nationalist movement: women. By telling the riveting story of the lives of three women advancing their agendas of bigotry, Darby exposes the ways in which white nationalism hinges on the contributions of women."

—Ibram X. Kendi, author of *How to Be an Antiracist* and *Stamped from the Beginning*

"In delving into the stories of each woman, one of whom has defected from the movement, Darby offers an unnerving portrait of extremism." —Annabel Gutterman, *Time*

"A fascinating yet highly disturbing deep dive into the toxic world of female white supremacists." —EJ Dickson, *Rolling Stone*

"There is no more urgent story than that of the resurgence of violent white-supremacist groups in America. *Sisters in Hate* delivers an invaluable examination of the ideologies at this movement's core by tracing the stories of three women who found themselves seduced by lies of hatred. Darby provides the most in-depth reporting I've ever encountered on the role of women in this emboldened movement while unflinchingly dissecting the misogyny implanted at its ideological core. Those who've spent recent years wondering 'how' will find the unsettling answers within this book's pages."
—Wesley Lowery, author of *They Can't Kill Us All*

"*Sisters in Hate* offers us a critical insight into how political identities are formed in white-nationalist women. It stands as both an example of a thoughtful study inclusive of women and a reminder of the role of race in extremist excavations."
—Nimmi Gowrinathan, *Los Angeles Review of Books*

"A book that probes the architecture of 'the war embedded in the landscape' of the United States, American identity, and the oft-overlooked role of women therein." —Lauren Markham, *Literary Hub*

"Darby charts the lives of three women who were or are active in the white-nationalist movement. In doing so, she adds dimension to readers' understanding of the complex role that gender plays in bolstering the country's racial regime." —Brandon Tensley, CNN.com

"Trump 2016. Charlottesville 2017. How to understand the unavoidable fact of masses of white women at the core of white nationalism, a movement marked by misogyny? With enormous care, Seyward Darby discovers the hungers within white women's attraction to hateful conspiracy theories of anti-Semitism and racism. Hers is a riveting account that I could not put down."

—Nell Irvin Painter, author of *The History of White People*

"*Sisters in Hate* shows just how 'permeable' the line between mainstream America and white supremacy is."   —Sam Gillette, *People*

"Offers rigorous research about the rise of white nationalism, how it retains its relevance, and the various reasons white women, including those profiled in the book, are drawn to it."

—Evette Dionne, Bitch Media

"Darby's key intervention is to show just how far these women go in comparison to their male peers."   —Jo Livingstone, *New Republic*

"A brave, detailed, and insightful portrait of three women who came to advocate the alt-right's bigotry, but a portrait that is not simplistic. Especially valuable is its examination of the women's complex and contradictory ideas about gender and the appropriate place for women."   —Linda Gordon, author of *The Second Coming of the KKK*

"As engaging as it is adroit, *Sisters in Hate* offers an excellent explanation for the ascent of Donald Trump amid a triumphal resurgence of white supremacy, sexism, and xenophobia."

—Michael Henry Adams, *The Guardian*

"This book is eye-opening and incredibly timely."   —*Booklist*

" 'Women are the hate movement's dulcet voices and its standard bearers,' Seyward Darby observes in *Sisters in Hate*—a timely, deeply reported, and chilling exploration of the role that women play in promoting white nationalism. By exploring the lives of three different women who have embraced white supremacy, Darby holds a mirror up to American society, illuminating the forces at work within our culture that continue, to this day, to lead to radicalization and violence. *Sisters in Hate* is a warning cry for the future while also suggesting the possibility of another, better path forward."

—Pamela Colloff, senior reporter at ProPublica and
staff writer at the *New York Times Magazine*

"A gripping, terrifying look at the white women who are pumping racist hate into the heart of their communities. Darby's clear-eyed and nuanced insights are essential for ending the racial hate movement in America."　　　—Kathleen M. Blee, author of *Women of the Klan*

"Seyward Darby's *Sisters in Hate* is a masterfully reported and incisive look at the virulence of American extremism, as seen through the eyes of three white women who trafficked in monstrous prejudice. Now more than ever, it's important to comprehend, and not look away from, the unspeakable damage caused by the far right, and Darby's book helps us understand the critical role women play in spreading such dangerous ideas."　　　—Sarah Weinman, author of *The Real Lolita*

"Darby writes with a clear sense of purpose and makes a concerted effort to understand why women would 'fight against their own interests.' The result is a disturbing and informative must-read."

—*Publishers Weekly*

"This book is essential reading for anyone seeking to understand the origins and depths of modern white supremacy. With dogged reporting and exacting prose, Seyward Darby not only paints a gripping portrait of the women enmeshed in hate movements but reveals how seeds of racism take hold in minds and communities. *Sisters in Hate* is terrible and mesmerizing, a book perfectly pitched for this moment."

—Evan Ratliff, author of *The Mastermind* and
cohost of the *Longform* podcast

Sisters in Hate

Sisters in Hate

American Women and
White Extremism

SEYWARD DARBY

BACK BAY BOOKS

Little, Brown and Company

New York   Boston   London

Back Bay Books / Little, Brown and Company
Hachette Book Group
1290 Avenue of the Americas, New York, NY 10104
littlebrown.com

Originally published in hardcover by Little, Brown and Company, July 2020
First Back Bay trade paperback edition, October 2021

Back Bay Books is an imprint of Little, Brown and Company, a division of Hachette
Book Group, Inc. The Back Bay Books name and logo are trademarks of Hachette
Book Group, Inc.

The publisher is not responsible for websites (or their content) that are not owned by
the publisher.

The Hachette Speakers Bureau provides a wide range of authors for speaking events.
To find out more, go to hachettespeakersbureau.com or call (866) 376-6591.

Excerpts: (p. xiii) "Worstward Ho" copyright © 1983 The Estate of Samuel Beckett.
Used by permission of Grove/Atlantic, Inc. Any third-party use of this material,
outside of this publication, is prohibited; (p. 3) "Lynchburg" from the book *Breaking the
Fever*. Copyright © 2006 by Mary Mackey. Permission granted by Lowenstein
Associates, Inc.; (p. 91) "Persephone the Wanderer" from *Poems 1962–2012* by Louise
Glück. Copyright © 2012 by Louise Glück. Reprinted by permission of Farrar, Straus
and Giroux.

ISBN 9780316487771 (hc) / 9780316487788 (pb)
LCCN 2020933326

Printing 1, 2021

LSC–C

Printed in the United States of America

For my family

CONTENTS

There is no time for despair, no place for self-pity, no need for silence, no room for fear. We speak, we write, we do language. That is how civilizations heal.

—Toni Morrison, *The Nation*

Ever tried. Ever failed. No matter. Try again. Fail again. Fail better.

—Samuel Beckett, "Worstward Ho"

PREFACE TO THE PAPERBACK EDITION

I wish I were not writing this preface.

The truth is that America is not well. And the sicker it gets, the more urgent the subject matter of *Sisters in Hate* becomes.

In the months immediately preceding the book's publication in July 2020, the novel coronavirus began battering the country, abetted by a White House that refused to acknowledge the threat, much less take the steps necessary to fight it. In the months that followed, COVID-19 continued to do its worst while another virus snaked its way into the minds of millions of Americans: the lie that the presidential election was stolen from Donald Trump and that the only way to prevent the outright destruction of the nation was to stop Joe Biden from taking office. Embedded in the DNA of that lie were other falsehoods predating the Trump administration by years, decades, even centuries: that America belongs to white people; that the BIPOC struggle for liberation is terrorism; that progressive politics are a vise tightening around individual freedom; that patriotism sometimes means sacrificing democratic norms on the altar of nationalism.

On January 6, 2021, incited by Trump himself, a mob stormed the U.S. Capitol, endeavoring to disrupt the counting of Electoral College votes. Far more than a riot, what happened that day was a coup attempt. But while the first major breach of the Capitol in more than two hundred years caught many people and institutions—from politicians to law enforcement to the media—off guard, it shouldn't have. For all the ways it was historic, the insurrection was also predictable, and not only because Trump's most fervent acolytes had telegraphed on social media and at political rallies exactly what they were going to do. As I wrote in an op-ed the day after the violence, "This moment...is a culmination, but it is not an ending. It is not, as some pundits have suggested, white supremacy or Trumpism's 'last gasp.' It is the manifestation of a long-held right-wing fantasy."

That fantasy is one in which patriotic white Americans rise up and reclaim *their* country. The pipe dream has been regurgitated since at least the Civil War by the Ku Klux Klan, neo-Nazis, far-right militia members, and other proponents of white supremacy. It has been the subject of fringe candidates' electoral platforms and mass shooters' manifestos, propaganda films and popular underground novels. The fantasy has fed on entrenched mythologies and simmering resentments, and it was only a matter of time before—accelerated by a charismatic leader, seismic social change, and powerful engines of disinformation—it burst into mainstream consciousness.

What happened on January 6 wasn't a blip. It was plotted—chaotically, yes, but also relentlessly.

As of this writing, more than four hundred people have been arrested for their roles in the attack. Among them are members of hard-core paramilitary groups such as the Oath Keepers; Proud Boys and other neofascists; Holocaust deniers and national socialists; and followers of QAnon, the movement centered around the conspiracy theory that Satan-worshipping, cannibalistic elites run a global sex-trafficking operation. Other participants in the insurrection don't outwardly identify with extremist ideologies or organizations, but they fall on the same political spectrum as those who do. Trump is what unites them—or, really, Trump*ism*.

Research conducted at the University of Chicago has found that more than 90 percent of the people arrested or charged in the insurrection are white. More telling is another data point: According to political scientist Robert Pape, "The people alleged by authorities to have taken the law into their hands on Jan. 6 typically hail from places where non-white populations are growing fastest." Based on national surveys, what fuels their rage is a fear of "the Great Replacement." Researchers of white nationalism, myself included, know this concept all too well: Right-wing extremists have long warned that America's white majority is being systematically, even intentionally, diminished by mass immigration and low birth rates.

Today, fear of racial replacement is the beating heart of Trumpism, a populist politics of white anxiety and resentment. Trumpism prioritizes white needs and wants over collective well-being, and white feeling over hard fact. Permissive of white bigotry and cruelty, it forces a narrow vision of America onto policy-making and storytelling.

Now isn't the moment to become complacent, to comfort oneself with the idea that, with Trump out of office, America is headed back to "normal." Trumpism isn't going anywhere. Polls make that much clear, as does the Republican Party's continued embrace of the ideology—and the man—since January 6. There will be another Trump, a leader who may not share his name but who will don his mantle. Someone who taps into white fear, someone with the capacity to ignite a popular assault on democracy, should they choose.

Above all, perhaps, we must remember this: Just because the last insurrection failed doesn't mean the next one will.

There were so many women there! I heard this exclamation more times than I can count in the wake of January 6, as law enforcement and the media identified participants.

Corinne Lee Montoni, thirty-one, of Lakeland, Florida, wore a Trump hoodie as she marched into the fray, shouting, "We're in the Capitol 'cause this is our house....Let's go!" Victoria White, thirty-nine, of Rochester, Minnesota, wrote on Facebook after the attack, "I am not afraid. . . . Come get me." Jenny Cudd, a flower shop owner from Midland, Texas, made headlines when, after her arrest, she asked a judge to let her take a prepaid trip to Mexico. Jenna Ryan, another Texan and a real estate agent, notoriously took a private plane to Washington for the event. Annie Howell of Swoyersville, Pennsylvania, wore a "Keep America Great" ball cap while she was inside the Capitol but later claimed online, in keeping with lies spread by many Trump supporters, "ANTIFA LEADER IS THE ONE WHO BROKE INTO THE CAPITAL [*sic*]!" Therese Duke was punched in the face when she tried to snatch a black security guard's cell phone, and she was outed on social media when her daughter, Helena, tweeted footage of the encounter: "hi mom," Helena wrote, "remember the time you told me I shouldn't go to BLM protests bc they could get violent . . . this you?" And then there was Ashli Babbitt, the thirty-five-year-old Air Force veteran shot and killed by police as she attempted to climb through an interior door of the Capitol. Not long before her death, Babbitt tweeted, "Nothing will stop us . . . they can try and try and try but the storm is here."

Many more daughters and mothers and sisters entered the Capitol on January 6, but that wasn't the only way women participated that day. Before the storming, there was a rally held nearby, organized by Women for America First, a pro-Trump group helmed by a mother-daughter team: Amy and Kylie Kremer. It was at this rally that Trump delivered his speech inciting his supporters to act. Amy Kremer spoke too. "We know that there was voter fraud, we absolutely know it and that's why we're here, to stop the steal," she told the crowd. "You guys, we cannot back down." By then, the Kremers had been hard at work for several weeks. Women for America First had staged a twenty-stop bus tour across the country, promoting disinformation about the election and encouraging people to "stop the steal." A now-deleted website about the tour stated, "We will do whatever it takes to ensure the integrity of this election for the good of the nation."

(After the insurrection, Women for America First released a statement denouncing violence.)

There were so many women there!

What's striking isn't the statement's verity—it's the air of disbelief with which people said it. The sense of surprise is frustratingly familiar. It colored many people's reactions to 2016, when Trump won a plurality of white women's votes, and to 2020, when history repeated itself. *How could they?* That was what the incredulous camp wanted to know about white women who supported a racist, sexist demagogue. But what people should have been asking was *Why wouldn't they?*

As *Sisters in Hate* shows, women have always been vital to the project of upholding white supremacy. They have been powerful right-wing activists, both behind the scenes and on the front lines of various political and social battles. For too long, powerful people and institutions have failed to recognize this fact. The reasons are sexist, and the impact is pernicious. We have no excuse to let it go on, no justification for being surprised.

To drive the point home: The next Trump might well be a woman. If she is, there will surely be a public narrative that she came out of the blue: *What a shock!* In truth, for anyone willing to pay attention, a female Trump will always have been an inevitability.

Since *Sisters in Hate* was published, I have heard from many readers. Some have been congratulatory, while others offered critiques. There were also messages from white supremacists eager to tell me—with no evidence to support their claims—all the ways the book was wrong about them, about whiteness, about America. But by far the most memorable missives were from people with a personal connection to the stories the book tells.

A former acquaintance and romantic suitor of Lana Lokteff told me he couldn't understand how the interesting, eloquent, intelligent young woman he'd known some twenty years ago had become so hateful. He'd tried to talk to friends about her but always felt that he came up short. "It's easy to explain the monster she became—her revolting Twitter feed tells that story for me—but it's much harder to say *how* she became one (and god forbid, whether I played even a minor part and/or could have helped prevent it)," he wrote to me. What had he missed, and what did that say about him?

More recently, I heard from the mother of a teenage boy who, while cooped up at home during the pandemic, had become radicalized by white-nationalist videos he'd found on YouTube. "Started with arguments against BLM movement, couple of incidents in his school over racial intolerance," his mother wrote in an email. "Over the summer he refused to go out because he is scared of the non-white people living in our neighborhood, and now he is refusing going to school." Among his favorite racist pundits was Lana—by whom, his mother told me, he was "deeply touched." She continued: "It is natural that my teen explores his identity, but it has gone too far. I also know that his attitude is not only to aggravate me and his dad. He really believes that the whites are entitled to be privileged. The videos online give teens certain empowerment that is very appealing to them at the age when they examine themselves. There is barely any censorship on the social media and now with COVID-19, YouTube is the educator."

In the case of Lana's onetime admirer, I told him what I had learned in writing *Sisters in Hate*: that the warning signs of radicalization aren't necessarily glaring—people who turn to racist extremism do so over time, and for various reasons, and not necessarily because of a particularly deep animus for individuals who aren't white. Their personal circumstances combine with the ready source of white supremacy that America offers to curdle their worldview. As for the "worried mom," as she signed her first email to me, I put her in touch with a deradicalization expert—a former white supremacist and a mother herself. She's made it her life's mission to expose the lies white extremists peddle and to encourage people to choose a different path. Because they can. We all can.

As I sit writing these words, yearning for a clear way to stop the spreading scourge of right-wing extremism, I can only hope this book will inspire readers to craft their own solutions. Ones that fit the needs of their circumstances and communities. Ones they can share, and build on, and grow. What America faces, this ailment eating the country alive, is congenital but treatable. It is within our power—and only ours—to make our nation well.

Sisters in Hate

INTRODUCTION

The Fun-House Mirror

Once a battlefield, ever a battlefield—so goes the story of this land. During the Civil War, the North and South fought fiercely in the Shenandoah Valley, clashing in places with quaint names like Tom's Brook and New Market. In 1862, Stonewall Jackson advanced north through the region to threaten Washington, D.C., and the Confederacy held the Shenandoah with such a firm grip for so many months that it became known as "the valley of humiliation" for the Union. Then the tide turned, flooding southward. In 1864, the Union waged a scorched-earth campaign to destroy everything the Confederacy had built and sown.[1]

The war became embedded in Virginia's landscape. Poet Mary Mackey writes of bodies revivified in nature:

the Confederate boys made themselves
into grass
and the Yankee boys made themselves
into gravel roads
they made themselves into cold fronts
coming in from the north
and tornadoes
sweeping across from the west

and hurricanes blowing in
from the Gulf
and sycamores
and pines
and red dirt.[2]

I visited Virginia in November 2016, on the cusp of winter, the time of year when the midday sun slants sharply against the Appalachian foothills and chilly air pricks the lungs. The news on the car radio felt just as piercing: Donald Trump had won the presidential election. Hillary Clinton had taken Virginia by five points, but the state's electoral map, carved up into counties, showed far more red than blue. In the Shenandoah, people had voted overwhelmingly for Trump.[3] On roadsides and in yards, MAGA signs stood alongside Confederate flags.

One of the flags was huge—twenty by thirty feet, strung up an eighty-foot pole—and already infamous. A month after white supremacist Dylann Roof murdered nine black people in a South Carolina church in 2015, the flag's owner bought advertising space in a Virginia newspaper. "Because of all the trouble the democrats and black race are causing, I place this ad," the text read. "No black people or democrats are allowed on my property until further notice."[4] Since then, the owner had doubled down on his political messaging, painting the phrases "Vote for Trump" and "Lock Her Up" on the side of his barn.[5]

My husband and I were in the Shenandoah for Thanksgiving, seeing family. When it was time to go, our last stop before snaking north of the Mason-Dixon was a gas station near the city of Harrisonburg. I went inside to get a bottle of water. At first, the only other customer was a black woman who had come in with two little girls; she was waiting while they used the bathroom. Then the station's glass door opened. I heard the sucking noise of its rubberized edges giving way and the weak ding of an automatic bell. A white woman stormed inside. Her hair was in a loose ponytail, and she wore a burgundy sweatshirt. She looked to be in her thirties, around my age. She began yelling at the black woman.

*Don't you know how gas stations work?** she demanded. *Or are you just lazy and stupid?* She was driving an SUV and needed to pump gas. Apparently, the black woman had parked her sedan next to the only available tank.

The white woman turned her ire on the two female cashiers— also white—behind the store's counter, demanding to know why they didn't do something. She threatened to never buy gas there again. She said that she was a longtime customer; the station would lose her good business.

The encounter couldn't have lasted more than a minute. The white woman turned on her heel and shoved the door open. Sucking sound. Weak bell. And a parting insult.

Fucking nigger!

She said it without looking back.

The women behind the counter said nothing. The black woman's face revealed only mild surprise—or maybe it was practiced defense. Just then, the little girls returned from the bathroom. Before she left the station, I asked the woman if she was all right. *She could've just asked me to move my car,* she replied with a shrug.

NINE MONTHS LATER and a short drive away, hundreds of demonstrators gathered after sundown on the campus of the University of Virginia. The tiki torches they carried glowed bright against their white skin and the inky night sky. The group kicked off their march with a collective yell that coursed through their winding formation of bodies: two by two, shoulder to shoulder, trooping forward.

---

* Throughout the book, quotes drawn from memory—mine or that of a source— are italicized.

The iconic images from August 11, 2017, the eve of the Unite the Right rally, show illuminated male faces—grimacing, grinning, threatening. Women were there too, but in fewer numbers than men. Amid chants of "You will not replace us" and "One people, one nation, end immigration," some marchers broke ranks to scream at people recording or protesting the event. In one moment, captured in a shaky video that was later posted on the internet, a woman stepped out of line. She wore a loose-fitting white top and jeans, and her long blond hair gleamed. She stood facing a manicured lawn that stretched toward one of UVA's signature white colonnades.[6]

"You sound like a nigger!" she shouted.

The target of her ire, presumably a critic of the march, wasn't visible on camera.

"You sound like a nigger!" the woman yelled again.

Five words that spoke to nearly four hundred years of accumulated racial privilege and contempt. The slur rang harshly, and "like" spoke volumes. Was the unseen person white? The woman's sneering sentence sounded like an accusation of tribal treason. She seemed disgusted that someone would debase themselves instead of standing with their own kind.

The woman repeated herself a third time before falling back in step with the marchers. She held her shoulders back, chin up, and torch aloft as she strode away. She looked proud.

BY THE TIME Charlottesville happened, I was already researching women who support white nationalism—the belief that America should remain a predominantly white country, led by white people. I had embarked on the project right after Trump's election, when exit polls showed that more than half of white women nationwide had voted for the president. The women I was observing and interviewing were like the one caught on camera at Unite the Right, the most prominent display of organized racism in recent memory. But I was also interested in women like the one at the gas station. Her banal malice was a paradox, so similar to what was chanted and championed in Charlottesville yet so unremarkable that it scarcely rattled the other people in the store. That scene planted a seed in my brain about white women's singular capacity to sow hate in ways both loud and quiet, blatant and not.

White Americans are often quick to distinguish between everyday prejudice and radical bigotry, between what I saw in Harrisonburg and what happened in Charlottesville, almost as if one doesn't have anything to do with the other. It's a convenient distinction, if a false one. "We like to think that the white-supremacist movement is in fact a 'lunatic fringe.' Yet the vitriol of hate groups is not so much an aberration as it is a reaffirmation of racist and gendered views that permeate society," writes sociologist Barbara Perry. "The political rhetoric of hate does not fall on deaf ears."[7] White nationalists make explicit ideas that are already coded, veiled, or circumscribed in the wider white imagination. Hate is what many white Americans would see if they looked in a fun-house mirror: a distorted but familiar reflection.

White nationalists have long exploited ideological intersections with the political mainstream. Recently, they have capitalized on the wide appeal of Trump's race-baiting and xenophobia. Around the 2016 election, many of them identified as part of the alt-right, a motley movement of racist pseudointellectuals, nihilistic internet trolls, conspiracy theorists, neo-Nazis, and other extremists. The alt-right tried to seem cutting-edge. It had its own slang, operated in every corner of the internet, and projected a smug, exclusive vibe. But it was merely laundering the old tenets of white nationalism, the hand-me-downs of scientific racism, anti-Semitism, antifeminism, and other forms of intolerance. "There's not really anything 'alt' about it," sociologist Kathleen Blee, one of the foremost experts on organized hate, told me in 2017. The scavenged worldview of the alt-right drew from America's paleoconservative movement and France's Nouvelle Droite

(New Right), among other extremist philosophies. In railing against a purported white genocide and rhapsodizing about ethno-states, they echoed terrorist groups like the Ku Klux Klan and Aryan Nations.

Polling in 2016 and 2017 suggested that between 6 and 10 percent of Americans supported the alt-right's ideology.[8] Still, it was hard to say how big the movement really was. It's just as difficult now, a few years down the line. People aren't necessarily forthcoming when pollsters ask them about controversial beliefs or affiliations, and gauging the strength of a diffuse social crusade is a nearly impossible challenge in the digital era. There's no centralized membership database; counting heads requires wading into an abyss of avatars, bots, and pseudonyms, where nothing may be what it seems. J. M. Berger, a researcher of extremism, attempted to tally the number of alt-right believers on Twitter, and the best he could come up with was an "extremely conservative" baseline of two hundred thousand. "The broader far-right community on Twitter," he concluded, "almost certainly runs into the millions."[9]

The mainstream media response to the far right has centered on male figures like Richard Spencer, who is college educated and telegenic, partial to dapper suits and hair gel. "He's able to be mainstream because he looks like a freaking weatherman," a former white nationalist told me.[10] At a conference in late 2016, Spencer elicited a *heil Hitler* salute in honor of Trump's victory, and he later got socked in the face during a media interview, launching a thousand "punch a Nazi" memes. On the even more extreme end of the spectrum is Andrew Anglin, founder of the neo-Nazi website the Daily Stormer. Anglin has urged his readers to unleash torrents of online abuse—"troll storms," he calls them—against handpicked targets, including the first black woman elected as the student body president of American University.[11] Anglin once wrote, "I ask myself this, in all things: WWHD? (What Would Hitler Do?)"[12]

The journalistic coverage of these men has been, by turns, fair, glib, or naive. Meanwhile, there has been a comparative shortage of reporting—good or bad—on the women of the far right. There seems to be a loose consensus that while protesters in pink pussy hats have become icons of the resistance to Trumpism, women aren't nearly as significant on the other side of the battle for America's soul. The relative paucity of women in Charlottesville has advanced this narrative. So has white nationalists' cross-pollination with misogynists—men's rights activists, men going their own way, incels, and other groups—to the point that they share lingo. "Red pill," a term that originated on chauvinist message boards, is a reference to *The Matrix,* in which Neo, the protagonist played by Keanu Reeves, must choose between swallowing a blue capsule that will allow him to live in ignorant bliss or downing a red one that will reveal a terrible conspiracy against humankind. Online, "red-pilling" has come to mean accepting the truth—a wholesale myth, in fact—about the oppression of men and white people at the hands of a liberal, multicultural establishment intent on wiping out America's heritage. To be red-pilled is to know that white people are under threat in a country that's rightfully theirs and, as Spencer once suggested, that women's "vindictiveness knows no bounds." It is to believe, in Anglin's words, that black people's "biological nature is incompatible with White society" and that a white woman who wastes motherhood on mixed-race children is a traitor. "It's OUR WOMB," Anglin once wrote. "It belongs to the males in her society."[13]

Washington Post gender columnist Monica Hesse summed up well the popular sentiment about these repellent gender politics. "It's hard to imagine a woman volunteering to be the backroom support staff for a group that believes women's liberation contributes to the deterioration of civilization,"[14] she wrote in 2019. There are at least two assumptions here: that women likely wouldn't fight against their own interests, and that if they did, their power and influence would not rival that of the men in their orbit. Neither, however, is accurate. We don't have to imagine what is already true: Women have been in backrooms and classrooms, chat rooms and newsrooms, boardrooms and bedrooms. Far from being incidental to white nationalism, they are a sustaining feature.

When I went looking for the women of the far right, it didn't take long to find them. They'd been there all along. So had the legacies of white women whose racist advocacy dated back more than a century. This book tells their story.

"RACE IS AN idea, not a fact," writes historian Nell Irvin Painter. In America, the edifice of whiteness is as mutable as it is entrenched. Who counts as white—what they look like, where they come from, even what they believe—has shifted over time according to what Painter describes as "individual taste and political need."[15] White *supremacy*, however, is a constant.

It began with slavery and the extermination of Native people; endured in the wake of the Civil War; found footholds in the Reconstruction, Jim Crow, and Progressive eras; seeped into policies governing everything from education to immigration to incarceration; and shaped lasting cultural paradigms. White supremacy lurks in mediocrity and civility as much as it fuels slurs and violence. It conceals itself in the false promises of Christian kindness, race blindness, and *e pluribus unum*.

According to legal scholar Frances Lee Ansley, white supremacy is "a political, economic and cultural system in which whites overwhelmingly control power and material resources, conscious and unconscious ideas of white superiority and entitlement are widespread, and relations of white dominance and non-white subordination are daily reenacted across a broad array of institutions and social settings."[16] For the purposes of this book, Ansley's definition is a baseline. *Sisters in Hate* is about women whose raison d'être is the preservation of white supremacy. In their chosen cause, they imagine solutions to problems both political and personal—their frustration with contemporary feminism, say, or their sense of dislocation in a rapidly changing country. Their commitment to white supremacy is what makes them white national-ists, denizens of the far right, supporters of the hate movement.

White nationalism is not a monolith. Supporters come from varied social, religious, and political backgrounds. Some are comfortable with overt cruelty, while others are quick to embrace a narrow definition of bigotry in order to sidestep personal culpability in the suffering of others. What they share is an outlook defined by binary thinking and perceived victimization. Flattened and facile, white nationalism possesses a near-apocalyptic sense of urgency: The time is now or never for white people to protect their own kind. For women, that means bearing white babies, putting a smiling face on an odious ideology, promising camaraderie to women who join their crusade, and challenging white nationalism's misogynistic reputation.

Three women are this book's main subjects. They are among the most notable female figures to emerge on the far right in the new millennium. "The internet is full of strange people," Gawker wrote in 2010. "Corinna [Olsen] may be the strangest." Gawker was refer-ring to Corinna's interests, which included embalming, bodybuilding, amateur pornography, and neo-Nazi activism. It was a bizarre list but an intelligible one, if you knew her: Corinna is a seeker who craves extreme experiences that she hopes will give her life gravity. Ayla Stewart is also a seeker. A college-educated, Christian stay-at-home mother of six, Ayla is better known online as Wife with a Purpose. She once considered herself a liberal feminist, until she found the way, the truth, and the light of white nationalism. She became a proselytizer of traditional gender roles, white pride, and personal redemption. Among the catalysts of Ayla's hard right turn was the third woman featured in *Sisters in Hate:* Lana Lokteff. With her husband, Lana runs Red Ice, an online media platform that presents itself as a viable alternative to mainstream news. In reality, it's a propaganda machine that promotes conspiracy theories in the service of a far-right agenda.

Corinna cooperated fully with my reporting. Lana and Ayla did so for a few months, before deciding that I was a leftist, feminist journalist who couldn't be trusted. They were also loath to give up control of their image and message, which they can curate tightly on social media. I gathered additional information about all three women's lives from blogs, Twitter feeds, personal websites, and other digital sources, and from people who know them or once did. Taken together, their stories reveal how abstract, toxic ideas can become knitted into people's lives and how women in particular can be swept up in a cause that seeks to circumscribe their freedoms. Corinna, Ayla, and Lana have much in common, but their differences are also important. They offer avenues for examining the breadth and depth of female participation in white nationalism over time, and how closely those contributions have tracked with white women's wider impact on establishment politics and social mores.

Since its nascence, the hate movement has fed on social anxiety, offering racist explanations for seismic change that has rattled many white Americans. The KKK formed in response to perceived racial dispossession after the Civil War and reached its zenith in the 1920s, on the coattails of a national fervor for purity: social reform, nativism, Prohibition, eugenics. "Civilization's going to pieces," Tom Buchanan says in *The Great Gatsby,* published in 1925. "If we don't look out the white race will be—will be utterly submerged. It's all scientific stuff; it's been proved."[17] Meanwhile, the United Daughters of the Confederacy (UDC) found fuel in popular nostalgia. Established in 1894 by two Southern society women, the UDC worked tirelessly to perpetuate the lore of the Lost Cause. Its members edited school textbooks to teach children that slavery didn't cause the Civil War, rewarded students who wrote essays in support of the Klan, and erected some seven hundred Confederate monuments—the ones that people continue to fight over today. The UDC's work, undertaken during the entrenchment of Jim Crow, didn't soften the legal regime's cruel blow so much as suggest that there was none at all: America was merely recreating the halcyon days of noble white overlords, dependent blacks, and national peace.

Neo-Nazism was born amid the Red Scare of the 1950s, and a woman was among its most influential ideologues, helping to imprint the doctrine, policy, and symbolism of the Third Reich on America's far right. White Citizens' Councils and other organs of resistance emerged in reaction to the civil rights movement; women were among the backlash's most important proponents. By the 1970s, outright bigotry was less socially acceptable than ever before, giving way to Lee Atwater–style dog whistles. White nationalism became an iconoclastic project, a platform for wannabe revolutionaries, warriors, and prophets with a vision of the future that looked strikingly like the past. It was nourished by other forms of social upheaval, including second-wave feminism and its discontents, veterans' mass return from the failure of the Vietnam War, and the rise of the new Christian right.

The three women at the heart of *Sisters in Hate* were born in 1979, a year of profound geopolitical significance. The United States and China established diplomatic relations. The Soviets invaded Afghanistan. The Shah fell in Iran, prompting a global oil shock. The year was also a critical one in the history of white nationalism. On November 3, the day before the Iran hostage crisis overtook headlines, a group of white supremacists attacked an antiracism event organized by members of the Communist Workers' Party in Greensboro, North Carolina. Four white men and a black woman were shot and killed. The perpetrators were acquitted in both state and federal court. Among them were neo-Nazis and Klan members who found common cause in their opposition to liberal politics—"distinctions among white power factions melted away," writes historian Kathleen Belew, and "anti-communism was used as an alibi for racism."[18] The alibi stuck, and others followed: Heritage not hate. It's okay to be white. All lives matter.

The organizers of the Greensboro Massacre dubbed themselves the United Racist Front, much like, some four decades later, the white supremacists in Charlottesville would call their event Unite the Right. In the intervening years, enterprising groups and leaders had packaged white nationalism as what Barbara Perry calls "button–down terror"—a seemingly modern, palatable version of the movement. It was intended to appeal to Americans who didn't want to be skinheads or separatists but who agreed that the country would benefit by doubling down on white supremacy. White nationalists had also mastered the internet, an infinite, unbridled space where they could communicate and recruit, evading scrutiny and the countervailing influence of reason and facts. Combined with epochal events—the September 11 attacks, two endless foreign wars, the financial crisis, the election of a black president, rising immigration, Trump's populist candidacy—the digital revolution heralded white nationalism's next groundswell. National unease, for reasons both real and imagined, was rampant. Recoil was all but inevitable. And women were likely to be on the front lines.

BY THE TIME Unite the Right happened, Corinna Olsen had renounced the hate movement. Ayla Stewart was invited to deliver a speech at the rally. Lana Lokteff wasn't there only because she had a new baby to care for.

I wasn't in Charlottesville either. I followed Unite the Right from afar, refreshing my social media feeds obsessively for the latest news about an event that would ultimately leave one woman murdered, two police officers dead in a helicopter crash, dozens of people injured, and countless more traumatized. I was angry, sad, and scared, but I wasn't surprised.

Because *Sisters in Hate* is about identity and ideology—how each can reinforce the other—I want to give a plain accounting of the personal lenses through which I view the material. I am a white woman married to a white man. I am a feminist and a progressive. My middle name, Lanier, comes from the poet Sidney Lanier, an ancestor of mine who, in addition to writing pleasant verse, was a private in the Confederate army. Several of my forebears fought on the wrong side of the Civil War, and most of my family still lives in the South. I was raised in North Carolina, in a small city a few hours east of Greensboro. A Confederate monument standing in front of the county courthouse a half mile from my childhood home honors "the heroes of 1861–1865." It was erected by the UDC. My parents are liberal; the place where I grew up is not. I once had a babysitter who referred to the predominantly black side of my hometown, situated across a set of railroad tracks from where she and I lived, as "Niggertown." A college coliseum a short drive from my parents' house is where, in the summer of 2019, a fervent audience chanted "Send her back" at a Trump rally, referring to a woman of color serving in the U.S. House of Representatives.

America is at a precarious juncture, and not only because of Trump's demagoguery and disdain for democracy. By the middle of the twenty-first century, white people will be a minority in America. White nationalists claim that this demographic shift is evidence of a determined attack on their race, waged by an army of liberals, feminists, immigrants, Muslims, Jews, and supporters of Black Lives Matter. This is magical thinking—there is no grand plot against white America—but it resonates with a real trend. Concerns about growing diversity "have driven some whites to turn inward, to circle the wagons," writes political scientist Ashley Jardina. "Whites are bringing their racial identity to bear on their political attitudes and behavior in important ways."[19]

Jardina's groundbreaking research shows that some 20 percent of white Americans—roughly forty million people[20]—now have "strong levels of group consciousness," meaning they "feel a sense of discontent over the status of their group." These people tend to be less educated but not financially vulnerable. "Most own houses, have average incomes similar to most whites in the United States, are employed, and identify as middle class," Jardina writes. And white *women* are more likely than white men to hold "exclusionary views about what it means to be American, preferring boundaries around the nation's identity that maintain it in their image."[21]

Having group consciousness doesn't automatically translate into prejudice, but they are two sides of the same coin. To further their agenda, white nationalists may well exploit the grievances and fears shared by a growing number of white Americans. In his seminal history of the movement, journalist Leonard Zeskind notes that its supporters have never been "paranoids or uneducated backwoodsmen with tobacco juice dripping down their chins, the 'extremists' of popular imagination. As a movement, white nationalists look like a demographic slice of white America."[22] What happens when their proximity to the rest of the pie proves more important than the thin lines that separate them from it?

Hate in America is surging. As of this writing, the Southern Poverty Law Center (SPLC) is tracking 940 hate groups nationwide.[23] In 2018, the number of murders committed by people who identify with the far right reached its highest point since 1995, the year of the Oklahoma City bombing.[24] We know relatively little about how to combat hate effectively; while scholars of the subject have toiled in the margins, the federal government has cut funding for programs to counter right-wing extremism and blocked the dissemination of data on the subject.[25] Only in 2019 did the Department of Homeland Security (DHS) acknowledge that white supremacy is a national security threat.[26]

The gaps in knowledge mean that journalists, politicians, and concerned observers too often rely on flawed assumptions—for instance, that white nationalism is the province of "angry white men" intent on being seen and heard. Men are the far right's most recognizable evangelists, and bombings, shootings, and rallies are the most obvious manifestations of the movement's strength. But there is other work keeping the flames of hate alive. That work is often done by women.

Sisters in Hate is about this truth. Any errors in the telling of it are my own.

Part I

CORINNA

The Grieved—are many—I am told—
There is the various Cause—
Death—is but one—and comes but once—
And only nails the eyes—

—Emily Dickinson, "I measure every Grief I meet"

1.

When I met her, Corinna Olsen lived in a salmon-pink house with two balconies and a three-car garage. It wasn't her house; she rented a wing—a studio apartment—from the elderly woman who owned it. Her only roommate was a Japanese Chin named Smithers, a small dog with silky fur and a lolling tongue. Corinna had adopted him off Craigslist because she wanted something cute to take care of.[1]

The pink house sat at the bottom of a steep hill in a quiet middle-class neighborhood of Tacoma, Washington. At the crest was a panoramic view of the city's harbor. It was early morning when I arrived to spend a day with Corinna. In the distance, the ocean looked gray and somnolent.

Corinna didn't invite me in. She heard me pull up in the driveway in my rental sedan and came out the front door, stiffly clutching her keys and purse. Over time, I would realize that she often looked inflexible, like doing even the most ordinary things was unnatural. She moved through the world as if it didn't feel like home. The only time I would see her at ease in her body was when she handled dead ones.

It was a workday for Corinna, a professional embalmer, and she wore all black—a suit jacket, a knee-length skirt, tights, and ankle boots. A faux-pearl barrette kept her bright blond hair out of her face. When Corinna greeted me, her voice was deep and steady. She had square features beneath a straight brow line. Her countenance was severe, even when she smiled, which almost always happened a beat after I expected it, as if she had to remind herself, *This is what people do.* Corinna was petite—just over five feet tall—but strong. She once competed in bodybuilding, which prizes sharp lines, bulbous contours, and cartoonish movements. To be attractive in that world is to be awkward by any conventional standard of beauty. By the time I met her, Corinna hadn't done bodybuilding in a few years; her health couldn't take the wear and tear. She stayed in shape by going to the gym and by lifting corpses and caskets.

We climbed into her Dodge minivan, and Corinna scooted close to the steering wheel. A gallon of distilled water sat on the passenger-side floor next to a dog-eared trade paperback. There were no seats in the back of the van. Corinna had removed them to make room for side-by-side stretchers, where she strapped the bodies that she ferried from morgues to funeral homes. An empty orange can, which once held a sugary energy drink, was lodged in the console between us. Corinna had kicked drug and alcohol addictions, leaving caffeine as her vice of choice. We stopped for a fresh round at a gas station. She dispensed hot coffee into a Styrofoam cup, then sipped it through a straw.

"So where is this body?" I asked, referring to her first appointment of the day. The deceased, Mr. Ford, was a man in his late thirties. He'd passed away about twenty-four hours before, and he was now at the office of the Pierce County medical examiner, a squat, square white building that looked like it might be a storage facility. Which, in a way, it was.

"When somebody calls and says, 'We need you to come get this body,' are you provided information about what happened to them?" I asked.

"Not usually," Corinna said. "They say in school, 'Ask yourself not of what the subject died, but rather what conditions exist.'"

"In what conditions they existed?"

"In what conditions is the deceased body *at present,*" Corinna corrected me. Her right foot tapped the accelerator so often that it seemed like a tic.

Take an autopsy, Corinna continued. Without the organs inside a body, she couldn't follow the usual steps of her work: injecting embalming fluid into the carotid artery and pumping it through the vascular system, replacing blood that simultaneously drained through the jugular vein. An autopsy necessarily means that a body's blood circuitry has been disrupted, so Corinna would have to access several major arteries to make sure the fluid got distributed. Then she would have to treat each extracted organ individually and return it to the body cavity. An autopsy was the difference between her work taking a couple of hours and it taking half a day. The same went for organ donation.

Corinna became an embalmer because, in a way, she had to. In the mid-aughts, after spending a few years at home with her two young daughters, she needed to make money. She had never finished college and didn't have any demonstrable professional skills. She could have worked retail or another job requiring minimal training, but she decided that she wanted a vocation. Corinna had always been fascinated by rituals and what she called "the misunderstood"—subjects that were taboo or macabre. Embalming fit the bill. It was an essential field that made people cringe; they needed it but didn't want to talk about it.

Corinna also had a personal connection to it because of her younger brother, Harley. He was everything she wasn't: sociable, fun, well-liked. Harley was tall and blond, with a handsome, goofy face and hair he sometimes wore gelled into a Mohawk or slicked down into a swoop over his forehead, Flock of Seagulls–style. He was a self-proclaimed anarchist who wore black combat boots and hung out with skinheads sporting studded leather jackets. He liked the Misfits and other punk bands. After graduating from high school, he took cooking classes at a community college, hoping to become a chef.

On June 10, 2001, Harley was supposed to help Corinna move into a new apartment. When he didn't show up on time, Corinna called a few of his friends. They told her that he'd blown her off to go canoeing at Crescent Lake, a body of water covering seven square miles and shaped like a half moon, with fir trees lining its picturesque shores. That day, strong, chilly winds turned the lake's flat waters into swaths of chop. There weren't many boats out, but twenty-year-old Harley and two teenage friends, feeling invincible in the way only young people can, paddled out several hundred yards. Suddenly a gust tipped their boat over, sending them plunging into the lake. Their jeans and sweaters became soggy weights. They couldn't grasp the slick bottom of the boat, so they tried to swim to shore, yelling to anyone who might be within earshot. A fisherman in a motorboat saw them from a distance and sped over. By the time he reached the scene, only two people were treading water. Harley had vanished.

It took authorities more than a year to recover his body, which had sunk to a depth of 165 feet. Corinna, by then married with a new baby, wasn't able to view her brother's decomposed body. Harley was cremated, and that was that. As an embalmer, she liked to work on the most difficult cases—gunshot victims, bodies charred in fires, corpses with battered and broken faces—to give families one last chance to see, maybe even to recognize, their loved ones.

Mr. Ford was not one of those cases. He'd likely died of an overdose. After she backed her van up to the rear entrance of the Pierce County medical examiner's office, Corinna and a young man in a wrinkled white coat slid a long tray out of a refrigerated wall. The corpse was wrapped in several layers of opaque white plastic, and the shape of the bundle made it clear that rigor mortis had set in. Corinna peeled back the plastic to look at Mr. Ford's face and nodded, satisfied. She loaded him onto one of the stretchers in the back of the van, with his head directly behind my seat, then reinstalled herself at the steering wheel.

"How's he looking?" I asked.

"Good enough for a viewing," she said.

On the way to deliver Mr. Ford to a funeral home, a cloudless image of Mount Rainier bobbed in the rearview mirror. I could feel the weight of the body bumping softly against my back each time Corinna pumped the brakes on the highway. There wasn't an obvious conversational bridge between handling the dead and championing racism—the cause that had once defined Corinna's existence and that had brought me to her door. She saw one, though, and crossed it with characteristic conviction.

Harley, she explained, had inadvertently introduced her to white nationalism. On what would have been his twenty-seventh birthday, in March 2008, she had found herself wanting to know more about her brother and the things that had mattered to him. She went on-line and typed in the search term *what are skinheads.* Harley and his friends had often been drunk, loud, and rowdy. Was that what being a skinhead meant?

Corinna told me that, back then, she had no idea some skinheads were neo-Nazis—an all but unfathomable claim for someone who came of age in the 1990s counterculture of the Pacific Northwest. Harley made racist jokes sometimes, but who didn't? Corinna heard them at work, too. Her bosses, all of whom were white men, threw around comments like *Jews will tell you they don't have any money, but they do.* Or *Blacks never pay their bills on time, and they steal things if they can.* Meanwhile, Corinna saw the bodies of people of color on her metal embalming slab. They'd died in speeding cars, in gang fights, or from drug use. Wearing an apron and face mask to absorb the spattering of blood, bile, and other viscous fluids, she wondered if her mentors were right when they said *those people* were ruining Oregon, a state with a constitution that banned black people from living there until 1926 and that didn't ratify the Fifteenth Amendment until 1959.

Corinna had never thought too hard about whether or not being white defined her. She'd never had to. She'd grown up in a heavily white school district in Eugene, Oregon, and she didn't interact—not meaningfully, anyway—with people of other races until her late twenties, when she moved to Portland for her embalming career. She'd paid such little mind to race as a concept that there was a flatness to it, a uni-dimensionality susceptible to simplified reasoning.

When her search for information about skinheads led straight to the racist bowels of the internet, Corinna wasn't fazed. She landed on Stormfront, the oldest internet forum dedicated to hate. Founded in 1990 by Don Black, a one-time leader of Alabama's KKK,[2] Stormfront was initially a dial-up bulletin board system (BBS). Precursors to social media, there were once tens of thousands of BBSes in North America, used by people with shared interests and hobbies.[3] Hate groups saw the message boards as unique opportunities to disseminate propaganda outside traditional media channels and their restrictions on hate speech. "It may very well be that American know-how has provided the technology which will allow those who love this country to save it from an ill-deserved fate," an Aryan Nations newsletter declared.[4] Stormfront became a website in 1995, opening it to far more users. Don Black told the *Philadelphia Inquirer,* "The potential of the Net for organizations and movements such as ours is enormous. We're reaching tens of thousands of people who never before had access to our point of view."[5]

He was right. The number of Stormfront users grew, and so did the number of racist websites. By the end of the 1990s, the far right had a sprawling digital ecosystem of chat rooms, journals, newsletters, and audio programming. Many of the sites tried to cloak their agendas. A 2003 study of 157 sites found that only a small percentage "specifically urged violence" and that one-third "disavowed racism or hatred."[6] This made it difficult for unsuspecting internet browsers to distinguish between fact and fiction, news and propaganda. Cloaking was a matter of strategy, an effort to widen what sociologists call the Overton window—the range of ideas considered viable or tolerable in public discourse.[7]

By the time Corinna found Stormfront, it was byzantine in comparison to newer racist websites making a play for mainstream purchase. It was slow to load and clunky to navigate. Corinna didn't immediately know what it was, so she began to read the messages that populated her computer screen. Some users said vile things, but others talked about white pride and heritage. None of that seemed so bad. Black people could celebrate their roots, Hispanic ones too—it stood to reason, Corinna thought, that white people should be able to do the same. Stormfront users presented this as if it were a mathematical proof, not a notion freighted with racist, violent history. White power, they claimed, was maligned and misunderstood.

The barriers to the conversations unfolding in front of Corinna were minimal. Joining was as easy as a few strikes on her keyboard. She created a Stormfront profile under the handle NorwayLuray, a reference to her ethnic roots and her middle name. One of her first posts, published on March 21, 2008, was in the site's "General Questions and Comments" section:

Hello, I am new, so please forgive my ignorance.

A lot of the stuff I have read here says that WN [white nationalism] is not the same as supremacy and some members are adamant that they are not white supremacists.

But...maybe I am one? I believe:

—white people are generally more hard-working, honest, decent, dignified, and intelligent than nonwhites;

and I prefer:

—the company of white people over that of nonwhite people;
—to live among white people;
—to work with other white people (right now at work it's

mostly blacks and it has been a disaster with every new one that is hired);

—to have only white friends;

—to date and marry a white man;

—that my children (2 white girls . . . I am divorced) attend schools that are largely white, live in neighborhoods that are largely white, and have only white friends and date only white boys.

Is there something wrong with being a white supremacist? I don't outwardly profess hatred for other races; I have to work with them and also serve clients of other races in my industry, and I am very good at what I do. I don't advocate violence toward other races; to me going around saying "kill all [Negroes]" makes me no better than the races I am trying to avoid being like.

What is wrong with seeing our race as superior to that of the blacks? Don't we all?*

The responses were plentiful and affirming. "There is nothing wrong with having a personal opinion," one read. White supremacy is a term used "to slander Whites who believe in Collective White Rights," said another. A commenter with the handle Thoughtful Patriot wrote, "Let's face reality, people self segregate by race. . . . Race is an intrinsic part of who we are." Corinna thought these people seemed smart. Certainly, they knew more than she did about what it meant to be white. There was much to learn and many new people to talk to, all right there on her computer.[8]

This marked the beginning of Corinna's years-long encounter with white nationalism. It accelerated quickly: Within a few months she

---

* The book quotes many written sources found online. With very few exceptions, I have left errors of grammar, spelling, and syntax as I found them.

would be the leader of a neo-Nazi group in Portland. Within a few years she would be one of the most recognized voices on far-right radio. She would sacrifice access to her children and put her career on hold to live as an avowed racist. Then she would leave the world of white nationalism behind.

It was a bizarre and winding story. She promised to tell me the whole thing. First, though, we had to drop Mr. Ford off in another fridge, this one at a funeral home. Corinna would embalm him later that day. We headed to her next appointment, which involved a difficult case, her specialty. The deceased was a middle-aged woman. Cancer had ravaged her body, leaving her veins shriveled. That made Corinna's work particularly crude: She had to stab the body several times and use the wounds as portals for the embalming fluid. She hid the damage beneath a layer of shrink-wrapped plastic, now concealed by the deceased's clothing. Still, there was a chance that, in front of family and friends, the corpse might start to seep and stew. Corinna planned to sit in her van outside the woman's memorial service, just in case she needed to patch or plug the body. It was a point of pride for Corinna to stand by her work.

"I'm really strict on respect," she said. "Absolutely no joking, no derisive comments. I tell interns, 'Don't speak in front of the body in a manner you wouldn't if he was alive or if his family was standing right there.'"

I asked if, as a white nationalist, the same rules had applied.

"I served black families and Jewish families," Corinna said. "I always aimed to treat them as I would treat my own family." When fellow neo-Nazis said they were jealous that she got to cremate Jews, she told them that she didn't want to talk about it.

The funeral home where she was picking up the woman's body looked like a ranch-style house with an oversize garage attached. Corinna parked on a patch of gravel under a pear tree and slid out of the van to meet the director of the memorial service. I followed her across the parking area and stopped abruptly when she did, as if she realized that she'd forgotten something in the van. She turned to face me.

The dead woman, Corinna said, was black. So was the funeral director. Corinna often did business with him and his colleagues. "I actually don't know if they know about me," she mused, referring to her former, racist self.

She was saying—without saying—that I probably shouldn't explain why I was there.

2.

On her first day of kindergarten, Corinna wanted to stand out. Her mother collected pins from kitschy stores, street vendors, and political campaigns, including one from Jesse Jackson's bid for the Democratic presidential nomination. Corinna liked to hold the pins, and when it came time to get ready for school, she asked her mother if she could wear some. The answer was yes, and Corinna scurried to the familiar stash. Choosing a few pins proved too difficult, so she decided to wear as many as she could. Corinna paraded off to kindergarten looking like she was wearing armor. Only after she came home did her mother realize that one of the pins was shaped like a marijuana leaf.

Corinna's parents first met in California. When she pictures them back then, in the 1970s, she sees a beat-up van parked on the side of a San Francisco street. Folk music crackles from the tape deck, or maybe it emanates from a guy sitting cross-legged in the back, strumming a guitar. Everyone is smoking weed. Corinna's parents lived like nomads, she told me, until one day they decided to decamp to Oregon and start a more conventional life. They got married. In January 1979, they had Corinna. Harley followed two years later.

When Corinna was three, her parents split up. She and Harley stayed with their mom in the city of Eugene, while their father moved to Alaska "to start a new family," as Corinna put it. "I always felt closer to my dad. I always resented being forced to live with my mom," she said. "My dad had actually wanted to raise me with his new wife, but like many men he didn't want conflict with the ex-wife, especially in the early eighties." Her father had two more daughters, and they became his full-time kids. Corinna and Harley visited now and then. At home in Oregon, life wasn't easy. Her mother brought boyfriends around the house. Sometimes, Corinna said, when her mom got angry, she became abusive.*

Corinna was an unhappy child. Even as a toddler, she had trouble connecting with other people, a fact that she told me was attributed partly to her being somewhere on the autism spectrum. Her domestic situation didn't help. "I was a very angry, frustrated child, and I would hurt smaller children frequently," she told me. She said it in the only way she ever spoke—frankly and evenly, with very few pauses or "ums." Her distinctive voice had once prompted listeners of a racist radio show that Corinna cohosted to ask if she was a robot or a man using a voice modulator.

By middle school, Corinna was often suspended for being disruptive. She had a short fuse and was prone to kicking and punching anyone, or anything, that made her mad. Sometimes her little brother bore the brunt of her frustrations; she saw Harley, who was as affable as she wasn't, as an adversary. Getting in trouble was exactly what Corinna wanted. "I was determined to get kicked out of school," she told me. "I was really angry and wanted to let everyone know." That included her parents. "I wanted to feel like I actually had parents," she once wrote on a blog.

Corinna dropped out of school in the eleventh grade. By then,

---

* Corinna's mother did not respond to a request for an interview.

she was using drugs, including cocaine and heroin. Exasperated, her mother kicked her out of the house, and Corinna was living on the streets by the time she was eighteen. She fell in with a group of homeless kids who only cared about getting high and finding a place to sleep. Sometimes that place was a tent in an abandoned lot or the back seat of someone's car. On good nights, when the group was able to scrounge up enough money from panhandling, they shared a motel room. Eventually they moved into what amounted to a flophouse: a two-room apartment, paid for by one of the kids' parents, where a dozen or so people squatted. They shared drugs and slept on old mattresses and couches.

Sometimes Corinna went back to her mom's house to do laundry. She would see Harley, a teenager with a big smile and a personality to match. Gradually the siblings formed the friendship they hadn't had when they were younger.

One of the things I found most striking in listening to Corinna's story was that whenever she'd made a decision, she'd stuck to it, as if it were literally impossible to deviate from whatever path she'd chosen. That went for quitting drugs. When she was nineteen, Corinna decided to get clean. She went to an outpatient program for homeless people. When she finished it, she started going to twelve-step meetings.

She got a job working at a hospital and was healthier than she'd been in years. Still, Corinna struggled socially. She was blunt and unpredictable; personal warmth wasn't her strong suit. One day at a recovery meeting, she spotted a man who looked like he had made it only halfway out of his pajamas before leaving home and then forgot to take off his outerwear when he got to the meeting. Corinna thought he looked "like a total dork." She decided to say hello.

His name was Tom, and he was seventeen years older than she was. Despite his ungainliness, or maybe because of it, Corinna liked him. Tom's first impression of Corinna was that she seemed like most people who are new to recovery. "I would describe her as moody and edgy. I have to confess, there's something about that energy that draws me," Tom told me in a phone call. "I had been sober for a few years at that point, but I still had a tendency to want to rescue people."[1] They started dating, and after six months, Corinna found out she was pregnant. Shortly after that, Harley drowned.

Over the years, Corinna would populate social media with evidence of the wound Harley's death left in her life. She put up photos from childhood: Harley in a Cub Scout uniform around age nine, holding one of his stepsisters on his shoulders. Harley as a senior in high school, wearing a graduation robe and grinning next to his mom. Harley staring solemnly at the camera, a too-big black bomber jacket enveloping his thin frame. Corinna compiled several of the images into a YouTube video set to a melancholy Kenny Chesney song. She also filmed herself visiting Harley's memorial. One frame of the video shows her placing a manicured hand on the modest granite stone. "Hey, buddy," she says gently. A beat later, she adds, "See you soon."[2]

After Harley's death Corinna hoped that she could create the family she'd always wanted, even if she didn't love Tom yet. They spent five hundred dollars on their wedding, which was held outdoors and officiated by Corinna's sponsor from Narcotics Anonymous. Corinna wore a white backless prom dress. Her mother attended; her father didn't. "I don't think I really developed the ability to bond with other people," Corinna told me. "I always felt kind of distant, like I was playing a role." The same went for marriage. "I stuck with the husband," she said, "because I was willing to wait and see if a connection happened."

It didn't. "I'd never been through anything like that," Tom said of the lingering impact of Harley's death. "I guess the ways that I tried to help weren't very helpful, and she really resented me for that and held it against me for a long time. It really hurt her the way I didn't know what to do."[3] Corinna gave birth to a second daughter when she was twenty-five. She'd decided to be a stay-at-home mom because it felt, she said, like "the right thing to do." Postpartum depression struck so intensely that she feared she'd hurt her children. Corinna told me that she would put them in one room and then go into another one, where she'd sit on her hands, trying to banish bad thoughts and control herself until Tom got home.

Corinna searched for someone or something to blame for how unhappy she was. She and Tom had moved from Corvallis to Albany— both small cities north of Eugene—and she didn't like it. Tom was working as a church choir director and studying to be a teacher. Money was tight; they sometimes had to borrow cash from Tom's parents. Corinna thought that if only she'd made other choices—better ones—maybe she wouldn't be so miserable.

By her late twenties, Corinna's marriage was over. She started her embalming career, which required a two-year degree, an apprenticeship, and government exams. She was happy to have a new purpose that allowed her to support herself and share custody of her daughters, but she still felt alienated and isolated from the wider world. When she wasn't working or with her kids, she was lonely. One day, while reading a local tabloid, an ad caught her eye. It dangled the promise of cash, paid daily, to hot girls. The ad was inviting women in and around Eugene to make pornography. She found similar listings online.

Like embalming, porn was taboo to many people—not watching it, perhaps, but making it. Corinna wondered why. "It's just body parts," she told me with a shrug. She wanted to know more about the culture. What sort of people decided to have sex on screen for strangers' pleasure? What feeling or rush were they getting out of it? The questions sounded much like mine when I started reporting on Corinna and other women in the hate movement. I grasped, at least, the seed of her fascination with a world she didn't understand.

Corinna responded to an ad and began appearing in low-budget porn films. Many of them featured torture. She let people gag, beat, and electrocute her, and she made a couple hundred dollars per shoot. In the course of getting to know Corinna, I considered watching the films. Maybe they would teach me something about her. I ultimately decided not to because the particularities of violent sex scenes seemed far less important than her choice to engage in them in the first place. When I asked why she started out in torture porn, as opposed to more conventional fare, she said that she was too old—around twenty-seven when she started—and not pretty enough to get other roles. Plus, she thought it would be more interesting. "Instead of doing some escorting or stripping or something, I had to jump right in," she said.

This was an acknowledgment of a crucial, consistent fact of her character: Corinna never tried the shallow end of anything. She didn't see the point, when the deep end was right there, waiting. I wondered, too, if she hadn't been trying to feel something—anything—deeply by taking abuse while a camera rolled. Maybe she hoped pain or shame could pierce her emotional shield, the way talking about embalming a corpse made her face light up. Or maybe choosing to be hurt restored a sense of agency she'd lost somewhere.

As we drove past some teenagers skateboarding in a parking lot, risking their necks to do tricks none of them seemed skilled enough to do, I asked Corinna about the strangest deaths she'd seen in her job. Her energy ticked up as she ran through the catalog of her memory. She'd seen a suicide in which someone tied shoelaces around his neck and a bedpost. "The guy just kind of knelt. If he changed his mind at any point, he would have just had to sit up," she said. She showed me a photograph of a mangled car, indistinguishable from the motorcycle it had crushed. She'd had to reconstruct the face of a fifteen-year-old boy who'd been in the accident.

I asked how many bodies she handled in a week. "It can be as many as ten," Corinna said. "Or sometimes I get nothing." Did the number vary according to the time of year? "There's no trend, ever," she said. "People assume it must be winter, summers, holidays, but..." Her voice trailed off in a rare moment when she seemed to be searching the corners of her brain for the right phrase.

"People die all the time," I suggested.

She nodded. Her job was "just biology," Corinna said. Then, she reconsidered: "Biology and art."

WHITE NATIONALISTS HAVE long used the "just biology" argument to defend their worldview. It is the essence of scientific racism, a collection of theories about supposedly inherent differences among people whose skin isn't the same color. In reality, these theories are more like bad art masquerading as science—the stuff of design, interpretation, and emotion, subjective exercises rather than ones grounded in any fact or fairness. Yet no matter how many times scientific racism has been debunked, it has always found new adherents. It has even experienced a revival in the new millennium, featured as "dangerous" and "edgy" ideas in academic papers, Breitbart articles, and the op-ed pages of the *New York Times*.[4] "We keep looking back to race because of its familiarity," journalist Angela Saini writes in her book *Superior: The Return of Race Science*. "For so long, it has been the backdrop to our lives, the running narrative. We automatically translate the information our eyes and ears receive into the language of race, forgetting where that language came from."[5]

Debated less often than the language of race is that of hate. Many times while writing this book, I found myself explaining its subject to friends and acquaintances who then insisted that they already knew why white nationalists are the way they are. Wasn't it obvious? They have a consuming disdain for people who are not white. By this standard, hate is a nasty weed that takes root deep in the mind—or in a biblical sense, it's a matter of the soul: "Thou shalt not hate thy brother in thine heart" (Leviticus 19:17). People told me that hate is a pathology, a deviance, a poison. Surely there is an antidote or corrective, and if someone doesn't respond to it, they are probably beyond help.

One definition of hate is animus toward another person or group, but there is a more complex, useful, and frightening description. Hate can be understood as a social bond, a complex phenomenon that occurs among people as a means of mattering and belonging. It is a currency that arises "in particular social, cultural, political, and historical contexts, and it shapes the possibilities for future social interactions," writes sociologist Kathleen Blee. Hate, Blee says, is "encouraged" by "the organization of the physical and cultural world"—racial segregation, say, and negative caricatures of minorities. It is also "a process rather than an attribute," a thing achieved as much as felt or believed. People may arrive on the doorstep of the hate movement with racist impulses, but not necessarily ones any stronger than those of many other white people. Blee explains: "Social camaraderie, a desire for simple answers to complex political problems, or even the opportunity to take action against formidable social forces can co-exist with, even substitute for, hatred as the reason for participation in organized racist activities."[6]

This has always been the case. Take the 1920s Klan, the organization's largest, most powerful version, with followers across the country. "Its allures were manifold," writes historian Linda Gordon.[7] "They included the rewards of being an insider, of belonging to a community, of expressing and acting on resentments, of participating in drama, of feeling religiously and morally righteous, of turning a profit." Several years later and an ocean away, Germans who worked for the Nazi regime weren't necessarily rabid anti-Semites. Most of the five hundred thousand German women who worked in the eastern territories of the Reich, for instance, "identified with other convictions and ambitions," explains historian Wendy Lower. They wanted to travel, advance their careers, make money. Some were officers' wives, but women were also secretaries, teachers, and nurses. Once installed in the Nazi machinery, they reaped social and political rewards. And because the Reich's cause was genocidal, they were conditioned "to accept violence, to incite it, and to commit it."

The same is true in America's contemporary hate movement, where animus is justified, incentivized, learned, and performed. Hate abhors a vacuum. Ritual and action signal belonging and do harm in the same stroke. We see this when people burn crosses, scrawl graffiti on synagogues, or harass their critics. They are reinforcing their place in a community by inflicting terror. Before all that happens, though, they start out in a place familiar to most any human being: They are looking for something, even if they can't quite put their finger on what it is.

Researchers have described the "underlying force" of extremism as "the basic human desire to matter and have meaning in one's life." They call this "the quest for personal significance," and there are three main parts: need, narrative, and network. Everyone experiences feelings of need. What sets budding extremists apart is an imbalance, "the tendency...to privilege one need over the expense of others." This disparity "allows formerly constrained behaviors to become liberated" and "be considered as reasonable and permissible" in service of the big need, the nagging one, the one that a person's sense of self seems to hang on.

Maybe they sense a gap between who they are and who they imagine they deserve to be; maybe they want to feel stronger than circumstances allow; maybe they want to protect a privileged status. To explain their need—both its causes and its possible remedies—people look for a narrative, a framework for understanding the world that "directly promise[s] a sense of mattering and purpose to those who subscribe." The most alluring narratives are often those that "portray the world in clearly defined, black-and-white terms that allow no room for ambiguity or cognitively demanding nuances." Hate, certainly, offers a story like that, and the untethered behaviors it encourages— from exclusion to slurs to violence—arise from America's communal well of white supremacy.

A network, finally, is a group of "important others such as family members, close friends, or comrades [who] function as an epistemic authority." The network reinforces the narrative, and together they fulfill the need.[8] A cycle of nourishment sets in.

There is no single type of person who becomes part of the hate movement, no demographic profile that allows for accurate predictions of extreme belief and behavior. ("That would be comforting," Blee once quipped.[9]) Yet neither do white Americans suddenly "wake up one morning with a new desire to engage in radical action, whether violent or not," as a trio of criminologists writes. The socialization of hate can last weeks, months, or years, feeding on personal discontent and wider social anxieties to reach clarifying moments—"awakenings," the criminologists call them, that "might be likened to quenching a long-standing thirst for 'truth.'"[10]

In the digital age, this happens both online and off. A person might have a series of encounters with members of other races that they find unpleasant, and a real or virtual friend might suggest evaluating those experiences in the context of hate. Someone might read racist tweets or watch xenophobic YouTube videos and feel prompted to review their own life through a new lens, finding a seeming truth about their whiteness that they never knew was there. Or, as with Corinna, a person eager for human connection might find a racist community, present themselves as a potential ally by saying all the right things, and forge friendships that solidify their place in a cause. Hate becomes a cure for loneliness.

Rae,[*] another woman I met during my research, had a story similar to Corinna's. She attributed her involvement with neo-Nazis and skin-heads to feeling like she didn't fit in anywhere else. As an adolescent, she desperately wanted to be defiant and strong; bullying at school and her parents' acrimonious divorce had left her feeling vulnerable. When she met older guys who were happy for her to tag along when they spray-painted swastikas on walls, who shared their cheap liquor, who promised to beat up anyone who was mean to her, she figured it was better than being left out. When they said cruel things about people of color, she remembered the time in middle school when a group of Latina students had made fun of her jeans and called her a stupid white girl. One skinhead talked about Hitler and how white people needed to look out for one another. That made Rae feel safe and valuable.

---

[*] Rae is a pseudonym. She is no longer part of the hate movement and asked not to be identified.

She had anxiety, maybe depression, and sometimes she cut herself; she started carving little swastikas in her skin. When she moved around as a young adult, from the Southwest to Arkansas to Florida, Rae re-created her milieu by going to racist punk and rockabilly concerts. She told herself that she wasn't hurting anybody by hanging pictures of Hitler and a Confederate flag in her bedroom.[11] If her friends gave the middle finger to the world, so what? She had moments of doubt, like when her friends, whom she called her "gang," beat up strangers. Still, she stayed, got married, and had a child, because for a long time it all felt like a sure thing. Today, Rae looks back at her old life with regret but not bewilderment—she sees what happened, and why.

Hate is a failing, but not an isolated one. In a perverse twist on the cliché, hate takes a village. A seeker finds a creed and a community where they can test out how white nationalism feels to them, how the language of hate rolls off their tongues in conversation or flies from their fingertips onto computer screens. They can hear how it echoes back to them, delivering the validation that they've been craving all along.

POSTING ON STORMFRONT for the first time was a turning point for Corinna. She suddenly had people to talk to. She could get on-line whenever she wanted, say what other users wanted to hear, and strangers paid attention to her. "They seemed immensely interested in me and my life, and they wanted to be my friend," Corinna said. "To someone who grew up without friends, that was very appealing. It made me feel like I must be doing something right."

Sometimes she asked her new friends for normal-enough advice—how to find a safe, affordable apartment, for instance. But her language, parroting the rest of Stormfront, was racist. "I know that to find the white places you just have to look in the richer parts of town, so as a single white person who is pretty much lower-middle income, I've been trying to decide which is the lesser of two evils, blacks or Mexicans," Corinna wrote of her housing hunt in April 2008. "Mexicans have decent food they sometimes sell out of vans; but they have too many filthy kids who will probably play on my doorstep like the ones where I live now. Blacks, um, well, I guess I can't think of anything good about them...oh wait, at least they speak (a form of) English. But they play loud rap music and steal stuff."

Replies ranged from the empathetic to the dismissive. "To be able to live in an affordable apartment in any city in the U.S. it means living in an integrated neighborhood," wrote user Nick Smith, who said he was based in Minnesota. "I have wrestled with that problem many times for many years. The only answer that I can think of is for whites to force their own areas into being using the same tactics as groids used to force us out of our neighborhoods."[12]

Corinna also flaunted a newfound interest in the "serious" side of white nationalism, noting that she'd purchased a copy of *Mein Kampf* for a few dollars on eBay. She asked for book recommendations to learn more about white history and how white people were different than other races. Recommendations ranged from tracts by famous white supremacists like David Duke to more mainstream books like *The Bell Curve* and Pat Buchanan's *The Death of the West*. Corinna urged longtime users to be understanding of newbies like herself, because it could take time to come around to all of the hard truths that Stormfront revealed. "If someone is drawn to this site and to our cause," she wrote one day, "they should be encouraged to look around here some more and not automatically jumped on for saying things like 'But I have known some really nice black people...' Can't all white people have a place here, as long as they support our cause and don't come here to argue and convince us we shouldn't be so 'racist'?" Several users agreed and thanked her for making the point.

Through private channels, Corinna gave out her home address, and people started sending her white-nationalist magazines and other literature—"important papers from my important friends," she recalled. When she saw a beautiful blond woman on the cover of one publication, she thought, *This is how they see me.* Corinna wasn't always sure that she believed what she was saying when she echoed her new friends' views, but she wanted to. If playing a part graduated to instinct, maybe they would like her even more.

After several months of activity on Stormfront, Corinna submitted an application to a local chapter of the National Socialist Movement (NSM). Soon after, a member contacted her to say that the group wanted to meet her—not in a chat room, in real life. The invitation came with instructions. "Racist groups usually have what they call safety checkpoints. They don't give locations of the meeting," Corinna explained. "They'll make you wait until an hour before the event and give you an address, and they'll meet you there and give you another address." She did what the message told her to do. On an appointed weekend morning, she drove to a mostly empty supermarket parking lot on the outskirts of Portland. People pushed rattling metal carts to and from the store's entrance, loaded with hardware supplies and food in bulk. Corinna sat in her car waiting—for what, she wasn't sure.

Finally, she saw a man approaching. He was short with a shaved head and looked to be in his thirties, maybe forties. As he got closer to her car, Corinna saw that he had on combat boots, like the ones Harley had once worn. When the man reached her window, she noticed swastika tattoos on his thick arms. For a split second, she thought she'd made a bad decision. What if he tried to hurt her?

Follow me, the man instructed gruffly, then turned on his heel and walked back to his car. Corinna obeyed.

She tailed him for thirty minutes along a secluded highway, with central Oregon's green expanse stretching to the mountains in the east and the ocean in the west. Finally, they reached the entrance to a state park and drove to a picnic area. Corinna pulled into a parking space alongside her guide. More than a dozen people were milling around, drinking and socializing. Someone had set up a boom box, and racist punk music blared into the air. Swastika flags were pinned to some fir trees.

Never good in a first encounter, Corinna was nervous approaching the group. What did they know about her? Had they read her Stormfront stuff? Were they looking for a reason—any reason—to reject her application?

In fact, Corinna was an easy sell. She was a woman of childbearing age who already had two white daughters, giving her immediate value to the organization. Her children functioned as stamps of legitimacy. White nationalism's professed goal is protecting the white race from extinction, which necessarily requires having babies, and Corinna had already done her part. She was also articulate and presentable. "They needed someone to serve as the face of their group," Corinna told me. "I had a clean [criminal] record and a job and a normal appearance."

After the picnic, the NSM accepted her. It didn't take long for her to be promoted to the head of its Portland chapter, where she led regular meetings that a half dozen or so people would attend. Then came adrenaline-fueled protests and rallies in the name of white pride. "They're all saying the same things. They're all dressed the same," she said of people at neo-Nazi gatherings. "And you feel, *yes,* I'm part of this now. I have a home here."

THE ROOTS OF the NSM reach back to the German-American Bund, an organization founded in 1936 to promote a favorable view of the Third Reich in the United States. The organization peaked in February 1939, when twenty thousand supporters gathered in Madison Square Garden for a rally that celebrated German ancestry and condemned President Franklin D. Roosevelt and his "Jew deal." The Bund collapsed at the dawn of World War II; its founder, a German immigrant, was deported after serving several months in prison for embezzlement and tax evasion.[13] Still, sympathy for the cause lingered. What it needed was purpose and direction.

It found both in the 1950s. Communism was the national bogeyman. Karl Marx's Jewish heritage, the espionage convictions of Julius and Ethel Rosenberg, and some American Jews' involvement in left-wing politics helped stoke anti-Semitism. Meanwhile, the end of legal segregation fueled anxieties about the upending of America's white order. Into the fray stepped a man with a furrowed brow who liked to be photographed wearing neatly cut suits and puffing on a corncob pipe. His name was George Lincoln Rockwell.

The son of a vaudeville star, Rockwell grew up middle class. He studied briefly at Brown University, where according to his biographer, Frederick Simonelli, he was frustrated by "the liberal orthodoxy he saw stifling creativity and freedom."[14] Rockwell dropped out and joined the Navy. Later he worked in advertising. He launched *U.S. Lady,* a periodical for the wives of American ambassadors and civil servants living abroad, in 1955. Due to a falling-out with his financial backers, Rockwell sold the publication the following year. Although the new editors would later denounce Rockwell's racist and anti-Semitic views, on at least one count, they seemed to agree with him: Men and women inhabiting traditional gender roles was vital to any grand political project. Rockwell would carry that idea into his neo-Nazi activism. The magazine promoted it too. "A concept frequently articulated in *U.S. Lady* was that women were both helpmates to servicemen-husbands and soft-power resources in U.S. international relations who augmented U.S. hard power," historian Donna Alvah writes in her book *Unofficial Ambassadors: American Military Families Overseas and the Cold War, 1946–1965.* Alvah quotes the magazine's editors as writing, "Women pray for peace and work in the kindly way they know best to back up their men. They are living history and making history, and just like the million-man armies and complicated weapons, they too pack quite a wallop."[15]

While he was in the Navy, stationed in Iceland, Rockwell had read *Mein Kampf* several times and become a self-described national socialist. He founded the American Nazi Party (ANP) in the late 1950s and headquartered it in Arlington, Virginia. To signal the party's coming out, he organized rallies on the National Mall; riots ensued as ANP supporters clashed with counterprotesters. Rockwell opposed racial integration, and the media invited him to debate civil rights figures like Stokely Carmichael, the most prominent advocate of "black power."[16] Rockwell coopted the phrase, describing the ANP as promoting "white power" and writing a book with that title. He denied the Holocaust, condemned homosexuality, and allied with the inchoate Christian Identity movement, which mixed biblical teachings with a devotion to white supremacy. He was a showman who nurtured a cult of white struggle and heroism, while draping bigotry with the appealing camouflage of common sense, social tradition, and religious faith. Though Rockwell never held public office, Simonelli notes that "his significance is in the strategic legacy he bequeathed the racist right."[17] It is also in Rockwell's aesthetic—many prominent white nationalists, from David Duke to Richard Spencer, have since mimicked his wholesome, clean-cut presentation.

Rockwell wasn't the only figure after World War II who drew a blueprint for neo-Nazism. Also influential was a woman named Savitri Devi, who in 1962 joined Rockwell and others in founding the World Union of National Socialists. Devi was born Maximiani Portas in 1905, into a well-to-do family of Greek, French, British, and Italian heritage. A passionate supporter of the Third Reich, she took the name Savitri Devi after moving to India, believed by some racist thinkers to be the birthplace of the so-called Aryan race that migrated to Europe and established Western civilization. Devi was a vocal proponent of India's caste system because she believed it preserved racial purity.

Devi fancied herself a philosopher. She wrote a number of essays and books outlining what became known as esoteric Hitlerism, a bizarre ideology that fuses Hinduism, paganism, environmentalism, and national socialism. The key points are that Hitler was divine—an avatar of Vishnu—and appeared in the world at a critical time. Hindus call it the Kali Yuga, a period of some 432,000 years characterized by disease, depravity, and despair. Hitler was a "man against time," Devi claimed, who fought to end the Kali Yuga and usher in a golden age, only to be derailed by the forces of evil, selfishness, and multiculturalism. Devi described the result in her 1958 book, *The Lightning and the Sun*.

> Upon the surface of this unfortunate planet, which is losing with alarming rapidity its once so broad and thick mantle of forests; of this unfortunate planet, where whole species of proud wild creatures—the aristocracy of the animal world—have already been or are being, with no less speed, wiped away—killed off to the last—one notices an increasingly obnoxious and steadily expanding swarm of dreary (when not positively ugly) vulgar, silly, worthless two-legged mammals. And the more worthless they are, the quicker they breed. The sickly and the dull have more children than the healthy and bright; the inferior races, and the people who have no race at all, definitely more than the hundred per cent Aryan; and the down-right rotten—afflicted both with hereditary diseases and racially undefinable blood— are, more often than not, terrifyingly fertile.[18]

Devi and Rockwell corresponded in letters, archived today by Counter-Currents, a white-nationalist publisher. In one 1960 missive, Rockwell complimented Devi's books:

> They have...forced me to revise my opinion of lady philoso- phers. In all my experience of the world, and all my studies and reading, I have never found a feminine writer who could reach the profoundest depths and heights of thought with power- ful and penetrating original ideas—without being obnoxiously masculine. You have done this thing, and, were you the rankest Communist, which, thank God you are not, I would still salute you for the masterful performance.

The pair didn't always agree. Devi, for instance, didn't like the term "white" because it could theoretically encompass Jews; she preferred

"Aryan." And she was wary of the ANP's appeals to white Christian Americans, because she believed Christianity was at odds with a "racialist" worldview. "Christianity is essentially a creed aiming at the salvation of the individual soul in a hypothetical 'next world,' and despising the body—and therefore *race*," Devi wrote to Rockwell in 1965. Practically speaking, however, Devi's arcane neo-Nazism complemented Rockwell's all-American version. It widened the appeal of national socialism—and by extension white nationalism—particularly as the New Age counterculture blossomed.

By then, Rockwell was dead, assassinated in 1967 outside a laundromat in Arlington by a disgruntled acolyte. Other leaders followed in his footsteps, including David Duke, founder of the Knights of the Ku Klux Klan, and William Luther Pierce, founder of the National Alliance and the author of *The Turner Diaries,* a 1978 novel that imagines a seismic race war in which a white-power group overthrows the U.S. government.* The ANP remained active, if in a diminished capacity; some followers participated in the 1979 Greensboro Massacre. Devi lived until 1982, by which time esoteric Hitlerism had seeped into the wider hate movement.

As a pair, Rockwell and Devi stand as the prototypical example of how white nationalism came to embrace a veritable buffet of identities, so long as beliefs in the sovereignty of white people and the preservation of whiteness as power were central to their worldview. The white-power movement of the late twentieth century "demanded that partisans set aside their differences," according to historian Kathleen Belew. "Activists circulated among groups and belief systems."[19] It is fitting that the present-day ANP, called the New Order and based in Wisconsin, casts itself as a "religious" organization that worships at the

---

*   *The Turner Diaries* became a touchstone for many far-right extremists, including Timothy McVeigh. The bomb that McVeigh set off in Oklahoma City in 1995, killing 168 people, was "strikingly similar to one described in detail in the book," according to J. M. Berger.

altar of Hitler. Before it was taken down in 2019, the group's website had an FAQ page that included a section under the question "Do you believe that Hitler was a god?" The short answer was no; the full reply seemed pulled straight from Devi's writings:

> Once in thousands of years...a singular and unique figure appears, whose special mission it is to declare anew the Divine Will and to redefine human history. In so doing, he himself becomes a universal **symbol.** In recent time, this extraordinary, providential figure appeared in the person of—*Adolf Hitler.* With his miraculous appearance, a new age on Earth has begun. That is why we honor and *revere* him.[20]

CORINNA DOVE HEADFIRST into activism with Oregon's neo-Nazis. She got racist tattoos, including a swastika on her lower back and a detailed rendering of Hitler's face on one of her calves. For unit meetings, she sometimes donned a military-style uniform with Nazi insignia. She placed recruitment flyers announcing "Jewish people are ruining America" on windshields in parking lots like the one where she'd first made contact with a neo-Nazi. "We put signs on people's cars encouraging them to join our group, so they could also put signs on cars," she told me. The flyer drives served an additional purpose: They provoked fear. In at least one instance, Corinna distributed literature in the neighborhood surrounding Congregation Beth Israel, a Portland synagogue.[21]

In November 2009, she traveled with fellow neo-Nazis to Phoenix, Arizona, for a rally demanding the protection of U.S. borders—the group wanted the government to halt the immigration of anyone who wasn't white and expel people already in America who weren't white. The NSM dubbed the Phoenix rally "America First," a slogan that, in the early twentieth century, had been used by isolationist politicians and the Klan; Donald Trump would later invoke it in his race to the White House.[22] A few dozen NSM members clad in all black marched in a loose formation down a city street carrying American flags and riot shields emblazoned with swastikas. They chanted "America first" and *"Sieg heil"* while a lone drummer rat-a-tatted.

Videos of the event show numerous women in the neo-Nazis' ranks. Three female members of the "youth division" sang an off-key national anthem before the NSM's leadership delivered speeches. "We come here in defense of white America, to speak to white people, and to say that illegals must go home, these foreigners are raping and plundering our land, and the two-party dictatorship of the Republicans and the Democrats will not stand up to it," one man yelled into a microphone. "We are not afraid. Our forefathers fought and resisted tyranny in this country, just as we stand here today in defiance of illegals, in defiance of a corrupt system that would just as soon put a bullet in the back of the white man's head."[23]

Even when she wasn't at rallies, Corinna was conspicuous in her white pride. She wore T-shirts with swastikas on them in public. Maybe, she thought, someone would see the symbol and ask what it was all about; then she'd be able to recruit them. (This never happened.) At the gym, where she'd begun training in bodybuilding, she wore apparel emblazoned with racist jokes and slogans, including one shirt that advertised Auschwitz as if it were a summer camp for kids. After several warnings, the gym she belonged to kicked her out—the sort of incident Corinna could carry to a unit meeting as evidence that she was fighting the good fight.

When she heard other NSM members brag about committing violence, she convinced herself they were talking about things they'd done before joining the unit. She told herself the NSM was a legitimate political group with intellectual underpinnings—never mind that she'd never been able to convince another neo-Nazi to read *Mein Kampf* and discuss it with her. *I had a wild youth,* Corinna remembered thinking, *and maybe a lot of these guys, especially those who've been in prison, maybe they are reforming themselves, too, by working in this actual political party instead of beating up immigrants.* She didn't necessarily like using racist language, but she did it anyway because she wanted to fit in. "The N-word," she said, "was everybody's third word."

When her family and ex-husband learned of her neo-Nazi affiliation, she assured them that it wasn't a big deal. She was just being politically active. She didn't care if it offended other people that white families wanted to protect their own. There was nothing wrong with wanting a bright, happy future for her kids and her race.

Her family didn't try to intervene, Corinna told me. "I think they got tired of dealing with me," she said, "and their whole approach was just, let her do what she's going to do until she burns out." Still, they found ways to express their disapproval. Her half sister disinvited Corinna from her wedding. Corinna insisted that she wouldn't ruin the event—*I have the ability to behave in public,* she said—but the bride-to-be didn't care. There were Jewish people on the guest list, and she didn't want them to be upset or uncomfortable.

Corinna once gave her daughters a mixtape of songs about Nordic purity and other neo-Nazi themes. Tom, her ex, took it away before the girls could listen to it.[24] In another instance, Corinna took her daughters, then five and eight years old, to a Halloween party that her NSM unit threw for members with families. She wore an SS uniform. It troubled Corinna when her elder daughter, a towhead like she'd been at her age, fell silent and didn't want to talk or play with anyone. She was usually an upbeat kid. "They didn't have the words to explain why it was wrong," Corinna said of her daughters. "They just knew that they shouldn't be there, and I shouldn't be there."

Tom choked up remembering how the incident traumatized his daughters. "Believe me, I've been over and over that," he said. He was trying to be a nice guy and keep the mother of his children in their lives. Should he have done something else? Taken Corinna to court to secure a no-visitation order? Talk to her frankly about her new lifestyle and friends? "I never really confronted her about it. Maybe I should have," Tom told me. "I could've just said no. I could've just said no."

CORINNA WAS LIVING in America in 2009, not Berlin in 1939. How could she reasonably think that a neo-Nazi group was a legitimate, if fringe, political party? How could she wear a T-shirt with a swastika on it and expect a reaction from onlookers other than dismay or outrage? On the one hand, she'd led a relatively cloistered existence and her uncommon impenetrability meant that the emotions most people located in the mundane—happiness, camaraderie, anger—she found only in extremes. It also seemed like no one in her life wanted to have the uncomfortable conversation with her about what the hell was going on.

It's possible, too, that Corinna was recasting her story when talking to me. In their book *Mistakes Were Made (but Not by Me)*, social psychologists Carol Tavris and Elliot Aronson explain that humans are prone to self-justification of everything we say, do, and believe, no matter how wrong or cruel it may be, because "it allows us to create a distinction between our moral lapses and someone else's and blur the discrepancy between our actions and our moral convictions." In this process, memory is "an unreliable, self-serving historian," equipped with "an ego-enhancing bias that blurs the edges of past events, softens culpability, and distorts what really happened."[25] Corinna may well have been more aware of the ugliness of neo-Nazism than she would later admit to herself or to me when I interviewed her more than a decade after the fact.

Striking, though, was her willingness to accept and articulate responsibility. When she spoke to me about her choices—and she knew they were choices—Corinna was bitterly derisive. When she said that she hadn't known any better when she joined the NSM, I didn't get the impression that she hoped I would feel sorry for her. (I didn't.)

Rather, she seemed to be saying that she knew she'd been wrong. She *should* have known better. And she would have, if she'd cared to think harder about what she was doing and the impact it was having. "I didn't realize there were different degrees of racism," Corinna told me. "If somebody said he didn't like black people, or he told a racist joke, or he said illegal immigration is wrong, I assumed that must mean he would want to join my group."

On at least this point, Corinna's past self as she remembered it wasn't entirely wrong. Many white Americans rationalize their racism—or even refuse to call it that—by insisting that it isn't *as bad* as someone else's. They could spit on immigrants instead of complaining in private about foreigners stealing American jobs. They could put Jewish people in camps instead of muttering about how they have too much power. They could lynch black people instead of making jokes about their intelligence.

All true, and yet. "What does a racist joke do," writes journalist Joe Bernstein, "except create the cognitive distance necessary to do harm, dissolve the bonds of moral obligation?"[26] Talking about bigotry as a matter of degrees and justifying it by way of comparison is for the benefit of the people doing it. Corinna was mistaken in thinking that the white people at her Portland gym would see her Nazi T-shirts and want to be her friend. In that assumption, however, was a kernel of truth: Bigotry in America has many branches, some bigger and stronger than others, but they all derive from the same trunk.

3.

After several months with the NSM, Corinna discovered—or was willing to see—that fellow unit members had served time for crimes she couldn't abide: molestation, domestic violence, rape. And some of them were still committing violence. Shortly after midnight on March 27, 2010, a local antiracist activist named Luke Querner was shot in the torso while leaving a club in downtown Portland. Querner, who was celebrating his thirtieth birthday, survived the attack but was paralyzed from the waist down.[1] Friends immediately suspected that far-right extremists were to blame.

Corinna, who had also just turned thirty, was contacted by police; she figured it was because she so conspicuously flaunted her NSM affiliation. Maybe they thought she knew something, or someone who did. Cops showed her pictures of various neo-Nazis, some clad in uniforms and holding rifles, and they peppered her with questions about them. One officer asked Corinna how she could associate with such bad people. Be their unit leader. Date them. What did she see in a bunch of criminals? For once her stock responses—they read interesting books, they were a political party—rang hollow in her ears.

Corinna was also withholding a piece of information that she knew might be relevant. After Querner's shooting, a member of her NSM unit had asked her to help conceal the fact that he owned a gun. It was a 9mm, and Corinna had given it to him as a gift, even though he was a convicted felon. The man said he needed to make it seem like the weapon belonged to someone else. Corinna told me that she orchestrated a fake bill of sale with another friend. She could have gone to the police with the truth—that she didn't know who perpetrated the shooting but had information about a suspicious gun. The tip might have led to interviews of potential suspects, maybe even an arrest and conviction. It also might have put Corinna in danger, if the NSM ever found out. She made a calculation and said nothing. "I just figured," she told me, "if the police didn't know where the gun was, I…"

Corinna stopped short of repeating whatever excuse she'd used to justify her silence to the police—a deafening void in which Querner was confined to a wheelchair for life and raised money online to cover his medical bills. "Nobody was ever arrested," Corinna finally said.

Complicity in hate takes many forms, from acts to gestures to omissions. Hearing Corinna's story, I thought of a passage in Elinor Langer's book *A Hundred Little Hitlers,* about a murder perpetrated in 1988 by a skinhead gang in Portland; it is one of the city's most infamous hate crimes. Three men were arrested and convicted, including a white nationalist named Kenneth Mieske. Langer describes Mieske, then twenty-three, sitting in a car as a street brawl between his friends and three Ethiopian immigrants escalated. Patty Copp—nineteen years old, white, a community college student who worked for a chiropractor—was behind the wheel.

"WELL, aren't you going to do something about it, Ken?" Copp demanded.

Mieske grabbed a Louisville Slugger that belonged to Copp's father and beat a man named Mulugeta Seraw to death. Copp later sawed the bat into pieces, which she and Mieske burned at a beach. They tossed the ashes and remaining shards of wood into a firepit.

Mieske went to prison for his crime and died behind bars at the age of forty-five. Copp was questioned and investigated for her involvement in the crime. According to a police officer, "She turned out to be the most bullheaded of the group."[2]

WOMEN ARE SUPPOSED to be nice. It's a belief inscribed in our social gospel. There's even a name for it: the women-are-wonderful effect. Psychologists coined the phrase based on research showing that people tend to assign more positive attributes to women than they do to men, qualities like "happy," "good," and "nurturing."[3] To meet these expectations, women are conditioned to be polite and self-effacing. A study described in a 2009 book found that young girls "quickly learn to smile, work quietly, be neat, defer to boys, and speak only when spoken to."[4] The effect cultivates benevolent sexism, as women are pigeonholed as pleasing, civilizing, and selfless forces. They are told to absorb misogyny without complaint, and they are often policed and punished when they don't.

An extension of the women-are-wonderful effect is the assumption that they require protection, like some rare gem or helpless creature. This was a rallying cry of the Ku Klux Klan in its earliest days. Under the pretense of protecting the fairer sex from rape and murder at the hands of black men, white men in white robes terrorized communities of color. D. W. Griffith's blockbuster silent film *The Birth of a Nation* valorized Klansmen as saviors of white womanhood. The Klan was an oxymoron, a "respectable organization of terrorists," as historian Otto H. Olsen once wrote.[5]

Well into the twentieth century, defending white women's purity, honor, and goodness was used to justify all manner of wrongs, most brutal among them the lynchings of black men. In some cases, these men were accused of assaulting white women. In others, their alleged offense was a look, a gesture, or a word deemed disrespectful. Often, it was women who did the accusing.

This was true in one of the country's most devastating hate crimes. Fourteen-year-old Emmett Till was beaten, shot, stripped, mutilated, and weighted down in a river by a fan blade from a cotton gin that had been lashed to his neck with barbed wire, all because a white woman named Carolyn Bryant claimed that he'd grabbed her waist and said sexually obscene things to her. Bryant was depicted by the press as sweet and attractive—a "crossroads Marilyn Monroe," according to one journalist who covered the 1955 crime and its aftermath.[6] The killers were acquitted. One of them was later quoted in *Look* magazine saying, "When a nigger gets close to mentioning sex with a white woman, he's tired o' livin'. I'm likely to kill him."[7]

More than fifty years later, Bryant admitted that she hadn't told the truth about what happened with Till.* It was a searing reminder of another way in which the women-are-wonderful effect is problematic: It risks blinding people to the ways in which women can be terrible.

Disbelief about women's complicity in the worst forms of bigotry stretches across time and cultures. Feminist historians of the Holocaust have documented the postwar fable of "the apolitical woman," a victim of the Third Reich even if, as a proud German, she participated in its work. "Very few women were prosecuted after the war; even fewer were judged and convicted," writes Wendy Lower. "Many of the female defendants, especially those who appeared matronly and meek, did not seem capable of committing such atrocities." As a result, Lower concludes, "most got away with murder."[8] Similarly, many historians of the antebellum South posited that white women benefited only indirectly from slavery and that their patriarchal culture's veneration

---

* Carolyn Bryant, whose last name is now Donham, reportedly recanted in an interview with writer Timothy Tyson for his book *The Blood of Emmett Till*. Regarding her accusation that Till made advances toward her, Bryant is quoted as telling Tyson, "That part's not true." In 2018, the U.S. Department of Justice announced that it was reopening the investigation of Till's murder, prompted in part by Tyson's research. Donham's daughter has said publicly that her mother did not recant in her interview with Tyson; the author disputes the claim.

of femininity meant that they couldn't have participated in the worst aspects of human bondage. They were Scarlett O'Hara: cherished, cosseted, even glamorous. In 2019, drawing on thousands of interviews with former slaves conducted during the New Deal by the Federal Writers' Project, historian Stephanie E. Jones-Rogers revealed how deeply implicated white women were in the system of buying, selling, and exploiting black bodies. "When we listen to what enslaved people had to say about white women and slave mastery, we find that they articulated quite clearly their belief that slave-owning women governed their slaves in the same ways that white men did," Jones-Rogers writes. "Sometimes they were more effective at slave management or they used more brutal methods of discipline than their husbands did."[9]

Does faith in women's goodness also explain the relative erasure of female actors from the history of the hate movement? Does it explain the Portland cop's seeming dismay at Patty Copp's behavior after the Seraw murder? To some extent, surely it does. It also illuminates the ways in which women have positioned themselves in white nationalism. The SPLC noted in a 1999 report that women were "staking out their own territory" in the digital realm with websites featuring names like Women's Frontier, Women for Aryan Unity, and White World of Skinchick. Some sites hosted "a spirited debate on the role of women in the racist movement," while others stuck "to more traditional fare, from 'Aryan' recipes to parenting tips for white mothers."[10] Stormfront had similar content woven into its channels, including the Women's Forum, which promised "sugar and spice, and everything nice."[11] By 2005, there was a magazine targeting female white nationalists; called *Homefront,* it was available to download online and featured articles about organic diets alongside anti-Semitic diatribes.[12]

Female-focused content continued to expand, but its goal remained constant: promoting a racist worldview through the trappings of home, family, and sisterhood—wholesome spheres of female influence. The facade was, and still is, both a shield and a beacon, deflecting criticism and inviting curiosity. "Racist women understand that groups of women who seem innocuous can attract people to racist politics," writes Kathleen Blee.[13]

Today, the savviest white nationalists are aware of the blind spot that observers often have when it comes to women, discounting their contributions to abhorrent causes because they prefer to think of them as humanity's better angels. One of this book's subjects put it this way: "A soft woman saying hard things can create repercussions throughout society," Lana Lokteff declared at a white-nationalist conference in 2017. "Since we aren't physically intimidating, we can get away with saying big things. And let me tell you, the women that I've met in this movement can be lionesses, and shield-maidens, and Valkyries."[14]

AFTER THE QUERNER shooting, Corinna decided that the NSM was the problem, not white nationalism. She went looking, in her words, for "a better white supremacy thing." There were plenty to choose from. White nationalism has never been homogeneous; it is comprised of small outfits and personality cults, splinter factions and reactionary groups, alliances and feuding parties. In 2010, there were more entities than ever from which Corinna could choose, because "the radical right in America expanded explosively," according to the SPLC. For the first time since the organization began counting in the 1980s, the number of hate groups in the country exceeded one thousand. That figure also represented a two-thirds increase over the previous decade. The SPLC attributed the unprecedented growth to "resentment over the changing racial demographics of the country, frustration over the government's handling of the economy, and the mainstreaming of conspiracy theories and other demonizing propaganda aimed at various minorities."[15] America was also grappling with the fallout from the September 11 attacks, a financial meltdown, the election of a black president, and the expanding reach of alternative media.

Corinna found a replacement for the NSM in a member of the

racist old guard, who'd rebranded himself for the digital age. Harold Covington's extremist activity dated back to at least 1971, the year he joined both the U.S. Army and the National Socialist White People's Party, the successor to Rockwell's ANP, before it became the New Order. Covington spent time in South Africa and Zimbabwe—then Rhodesia—until he was deported for sending anti-Semitic letters to a local Jewish congregation.[16] He moved back to his native North Carolina, where he became powerful in neo-Nazi and Klan circles alongside the perpetrators of the 1979 Greensboro Massacre. The year after that bloody event, Covington ran for the Republican nomination for state attorney general and won almost 43 percent of the vote.[17] For tens of thousands of voters, open racism and adoration for Hitler weren't disqualifying attributes in a candidate.

Covington eventually made his way to the Pacific Northwest, where he fell in step with an idea popularized by Richard Butler, the founder of Aryan Nations, which since the late 1970s had operated out of a compound in Hayden Lake, Idaho. Butler and his followers believed that a swath of territory in Wyoming, Idaho, Oregon, Washington, and Montana should be a white homeland—a place without minorities, where Aryans could live in racial harmony. Covington supported the separatist agenda and eventually founded the Northwest Front (NWF) to promote it. He claimed that he officially birthed the NWF on November 5, 2008, one day after "black Tuesday," his description of Barack Obama's election. "My nigger Barry and his ho bought the White House," Covington later said in a radio broadcast, the Southern lilt in his voice all but erasing the *r* in the slur. "The disease was immediately followed by the cure."[18]

Though he described the NWF as an organization, it was mostly a propaganda machine. Covington produced a website and podcast— *Radio Free Northwest,* a mocking riff on the name of anti-Soviet programming during the Cold War—that championed white nationalism and invited white Americans to move to the Northwest. The NWF's work was premised on a manifesto written by Covington, which Dylann Roof would later cite as inspiration for his 2015 massacre of black parishioners at a church in Charleston, South Carolina. Covington's document reads in part:

> We as a people have wasted the past six decades on pointless, futile and impotent right-wing and kosher conservative organizations and strategies. The overwhelming majority of these past organizations and movements refused to recognize the vital central importance of race in all issues, and they refused to recognize the urgent need for state power in order to preserve the existence of our race. The few attempts that have been made to resist racial extinction by groups and personalities of an openly National Socialist or racialist nature have been led by men who were stupid, incompetent, dishonest, or some combination of all three. The result of the past sixty years of right-wing failure and impotence is that we are now out of time.

Corinna learned about Covington through one of her NSM unit members. Covington's intellectual trappings, conveyed in a booming baritone to his listeners on *Radio Free Northwest,* appealed to her. In addition to the manifesto and his long-winded radio scripts, Covington had written several novels, including *A Mighty Fortress* and *A Distant Thunder,* which imagined a near-future America in which white militias fought the government to gain freedom for their people. Covington also stressed normalcy: He believed that NWF acolytes should fit into wider society, which meant no Nazi insignia on their clothes or visible racist tattoos. By seeming run-of-the-mill, they might gain a foothold alongside millions of white Americans whose less strident racism was a cultural norm.

Corinna was eager to meet Covington. He was paranoid, so making contact with him was an arcane process—to get an invitation to visit the NWF's office in Washington State, you had to know someone who already knew him and could pass on your message of interest. This happened for Corinna, and a summons from Covington eventually arrived by mail. Corinna carpooled north with some NSM friends. Covington's apartment-cum-office was in Port Orchard, a small city situated on one of the jagged thrusts of land in the waters between Seattle and Olympic National Park. The space was on the second floor of a large, run-down housing complex. Trash and unwashed dishes were strewn on tabletops and stacked in corners.

A jowly man in his late fifties with a dark goatee and prominent pointy eyebrows, Covington often appeared in photos with a fedora on his head and a pipe between his lips—an homage, perhaps, to George Lincoln Rockwell. That day he wore a food-stained shirt to greet his guests. Still, Corinna was impressed. The office had a designated "literature room"—a converted bedroom—filled with racist pamphlets, books, and other printed material, including copies of Covington's novels. Here was a man who loved big ideas, Corinna thought. Later, once they knew each other better, Covington would tell her that he'd been waiting decades to meet her: *When I was fourteen,* Covington said, *I met you in a dream. You were an angel of the lord, who would lead the white race to victory.* Corinna had never heard anything so strange, or so flattering. "Who doesn't want to lead people to victory? Especially when it's divinely ordained?" she asked me.

Corinna wanted to move to Port Orchard and work with Covington right away, but she needed money. A job search at funeral homes didn't turn up anything in the Seattle area. Instead, she found an opportunity in Kalispell, Montana. The town of about twenty thousand people was more than five hundred miles from Covington's office, and even farther from Corinna's daughters in Oregon. Kalispell was located in a flat, verdant valley ringed by the peaks of Glacier National Park, expanses of kelly-green forest, and the largest freshwater lake west of the Mississippi River. It had recently become a hub for white nationalists, thanks to a woman named April Gaede.

BORN IN CALIFORNIA in 1966, Gaede was raised by racists. Her father owned a ranch near Fresno where he branded his cattle with swastikas. As an adult, she participated in neo-Nazi organizations, including William Pierce's National Alliance. According to the SPLC, Gaede "spent hundreds of hours posting racist and anti-Semitic diatribes, along with gardening and parenting tips, on white nationalist on-line message boards."[19] Over the years, in posts on Stormfront, she reminded women of the vital, powerful role they played as mothers in preserving white culture. She once recommended a 1943 children's book that "explains the differences between the races" and others that "are very non PC, show examples of only white families and children and teach old fashioned values. They are worth it for the photos alone."[20]

Gaede's biggest claim to fame was her daughters. In 1992, during the first of her three marriages, Gaede gave birth to twin girls, Lynx and Lamb. A decade later, she decided to deploy them as propaganda tools. With blond hair and delicate features, Lynx and Lamb appeared perfectly Aryan and equally innocent. Gaede began stage-managing them as a musical duo under the moniker Prussian Blue. The name was a reference to the color of the residue left—or not left, according to Holocaust deniers—by Zyklon B in Nazi gas chambers. The girls said in interviews that it was a pretty color, similar to that of their eyes.[21]

Lynx and Lamb sang while they played the guitar and violin. The vocals were nothing special, but skill wasn't the point—aesthetics was. Wearing medieval-style dresses that laced up the front, kilts and knee socks, or their Sunday best, the girls trilled folk-pop tunes about embattled white men and racial holy war (RAHOWA in white-supremacist lingo). Gaede booked them at county fairs and white-nationalist festivals. They had a website and music videos.

The scheme wasn't bizarre—at least, not in the tradition of white nationalism. Since at least the 1970s, capitalizing on the reach and power of popular music, far-right extremists had been founding racist bands and underground labels. Their targets were young, impression-able audiences looking for community and identity. Many of these musical endeavors developed in the punk and heavy-metal scenes, popular with rebellious, angry youth. Others took shape in more family-friendly genres. According to the book *Trendy Fascism,* "With its Neo-Nazi folk genre, the white power movement joins, coopts, and shifts the long-standing social reformist tradition of folk and protest music in America. It embraces folk music as a racially pure expression of white culture." On the surface, the sound was pleasing, even benign. It was also potent, like a gateway drug.[22]

Gaede was surely aware of these dynamics when she orchestrated Prussian Blue. Media attention would mean opportunities to demon-strate to a wide audience that her way of life wasn't so terrible. She was a plain-faced mom who homeschooled her girls, nurtured their talents, and taught them to respect their heritage—what was so scary about that? Such a simple, if misleading, question might serve as a bridge to mainstream America. According to Patricia Anne Simpson, a scholar of Germanic culture, Prussian Blue "projected racist messages through the megaphone of their own vulnerability and beauty." Their aesthetic was intended to "trigger the protective rhetoric of both Europeans and American radical groups: ones that lament the death of the white race, the loss of blond, blue-eyed beauty, and the hyperbolic commitment to fostering family, family values, and the increasingly urgent need to secure a future for white children."[23]

Lynx and Lamb were the subjects of a *GQ* article[24] and were featured on ABC's *Primetime.*[25] It seemed like exactly what Gaede wanted: publicity for white nationalism that, if not outright positive, was more curious than confrontational. She milked the public ogling. "What young, red-blooded American boy isn't going to find two blonde twins...singing about white pride and pride in your race...very appealing?" Gaede once asked.[26]

In the midst of Prussian Blue's run, Gaede decided to leave California. She compared the state's growing minority population to "watching a good friend die a slow death." Whiter pastures called to her. In 2006, Gaede jumped on the bandwagon of Pioneer Little Europe (PLE), a recently developed concept that encouraged "racially conscious" white people to form tightly knit communities in small towns, which in theory would prompt people who weren't white to leave.[27] Based on two visits and research on "demographics, schools, crime, etc.," Gaede packed up her family and moved to Kalispell, where she issued an invitation on Stormfront. "Come home," she wrote to other white nationalists. "Those of us who have already made the move will try to help and advise those who wish to do so as well." Gaede continued:

> We chose to leave California because of the increase in Mestizos who had changed the whole culture and community of our hometowns for the worse. We couldn't allow our teenage daughters to run around with their friends or even go to the mall without adult protection.... My parent's cattle ranch was over run with Mexican mafia who planted gardens of marijuana that the local deputies were scared to confront. We women could not longer safely walk or hike or ride on the ranch.

In Kalispell, Lynx and Lamb were able to "attend one of the best high schools in the nation and they can attend games and go to the ice cream store like kids did back in the 50s." Gaede was appealing directly to fellow mothers—white women who saw threats to their families and personal comfort lurking in the big, bad racially mixed world. Kalispell offered a balm that was as American as apple pie and as white as a dollop of vanilla ice cream.[28]

A group of concerned residents in Kalispell responded to Gaede's and her family's arrival by distributing flyers to local homes. "This letter is not written as a means to harass the family or to begin a witch hunt," the flyers read, according to the Associated Press. "We wish the family no harm. Our goal is to peacefully communicate that this kind of hate and ignorance will not be accepted here in our neighborhood where we live and raise our families." The flip side of the flyers, printed on fluorescent paper, declared in black block letters, "No hate here." People were urged to place the message in their homes' front windows.[29]

Gaede persisted with her propaganda. PLE took out a full-page advertisement in the *Flathead Beacon* newspaper featuring the photos of forty-seven babies—all but one with light-colored skin—recently born in the Kalispell Regional Medical Center. "What do the babies look like being born in your town?" PLE's website asked visitors. According to Media Matters for America, dozens of extremists answered the call and moved to Kalispell.[30]

Corinna bought into the mythology too. "Kalispell had this more wholesome image: happy white families, no facial tattoos, no stomping [on] things. Just good, wholesome, smiling people carving pumpkins together," she said. "I wanted to be in a group like that." And she was keen to befriend Gaede, a woman whom she described as a "racist Martha Stewart."

THE TWO WOMEN met for the first time at an IHOP in Kalispell, when Corinna came to town to interview for the embalming job. Over dessert, they got to know each other. They were both proudly independent and navigated the hate movement on their own terms— none of this *doing it for my man* business. Gaede pitched PLE to Corinna, assuring her that it attracted only the best kind of white people. In fact, most of the PLE members in Kalispell were women who got together and talked about cooking, raising children, and other mundane topics. They just wanted to have a nice, white life. Corinna could have one too.

By the end of the meeting, Gaede had invited Corinna to live with her if she moved to town. "It was one of those situations where you suddenly have an instant best friend," Corinna recalled. Gaede was kind to her, or maybe she was just savvy. "Those who recruit, they're good at attaching themselves to people," Corinna said, particularly "weird loners who spend too much time on the internet." Loners, that is, like her.

Corinna took the job in Kalispell. She told her ex-husband that she wanted to bring her daughters, or at least have them with her for part of the year. He was wary. He told her that, once she moved, he'd come with the girls to visit her. So Corinna packed up and drove from Portland to Kalispell, only to receive a rude welcome, courtesy of local bureaucracy. The funeral home told her that it needed her to have a particular state license; she didn't, which meant she couldn't do the job. In a panic, she contacted Gaede.

I don't have anywhere to live, Corinna said.

Of course you can move in, Gaede told her.

Gaede's house had several bedrooms, a dog and chickens in the yard, and a horse in a nearby pasture. Lynx and Lamb had finished high school, stopped making music, and moved out on their own, but Gaede had another daughter, Dresden, who was still elementary-school age. The interior of the house was tastefully decorated—no Nazi symbols were on the walls. Gaede preferred to keep the talismans of her activism tucked away. Sometimes she would pull out a shoebox filled with media clippings and tell Corinna the stories behind them. Recently she and the PLE had attracted attention for holding movie screenings at Kalispell's public library. The films were documentaries about the Third Reich, with titles like *Epic: The Story of the Waffen SS.*[31]

According to Corinna, Gaede bragged about a particular item under her bed: a container holding David Lane's ashes. Lane had been one of the most infamous white nationalists in the country, a key member of the Order, a violent organization that had robbed banks, racketeered, planted bombs, and committed murder before law enforcement caught up to it in the mid-1980s. The group took its name from *The Turner Diaries.* Lane, sentenced to 190 years in prison, maintained his influence on the radical right from behind bars. He coined the closest thing white nationalism had to a campaign slogan, known in the movement as the 14 Words: "We must secure the existence of our people and a future for white children."

Gaede and Lane were friends. He wrote lyrics for Prussian Blue and struck up a correspondence with the twins from prison. In a phone call, captured on film by a British documentarian, Lane described being out in the yard of the Colorado penitentiary where he was housed and seeing a cloud break such that it looked like a white circle with clear blue sky in the middle. Lane, in his sixties at the time, said it reminded him of Lynx's and Lamb's eyes. "When the girls were little, they were like daughters or something," he said, his voice muffled over the prison's landline. "Now they're growing into women, and being a natural male... they're like sisters, daughters, fantasy sweethearts, I don't know what else."[32]

When Lane died in 2007, Gaede was bequeathed his remains. She had him cremated, per his wishes. The plan was to distribute portions of his ashes to fourteen white-nationalist women, in honor of the 14 Words. Gaede told Corinna that, if she proved herself worthy, she might get some of the ashes one day.

Corinna already had a tattoo of Lane's slogan encircling one of her ankles. When she was in the NSM, she and other unit members had made a pilgrimage to the site where one of Lane's associates, Robert Mathews, was killed in a shoot-out with the FBI in December 1984. Whidbey Island, in the Puget Sound, was where Mathews made his last stand. It took Corinna and her friends six hours to get there from Oregon, and when they arrived, they weren't sure what they were looking for. Mathews's house, which caught fire in the shoot-out, had likely been bulldozed. They found a clearing where they thought the incident may have happened, paid their respects, and left to get food.

As a member of the NSM, Corinna wrote letters to surviving Order members, all of whom were in prison. One of them, Gary Yarbrough, wrote back in slanting script on blue-lined notebook paper. "You were only 5 years old when Bob [Mathews] and the rest of us sacrificed our lives & freedoms for our folk cause," he said in the letter, dated December 20, 2009, which Corinna shared with me. "Actually, it was for you & the as yet unborn, because our own generation was/ is totally unworthy of the losses we suffered & still suffer." Yarbrough continued, "The conflict of the ages is upon us, keep your head up & keep up the good fight!" The exclamation point was shaped like a lightning bolt. "Our victory is destined, we cannot fail," he said. "See you at the victory fest."*

In Kalispell, living with Gaede, a personal friend of Order members, Corinna felt like she was moving up in the hate movement. The decision to leave Portland's NSM chapter and relocate to Montana felt like the right one. Her ex had even followed through on his promise to bring the girls to visit. "I took the kids to the house and I met them," Tom told me, referring to Gaede's family. "They seemed nice enough."

THERE WAS NO single cause of Corinna and Gaede's relationship curdling. In Corinna's recollection, Gaede grew annoyed with her assertiveness. Corinna may have been awkward, but she wasn't a shrinking violet, and the independence that had initially bonded the women became a problem. Once, when Gaede had people over for a loved one's birthday, Corinna asked what the guest of honor's favorite dessert was. The answer was strawberry-rhubarb pie, so Corinna made several with help from Gaede's daughter Dresden. They carved swastikas in the crust.

---

* Unlike some other Order members, Yarbrough wasn't charged with murder; his crimes were illegal possession of weapons and the assault of FBI agents. When asked in a press conference after his 1984 arrest who did kill a Jewish target of the Order, Yarbrough answered, "God." Gary Yarbrough died in April 2018, at the age of sixty-two. He was still serving his prison sentence.

Gaede wasn't impressed. She refused to eat the pie, Corinna recalled, and complained that there was too much food in the house. A man who attended the party mused to Corinna that she'd stepped on the alpha female's toes.

It wasn't the first time Gaede's opinion of other women in the movement had soured. After Lane's death, she'd feuded over his remains with members of Women for Aryan Unity, a self-described network of "European women who have chosen to support the advancement of their Folk and to be productive participants in our movement."[33] Corinna, however, lived under Gaede's roof. Gaede, who'd once floated the idea of starting a matchmaking service for white nationalists, wondered why Corinna was dating but not trying to have more children. She was displeased when Corinna said that her tubes were tied, a decision she didn't plan to undo. In Gaede's eyes, according to Corinna, her value as a white woman plummeted.

The final straw, perhaps, was an online exposé. In July 2010, antiracist activists in Portland published an article revealing Corinna's history with low-budget porn. She had worked under names like "Slave Corrylu" and appeared in films called *Handjobs Across America #18, Deepthroat Virgins #21,* and *Corrylu's Correction.* Her work was available on DVD and websites like Bondage Auditions. Corinna had talked about porn on Stormfront but only to criticize it as degenerate—the sort of thing that was beneath the white race. "WN men can start encouraging other rites of passage for boys," she wrote on May 16, 2010. "How pathetic is it to look forward to getting to see a naked woman in a magazine? Many boys believe they are missing out if they don't get to look at one or go to a strip club."[34] She said nothing about her own history with the industry.

Other media picked up the story, including Gawker, which shared pictures of Corinna in her NSM uniform—swastika armband over the sleeve of a crisp white button-down tucked into a sensible black skirt, like the attire of a Nazi schoolmarm—and in bikinis she'd worn to amateur bodybuilding competitions. She carried so much muscle on her small frame, the result of a grueling weight-lifting regimen, that her fake-tanned skin looked painfully taut. In an interview with Gawker, Corinna said she was surprised about the attention being paid to her porn career, which she claimed to have abandoned after white nationalism showed her the error of her ways. "I didn't consider this to be some sort of secret," she explained, adding drily, "I raise gerbils, too."* Her quote prompted Gawker to declare, "She's a renaissance woman from hell."

Online, some white nationalists embraced the narrative of a porn star redeemed. "This is an individual who has grown up in the sewer that is the USA, and some of the sewage lapped up on her, but she pulled herself out of it. I would be happy to meet this woman and shake her hand," one user wrote on a Vanguard News Network message board.[35] Others weren't convinced, including Gaede. When she got wind of Corinna's past, she told her houseguest that she was no longer welcome.

By then, Corinna had a boyfriend she could live with—a man Gaede had set her up with—so she wasn't homeless. But Corinna started to wonder if it was time to leave Kalispell. Another man in the town's white-nationalist community had told her that he thought it was wrong that her daughters were living with her ex-husband. If she wanted, the man offered, he could orchestrate the girls' kidnapping and bring them to Montana.

Legally or not, Corinna was no longer interested in having her daughters with her in Kalispell—not around the people she'd met there, and not after Gaede had cut her off. "I wanted my kids the hell away from this whole scene," Corinna told me. "People made disturbing comments about how, even though I couldn't have kids, I

---

* The gerbils comment was true. In fact, Corinna's screen name on a bodybuilding forum was 14gerbils88; the first number referenced David Lane's infamous saying, while the second represented *heil Hitler*—h is the eighth letter of the alphabet.

came with kids." She wondered if the people in Kalispell really wanted her around. Maybe her daughters, much like Lynx and Lamb, were the ultimate prizes.* "I began to realize that my kids are going to be turned into really miserable breeding stock," Corinna said.

She decided to leave Kalispell, where she'd never found steady work anyway, and move to Washington to work for Covington and the NWF. Her ex-husband had moved up near Seattle, so Corinna could be close by her daughters again, too. Just as she packed up to leave, however, a major snowstorm hit. The roads were so bad that she wrecked her car on her way out of town. While she waited for repairs and for the snow to melt, she stayed at a cheap motel. It was an extended-stay place where residents threw parties and got raging drunk. She hated it.

For all its natural beauty, Kalispell's luster and promise were gone. Corinna couldn't wait to get out. Covington and his literature room were at the end of the road, though not in the way she imagined.

---

* In 2011, Lynx and Lamb told media outlets that they no longer held white-nationalist views. In the years that followed, their Facebook accounts featured photos of them with piercings, tattoos, brightly dyed hair, and dreadlocks. Lamb is now married and has a daughter. A Twitter account that appears to belong to April Gaede—the bio reads, "Alt Right, Chief Cook and Bottle Washer"—includes a photo of Lamb with her baby, along with the hashtag #Whitemothersaremagic.

4.

"Hi, Robert!"

Corinna's voice was bright, like she'd just polished it on her sleeve. It was April 28, 2011. She'd been in Port Orchard, Washington, for a few months by then, and she was Covington's new sidekick on *Radio Free Northwest*. Her task on this particular broadcast was answering a question from a listener, a white man living in Afghanistan, presumably a member of the military. Robert wanted to know what, exactly, the "Jewish question" was.

"The Jewish question itself is pretty simple—them or us, because that's what it boils down to," Corinna said, reading from a script. "Are we going to continue to allow the Jews to do what they've been doing to the world for the last few thousand years, or are we going to do something to stop them?"

She ticked off anti-Semitism's stock-in-trade: Jews are immoral and materialistic. They seek to profit from the civilization white people have built, even if that means destroying it. They are behind the liberal agenda poisoning America. "Wherever there is organized degeneracy and corruption," Corinna declared, "wherever the white woman is cheapened into a sex object and her role as wife and mother is mocked and degraded, wherever our daughters and sisters are depicted in the arms of non-whites...wherever the white male and the Western civilization he created are abused, reviled, and subverted, there you will find the influence of the Jew—always the Jew."

Corinna's tirade was capped off with a song by the British white-power band No Remorse. Covington liked interspersing radio segments with racist music. This particular tune's screeching refrain was "Kill you, you filthy Jew!"[1]

When Corinna first arrived in Port Orchard, she hadn't intended to be on the radio. She'd left Kalispell with nothing, and Covington said she could sleep on the couch of the NWF office. In exchange, she could be his assistant while she got her embalming career back on track. Then Covington told her that the radio show needed new blood. Ideally, it would be a woman, someone female listeners could relate to. Corinna was skeptical. "I am one of those people who just plain do not like to talk," she later wrote on a blog. "One time I had laryngitis and literally could not make a vocal sound for an entire week. I was worried how this would affect my work performance at my regular job. As it turns out, no one noticed."

Still, she agreed to give radio a shot. Covington paid her a small salary. On air she became his "gal," Axis Sally. She took the moniker from a real person: Mildred Gillars. Born in 1900 in Maine, Gillars had a childhood marred by divorce, poverty, and abuse. She trained to be an actress but her career never took off. She relocated to Germany in the mid-1930s and became an assistant to actress Brigitte Horney, a star of Nazi cinema, and a radio announcer. "It must have seemed to Mildred that she was finally part of a world she long dreamed of," writes her biographer, Richard Lucas. Gillars stayed in Berlin during World War II. She remained behind the microphone on Nazi radio, catching the attention of Joseph Goebbels. Part of Goebbels's propaganda strategy for the regime was radio content targeting American audiences. Gillars began hosting a program called *Home Sweet Home* that was "designed to arouse homesickness in soldiers," according to Lucas. She became known as Axis Sally, "the vixen behind the microphone, taunting the men on the front lines and casting doubt in their minds about their mission, their wives and girlfriends, and their prospects after the war."[2] Her program also spoke to U.S. women, urging them to see the war as contrary to their interests. Didn't they want their lives to go back to normal? Gillars's plea to women—namely white women—was one of self-preservation draped in patriotism:

> The enemies are precisely those people who are fighting Germany today, and in case you don't know it, indirectly against America too.... We are shedding our good young blood for this 'kike' war, for this British war. Oh, girls, why don't you wake up? I mean, after all, the women can do something, can't they?

After the war, Gillars was arrested by U.S. forces. She claimed that she didn't support the Third Reich so much as she opposed the war and that the Nazis had intimidated her into fame. According to the *New York Times,* at her 1949 trial, Gillars "cut a theatrical figure in tight-fitting black dresses, long silver hair, and a deep tan. She had scarlet lips and nails." Gillars was found guilty, becoming the first woman convicted of treason against the United States. She served twelve years in prison, was paroled, and moved back to Ohio, where she lived reclusively until her death in 1988.[3]

As it had for Gillars, being Axis Sally gave Corinna new power. Listeners wrote and called in to say how much they liked her. Phrases like "keep up the good work" and "a definite asset to our cause" peppered the show's online comments section.[4] Covington let her write her own material, and she injected it with wicked humor, setting her apart from her mentor and his bloviating monologues. In one broadcast, Corinna claimed she was endorsing a "lemonade revolution" after law enforcement in Midway, Georgia, stopped three young girls from running a lemonade stand, on account of their not having a business license or permit. What was America coming to,

Corinna wanted to know. She told audiences that she'd looked up the chief of police in Midway, a woman, and had only one thing to say: "Why do ugly bitches always have to ruin everyone's day?"[5] The segment was a knock against political correctness and feminism as much as it was a lament about the purported demise of American culture. The wholesome kind. The white kind.

Corinna, however, was hiding the truth from her fan base, and not only by repeating racist lies. Like Gaede, Covington had quickly disappointed Corinna. He insisted that she bring her daughters to the NWF's Washington office, so that he could put eyes on two Aryan girls. The thought of an aging man sizing up her daughters made her sick to her stomach, the same way the idea of kidnapping the girls had when she was in Kalispell. Corinna said that Covington also "got on [her] case" for not "having more white children."

For some people, that might have been reason enough to quit the NWF. But in her telling, Corinna's breaking point had to do with violence. Not the theoretical kind that she and Covington mused about on *Radio Free Northwest* as one day being necessary to defend a white ethno-state from its enemies. The kind that was already happening.

THE PIPE BOMB was tucked inside a black Swiss Army backpack and left beneath an empty city bench. It held 128 lead fishing weights—that was the shrapnel. The weights were coated with rat poison, which impedes blood clotting, and human feces, which teem with infection-causing bacteria. The bomb's engineer wanted to kill or maim as many people as possible when he remotely triggered the explosion in the middle of the annual Martin Luther King Jr. Day parade in Spokane, Washington.

At 9:25 a.m. on January 17, 2011, city workers spotted the backpack near the corner of North Washington Street and West Main Avenue, an intersection surrounded by office buildings, parking garages, and Hills' Restaurant, a family joint that was famous for its elk burger. The morning was balmy, and the workers were clearing the streets of trash and debris before the parade arrived. Suspicious of the unaccompanied bag, they peeked inside. They saw wires poking out from underneath T-shirts. The workers called law enforcement, who raced to the scene. Officers rerouted the parade and defused the bomb.

After a nearly two-month manhunt, on March 9, federal agents arrested the bomb's engineer in a rural town in northeastern Washington. An Army veteran, thirty-six-year-old Kevin Harpham had reddish-brown hair and scruff on his chin to match. His neighbors knew him as a loner. He was also a white nationalist who had once been a member of the neo-Nazi National Alliance. Harpham would eventually plead guilty to attempted use of a weapon of mass destruction and to a hate crime. He said in court that he'd intended for the bomb to be a protest against multiculturalism.[6]

Nationwide, Harpham's plot and arrest were relatively minor news stories, and not only because the bombing failed. Since the September 11 attacks, domestic terrorism had come to mean something different than it had in the era of the Unabomber and Timothy McVeigh. Now, almost exclusively, it meant radical Islam: al Qaeda, suicide bombers, lone wolves who found recipes for explosives on the internet. This was certainly *a* danger to the world, but American policy makers' frenzied focus on radical Islam diverted attention from other homegrown threats that fed on simmering resentments—the kind embedded in the country's existence, liable to flare up under the right conditions.

According to a 2009 DHS report, "unique drivers for rightwing radicalization and recruitment" had recently emerged, including the recession, stricter gun regulations, and the large number of military veterans struggling to acclimate to civilian life. Most visibly, the occupant of the White House was a black man. "Rightwing extremists are harnessing this historical election as a recruitment tool," the report noted. "[They] have capitalized on related racial and political prejudices in expanded propaganda campaigns, thereby reaching out to a wider audience of potential sympathizers."[7]

The report, authored by an analyst named Daryl Johnson, was talking about material disseminated through venues like *Radio Free Northwest* and Stormfront, which saw a surge in users after Obama's election; there were more than one hundred thousand registrations on Stormfront in 2009 alone.[8] Johnson was also referring to discussions and messaging on newer digital platforms, including Facebook, YouTube, and Twitter. Yet many politicians were loath to acknowledge the truth. In response to anger from conservative lawmakers, the DHS backed off the report, publicly repudiating Johnson's work. Over the next few years, the federal government cut resources dedicated to tracking the far right. Johnson, for his part, left the DHS in 2010, after it dissolved the team he worked on.[9]

The following year, Republican congressman Peter King delivered impassioned remarks pledging that the House Homeland Security Committee, of which he was the chair, would not investigate far-right extremism in any hearings on domestic terrorism:

> This committee cannot live in denial, which is what some would have us do when they suggest that this hearing dilute its focus by investigating threats unrelated to al Qaeda. The Department of Homeland Security and this committee were formed in response to the al Qaeda attacks of 9/11. There is no equivalency of threat between al Qaeda and neo-Nazis, environmental extremists, or other isolated madmen.[10]

Except they weren't isolated madmen (or -women, for that matter). Even if they acted alone in specific instances of violence, a vast, pernicious apparatus of punditry and disinformation fostered their beliefs and choices. To access it, all they needed was an internet connection.

As it happened, King made his speech the day after Kevin Harpham's arrest. Harpham was a known presence on at least one of the hate movement's digital venues. He had posted more than one thousand comments on the Vanguard News Network. In a 2009 post, amid the financial crisis, he wrote, "A lone Wolf would be hard pressed to compete with the level of destruction the jew bankers are doing to the country right now."[11]

Corinna, who was in Port Orchard when Harpham was detained, heard talk that he'd once visited Kalispell. Gaede posted online that she'd never met him.[12] Covington claimed that he didn't know Harpham either. Still, on *Radio Free Northwest,* Covington regurgitated a favorite trope of the hate movement: He said the guy was surely being framed by the FBI, a longtime enemy of the white race. Maybe it was all a conspiracy and the bureau had orchestrated the attack, never intending for it to succeed, just so the federal government could bad-mouth the good people of the white-power cause. In an email to several NWF followers, Covington called Harpham "the poor shlub the FBI has decided to drop into the frame for the mysterious Bionic Backpack incident in Spokane." He also encouraged the message's recipients to consider no longer posting on Stormfront and the Vanguard News Network. "The enemy does monitor these things," Covington wrote, "and anything you say online can and will be held against you, sometimes years later."

Privately Covington went off-script. *At least he did something,* Corinna remembered Covington saying of Harpham one day in the NWF office. He added disparagingly, with a gesture at Corinna and other people in the room, *None of you do anything.*

Corinna told me that she pushed back, saying that a bombing in a city would do more than kill the enemies of white nationalism. It would also kill innocent white people, potential allies. Covington waved her off. *In times of war,* he said, *extreme measures are sometimes necessary.*

A switch didn't flip, exactly: Corinna hadn't liked the NSM. She hadn't liked April Gaede and the PLE. She no longer liked Covington and the NWF. What white nationalism had promised her—meaning and camaraderie—it was no longer providing. The accumulation of disappointments had left her disenchanted and disgusted. Still,

Corinna would later pinpoint Covington's *in times of war* comment as the moment she decided she was done with white nationalism. She wanted out.

Corinna was in so deep that white nationalism had become her livelihood; she didn't have an embalming job at the time. There was also a chance that, in extricating herself, she'd place herself or her daughters in danger. Corinna knew that the FBI had contacted Covington about the Harpham case. She also knew that Covington loathed nothing more than government informants. When a traitor was right under your nose, Covington once said on *Radio Free Northwest,* you should recognize the smell.[13]

One day late in the summer of 2011, while Covington was out, Corinna searched through his shambolic office. Opening stuffed drawers, pushing aside scrap paper on which he drafted scripts, she looked for the card of the FBI agent who'd spoken to Covington. She found it, and on the cusp of dismantling her life, Corinna was calm. When she made a choice, she stuck to it—no second-guessing, no backing out. As soon as she got the chance, she logged into her personal email account and sent a message to the FBI.*

An agent replied. Corinna explained who she was and what she wanted: the bureau's help leaving white nationalism. The agent told her to fly to Spokane that afternoon. She didn't even pack a bag. She caught a flight from Seattle, and men in an SUV with tinted windows picked her up at the airport. One of them she later remembered as

---

*   The FBI's public affairs office declined to confirm or deny Corinna's work as an informant, citing "strict policy." Corinna gave me the names of her FBI handlers. In July 2018, I reached out to one of them. I followed up a few times over several months but never received a reply. Then, unprompted and without my telling her that I had tried to make contact with the FBI, Corinna emailed me in December 2018. "Hey, strange thing happened today," she wrote. "I was contacted by Tacoma FBI who asked to meet with me to discuss my history as an informant. They mentioned you had contacted one of the offices and mentioned the names of the agents I'd worked with. They asked if I could reach out and see if you could change any names or identifying details in the book." I have obliged that request.

being tall with movie-star good looks. He talked to her the most of everyone she met, first over food and later in a conference room in a building not far from where Harpham had left his explosive-laden backpack.

The agents delivered what sounded like a rehearsed speech: *We believe in the First Amendment, and if you want to put flyers on cars that is perfectly fine with us, but we can't have people planting bombs out there.* "I just waited for them to get through it," Corinna told me. "Then I said, 'So how can I help you?'"

The agents said they'd been aware of her for some time. They knew who she was, where she came from, and what she did with the NWF. Before she left white nationalism, they wanted to know if she'd work as an informant. She would provide regular updates on Covington's work and associates. She'd get paid in cash, a few hundred dollars at a time. She'd sign a statement with her code name (Frankie) to acknowledge the payment.

Corinna needed the money. Plus, she'd be a rat under Covington's nose, the ultimate humiliation. She agreed to go undercover.

EXITING HATE IS similar to embracing it. It involves a search for place and purpose, born of personal need. A person doesn't necessarily exit because a veil lifts and they are suddenly able to see hate for what it is. They leave because it makes sense to them and for them. Corinna seemed to know this, writing once on a blog she kept as Axis Sally, "The reality is, people rarely change their personality or ideals during adulthood, and if they do, it needs to be something they do on their own, for themselves."[14]

Leaving white nationalism demands a replacement for the value that hate provides, which sociologists studying deradicalization have described as "an alternative source of self-worth and affirmation." The less stable or available this source, the longer the residue of hate can linger. A person who claims to no longer be in the movement may still display the behaviors that once validated their participation. It isn't unlike the challenge of kicking an addiction: A person may desire change but still feel compelled to do the thing they've always done. With addiction, that might mean sneaking a cigarette or a shot of whiskey. With hate, it can mean acting out animus. A former neo-Nazi, a woman called Bonnie, told researchers in a 2017 study about an incident at a Jack in the Box restaurant where, in her recollection, a Hispanic server got her order wrong and then refused to address the problem. Bonnie's response was to yell, "Fuck you, you fucking Beaner, get out of my country." She also said, "White power!" and even threw a Nazi salute. "Leaving can be a very ambiguous process with no clear demarcation about when it begins or ends," the researchers concluded, "at least partially due to deeply held and felt aspects that reside outside conscious control."[15]

Corinna's exit dragged on for a year and a half. She continued working for the NWF while reporting to the FBI. She sent the bureau emails and handed over her computer for days at a time. She met with agents for meals in Seattle neighborhoods with large LGBTQ or Hispanic populations, places where white nationalists probably wouldn't hang out.

She didn't have actionable information. Covington had the legal right to say what he wanted, and talking seemed to be all he really did. Still, Corinna was able to give the FBI intelligence about how the NWF functioned—a list of donors, for instance, with mailing addresses. Some were in white-nationalist hotbeds like Kalispell and Hayden Lake; others were in Brooklyn and Berkeley. Corinna also provided information about communications between the NWF and white nationalists scattered across the Pacific Northwest, including a married middle-aged couple in Oregon who a few years later would attract media attention with protest signs declaring "Jew Lies Matter" and "Trump: Do the White Thing."[16] She talked about people who contacted her because of her role on Covington's podcast. The FBI "wanted my input on whether these people seemed truly dangerous or were just racist loners," Corinna said. "They had me take a lot of photos of just return addresses on envelopes."

Covington was worried about the NWF's money and membership. "We have a small core of regular and faithful followers who keep me going, many of them elderly people who can't be counted on for too much longer, and we have a few people coming into the area, but they are economically marginal, like so many Whites," he wrote in a May 2011 email to an admirer who hoped to come work, for a salary, with the NWF. Corinna suspected, too, that Covington was unwell. "I've been seeing a few more signs that he's just generally losing it—misplacing money and books; sending people thank-you letters for donations they did not send; and greater-than-usual hypochondriac fits," she wrote in a message to the FBI, which she shared with me. "He also said that at this time next year, the NVA"—the Northwest Volunteer Army, which Covington claimed would lead an insurgency against the U.S. government—"will be fully formed and operational. I haven't known him long enough to say if this is a claim he makes every year or not, but I guess we'll know more later."

Juggling reconnaissance with life inside the NWF was a study in tension. As Axis Sally, Corinna continued to deliver monologues thick with vitriol. On her blog, she dispensed radical advice, often to women. "The white race is going extinct and we must increase our numbers at any cost," she wrote in one post. "There is no excuse for a white woman to look like ass. Women of our race should, on average, be more attractive than women of other races," she declared in another. "If you don't love what you see in the mirror every day, you're doing something wrong and it's your own fault. So fix it." Complacency about physical appearance, Corinna continued, meant less chance of finding a man to have white children with. Plus, it gave degenerates an opening. "One day, some guy is going to walk by you in high heels and everyone will think he looks better than you," she wrote, referring to transgender women.

The FBI wanted her to cool it. If a white nationalist committed violence and claimed Axis Sally as inspiration, the agency would have some explaining to do. She told me that her handlers said she could keep doing the podcast and writing online, but that she needed to soften her rhetoric. Problem being, her followers didn't want that. Neither did Corinna. If she had to be Axis Sally, she wanted to be good at it—scarily good, the kind of good that prompted complimentary emails, good to the point that listeners thought she should have her own show. For Corinna, as ever, it was all or nothing.

In the summer of 2012, she stopped appearing on *Radio Free Northwest*. By then she had more stability: She'd started working as an embalmer again, and she had her own apartment. She saw her kids now and then. She kept posting on her blog, inhabiting the role of an outspoken white nationalist, but her tone grew taunting. "Why is it that no matter what a skinhead does, he considers himself to be 'fighting on the front lines'?" she wrote in a September 2012 post. "Whether it's playing foosball with the bros, whining at his mom that he needs more clean laundry or knocking stuff off the shelves at 7-11 in a drunken fit at 3am, he is ON THE FRONT LINES!!! Fighting for the GREAT WHITE RACE!!!" In another message she asked coyly, "What parts of the things Axis Sally says are Corinna's own feelings, and what are things that just go perfectly with the Axis Sally persona you all know? Of course I'll just say, 'If you can't tell, why should I?'"

She let other interests fill more of her time. She wrote on her blog that she was training for bodybuilding competitions more intensely than ever. "I realized, the only way to protect my family is to be bigger than those who would try to hurt them," she once said. "I could carry weapons all the time or learn martial arts. But personally, I would rather prevent an altercation in the first place. What's better: kicking the ass of someone who grabs your child, or looking so damn scary they never touch your kid in the first place? Why not ask the child?" She started to pack on muscle by going to the gym for at least two hours every day and maintaining a strict high-protein diet.

Bodybuilding gave Corinna's life order. She penciled competitions into her calendar, including many that she went on to win. "It was one of the few things I was good at," she told me. "I was being seen. I was getting attention." She had a coach and acquaintances in the bodybuilding community, including people of color with whom she was in close proximity backstage at shows, slipping into spandex and lathering on bronzer. She didn't mind; she even went on dates with a few black men, reveling in the fact that Covington had no idea she was defying him. Whereas once Corinna might have flexed her muscles for judges in time with a white-power rock soundtrack, now she was annoyed that she had to spend time covering her racist tattoos with heavy makeup.

In late 2012, she told her FBI handlers that she wanted to stop working as an informant. But Corinna didn't slink away from white nationalism. She wanted payback and, perhaps, a last dose of the attention she'd basked in as Axis Sally. She took her listeners' advice and twisted it, producing a new website and podcast, which debuted in January 2013. The first episode, entitled "Axis Sally Comes Clean," described her disillusionment with Covington and white nationalism. In no uncertain terms, she described the far right as a bunch of idiots and criminals too inept to launch a political movement of any kind, mired in petty resentments of everything and everyone they saw as holding white people back—including one another.

Covington told his followers that he barely knew Corinna and continued running the NWF as if nothing had happened.[17] Other white nationalists were furious. Hundreds of comments accumulated online, calling Corinna a slut, a race traitor, and a Jew. One racist troll took to calling her Axis Skanky, insisted that she was an "off-breed mongrel," and said that her daughters, whom men in the movement had sniffed around for so long, probably weren't even white—their bodies were wasted commodities.

For all the anger, however, no one came after Corinna. Maybe it was because her podcast didn't rank as a damaging concern when she could be dismissed out of hand as a degenerate. Corinna didn't admit in her tell-all episodes that she'd been an FBI informant. That was a secret she decided to keep, at least for a while.

5.

In the summer of 2013, the SPLC came calling. It interviewed Corinna about her exit for its flagship publication, *Intelligence Report*. A young man was interviewed too: Derek Black, the son of Stormfront founder Don Black, who in college had renounced the movement of which he was a scion. Corinna appeared in photos wearing a patterned sundress—blocks of paisley alternating with swatches of floral print. Her hair was dyed brown, and her frame was bulky from the steroids she'd started taking for bodybuilding. Pink blush shone on her cheeks, and she gazed into the camera with heavily shadowed eyes.

Corinna outlined her life story and the reasons she'd decided to leave the hate movement. "I realized, okay, no, people of other races have never done anything to me or my children in the way white nationalists have. This is the real enemy," she told the SPLC. "I realized much too late that this entire movement is a huge waste of life."[1]

She wanted to make up for it. Corinna approached the Portland police to tell them what she knew about the shooting of Luke Querner in 2010. She got her racist tattoos covered up: a fairy over Hitler's face, an ocean wave over the 14 Words, a rose over *Sieg Heil* and the swastika. She had a portion of that last one surgically removed, but it never healed properly. One night in her apartment, Corinna ripped open the incision stitched up on her lower back. She was on pain-killers and had convinced herself that she could do the sutures better than a nurse or doctor. Blood oozed fast and crimson into her sink while Corinna sat on the porcelain edge, watching, with a scalpel in her hand. When the wound eventually scarred over, it looked like an ugly, twisting gash of pink.

For a while Corinna got lost again, this time in an obsession with her body. She wanted it to be big and tight and tan. She spent thousands of dollars on steroids and plastic surgery in preparation for bodybuilding competitions. "I was chasing perfection," she told me. "I had a twenty-three-inch waist—but what if it were twenty-two?" Liposuction. A breast enhancement. Two more after that. The anesthesia made her sick for days but she kept going back for more. She once had seven procedures done in a single surgery. At the last minute, before going under, she asked the doctor what she could get for another $1,800, all the money she had left to spend. The doctor offered to remove a mole from her face. "So instead of a mole, I have a scar," Corinna told me.

In 2016, her tank ran dry—of money, of health, of interest. She was doing so much to look good in other people's eyes, yet there was no one in her life she could ask to give her a ride home after surgery. Once again, she extricated herself from a culture that she'd let overtake her. She quit bodybuilding. To avoid feeling exposed for too long, however, she would have to slip on a new identity.

She'd started a new blog, *The Last Person You Want to Meet,* where she ruminated about death and the funeral industry. Sometimes she responded to other bloggers who wrote about the same topics, members of a new digital community. Usually, though, she wrote short personal essays. Corinna's prose was that of a loner burdened by the impulses of cynicism and empathy, which she struggled to reconcile. She didn't understand or relate to most people, but she felt connected to the dead and the people mourning them. "No one wants to know about my best day on the job; about times when I really came through for someone or went far above and beyond or made old Mrs. Jones smile when she saw that I remembered to put the teddy bear in the casket," she wrote in the blog's first post. "They want to hear things that will make them cringe and make them glad they work in an office with a desk and a lamp." Corinna continued:

> The worst things I have ever seen are the unlimited horrors one person can inflict upon another. Chances are, what you worry about possibly happening to your child, or your wife, I have seen. What you pay money to watch in a slasher movie, I can see just by showing up at work tomorrow.
>
> I never watch scary movies anymore. It's not entertainment. It's a personal tragedy that I will deal with from every angle. While you're watching people die or get dismembered on screen, I'm picking up the pieces. Literally. And still talking to the surviving family a year later.[2]

She described waking up crying from a recurring dream about Harley. She knew by then that Harley hadn't been a racist skinhead; he'd been a punk antifascist. In the dream, he wasn't dead. Corinna asked him what happened and how he survived, but he didn't speak. When she woke up with a start and realized the dream wasn't real, Corinna tried to go back to sleep so that she could see Harley again. "If you have ever asked anyone if your grief reactions are normal, I already know they are," she wrote on the blog. "Normalcy cannot be measured in how long you cry, how often you visit the grave, or how soon you go back to work. Normalcy is only about how you assimilate the loss into your life, as a permanent, unwanted, irreversible change, and what is normal for you may not be normal for another."[3]

Eventually, she wrote about the human impulse to find significance, no matter how difficult. "People are often forced to adapt and overcome," she said. "People serving life sentences can do things to find meaning and purpose in their lives. People who have become paralyzed, who are terminally ill, who suffer loss after loss can find something else that keeps them going and gives them a reason to get out of bed."[4] Corinna's reason was her work and her daughters, with whom she began to make amends just as the older one became a teenager. Adolescence—with its moods, navel-gazing, and defiance of authority—became a new source of distance, but a more normal one.

What Corinna didn't have was a community. She still yearned for the ritual, belief, and bond that hate once gave her. By the time I met her in 2018, she'd found it.

WHEN SHE FINISHED her to-do list of picking up bodies and attending funerals, Corinna drove to a busy intersection bounded by the colorful signage of chain stores: Safeway, Starbucks, Dollar Tree. She steered past the beckoning logos and eased her van onto a rocky driveway that led to a cluster of nondescript buildings. Nailed to one panel of brown siding was a small hand-painted sign. It had an arrow, pointing to the right, and a word written in both English and Arabic: *mosque.*

A few months before I visited her, Corinna had converted to Islam. She exhibited the requisite zeal of a convert. She attended prayers as often as possible, read biographies of the prophet Muhammad, and covered most of her body with clothing. When we arrived at the mosque, she went into the women's bathroom with an armload of fabric she planned to swap for her work clothes. She emerged wearing a hijab and a flowing patterned abaya. She had told me to dress conservatively, so despite the summer heat, I'd worn jeans and a long-sleeved blouse that day. But the outfit wouldn't be enough for the mosque, Corinna said. She loaned me a khaki trench coat and an extra hijab she always kept in the van, just in case.

We walked into the women's portion of the mosque, a spare, carpeted space with oscillating fans hanging above several windows, their blinds drawn. As women and children gathered, the air thickened, and the tallest people in the group reached high to click the fans on. It didn't do much good, but no one seemed to mind. I sat in the back against a wall, sweating and trying to be inconspicuous. Corinna made her way to the front and dropped to her knees. Other women—most of whom had black or brown skin—were loose, almost casual, going through motions they seemed to have done more times than they could count. Corinna, though, kept her legs and feet pressed tightly together and her core muscles clenched as she leaned forward to touch her forehead to the carpet.

When the prayers ended, the women chatted in a jumble of languages. The mosque was selling Styrofoam containers of chicken and rice as part of a fundraiser, and the smell of purchased meals wafted through the room. "Sister Corinna!" I heard several women crow happily when they saw her. She offered a slight but genuine smile in response to each greeting, along with *"as salaam alaikum"* (peace be unto you).

Why Islam? Corinna didn't seem to understand why anyone would find her choice strange. She liked how the religion gave structure to her days. The mosque was a place to go where there were people she knew. She liked that Islam was a topic she could learn about from books. Keeping her body covered meant that it was hers and no one else's. "It is freeing, actually, to feel like I'm taking something away from men," she told me.

Maybe, I thought, there were other reasons for her conversion. It made her conspicuous, and she knew it. "I'm 5 feet tall and probably the only white girl in a headscarf," she'd quipped in an email before we first met, letting me know how to spot her at the Mediterranean grill in a strip mall where we were getting dinner. Corinna was embracing a culture that she knew frightened or enraged many white Americans. "Meeting a journalist. Hope we don't get murdered," she tweeted before our dinner—her acknowledgment, it seemed, that Muslims and journalists can both be kindling for right-wing rage. Corinna was also sticking it to the racists she'd once considered friends. She bragged online about ordering a Black Lives Matter T-shirt and a Nike hijab to wear while working out so that she could "offend multiple people." For good measure she tacked on the hashtag #umadbro.

Corinna claimed that she tried to avoid news about the hate movement; it made her too mad. That summer, she found out a few weeks after the fact that Covington had died at the age of sixty-four. (She wouldn't gloat about his death, Corinna told me, but she wasn't sad either.) Her social media told a different story. She shared articles posted by the SPLC and mocked or lashed out at white nationalists. She called them names like "human garbage" and "crybabies." Sometimes she used the hashtag #killnazis.[5]

When I asked about the disturbing language, Corinna shrugged— she figured that most people reading or watching her content were white nationalists, so why not provoke them. But was she anxious about possible reprisals? "I have worried, but I guess it's one of those things where you can't just live in fear all the time," Corinna replied. "I figured whatever came my way as a punishment was something I deserved for the mistakes that I made."

Sometimes she trained her ire on people who had joined the hate movement after she left it. They claimed that they were different from the bigots who came before them because they had a powerful, attainable vision for America, one that any rational white person could get behind, one that the new president all but endorsed. "The aim of most of these groups," Corinna told me, "is making it normal."

She recognized their vision perfectly.

Part II

AYLA

Is she
at home nowhere? Is she
a born wanderer, in other words
an existential
replica of her own mother, less
hamstrung by ideas of causality?

—Louise Glück, "Persephone the Wanderer"

1.

As viral content goes, the photograph was a blockbuster, accumulating more than ten million likes and three hundred thousand comments on Instagram. First published on July 13, 2017, it showed music megastar Beyoncé cradling her one-month-old twins against her naked torso, standing beachside in front of an arch laced with lush flower blossoms. A pale teal veil was affixed to her rippling blond hair, and a sheer purple robe cascaded from her shoulders to her bare feet. Her head was tilted so that her face caught the sunlight beaming down from the clear blue sky. In the distance was a blurry horizon where ocean met air.[1]

The image was a visual echo of Beyoncé's famous pregnancy photos, released earlier the same year. The aesthetic was inspired by art dating back centuries: Beyoncé was Raphael's Madonna, Botticelli's Venus, the Virgin of Guadalupe. She was a black woman inserting herself into a canon that so rarely depicted figures of color, much less glorified them. "She appears as not one but many women—or, instead, maybe the universal woman and mother," an art history professor at New York University told *Harper's Bazaar*.[2]

When she saw the photo, Ayla Stewart had a different take.[3] She wondered why people had such reverence for Beyoncé, the kind Ayla believed should be reserved for the divine. A devoutly Christian mother of six with a round, dimpled face and wide blue eyes, Ayla decided to denounce what she saw as idolatry. As Beyoncé's image ricocheted around the internet, Ayla screen-grabbed it. She juxtaposed the photo with a painting of the Virgin Mary and an infant Jesus, encircled by gilded haloes. Ayla captioned the side-by-side comparison "Tubillardine Whiskey (1952) vs. Kool-Aid." Mary was the vintage; Beyoncé was the fake stuff.

Ayla shared the meme on Twitter, where she kept an account under the name Wife with a Purpose. Reactions were swift, and some were furious. "Girl, fuck you," one Twitter user wrote. "I haven't beat anyone up all year so I'm ready to fight."[4] The website Bossip included Ayla in a roundup of "mediocre mayo packets who spent their whole entire pay day splattering not-very-subtle racism all over Al Gore's world wide web" because they didn't like Beyoncé's photo.[5] In Ayla's case, the racism was in the association between Kool-Aid and African Americans, a long-standing stereotype implying that black people enjoy—or can only afford—cheap, childish, and unhealthy things.

Among friends, Ayla expressed dismay at the accusations that the meme was racist. "I honestly wasn't trying to be," she wrote in a private online forum, later leaked for anyone to read.[*] "It was a commentary on how they worship her." Ayla said that "black twitter" was coming after her, sending her "hundreds of threats." She was supposed to speak at a public event in a month. What if it wasn't safe for her to attend?

People told Ayla not to worry. "Black twitter doesn't even know how to navigate," wrote someone with the handle Americana—MD. "There's a reason no nigger ever set sail (unless we made them) or learned to navigate via celestial bodies."

---

[*] The chat logs were leaked by the left-wing media collective Unicorn Riot.

"But gps?" Ayla replied, punctuating the question with a laughing emoji.

"Don't lie @Americana—MD you KNOW those two nigres mathematicians put our men on the moon!!!" another user chimed in.[*]

"KANGZ!" Ayla wrote. "I love our folk." Later in the conversation, she said of Beyoncé, "She's the perfect poster girl for blacks going white when they have enough money to."[6]

In this exchange, context was everything. The conversation took place on Discord, a messaging app launched in 2015 to facilitate communication in the online gaming world; it could handle text, images, video, and audio.[7] Because Discord prioritized anonymity and privacy, it quickly attracted users who didn't necessarily care about gaming, including far-right activists hoping to disseminate information and organize events away from the prying eyes of critics. Ayla was using a server—how Discord referred to its private chat rooms—called Charlottesville 2.0. It was one of the main planning forums for Unite the Right. The August 2017 rally in Virginia was the event where Ayla was slated to speak, the one she was now nervous to attend. Charlottesville 2.0 had subservers dedicated to topics like car pools, lodging, and propaganda. "If you're good at making memes or promotional materials for events like this, please post your creations here," an organizer wrote in the forum #promotion_and_cyberstrike. "Use that meme magic to make Charlottesville OUR territory."[8]

Meme culture was key to understanding Ayla's use of the words "folk" and "kangz" in the exchange about Beyoncé. By 2017, both were staples of far-right internet lingo. "Folk" was a collective term for white nationalists. Nonthreatening on its surface, it connoted tribe and tradition. But it was also a less-than-subtle reference to the German term *volk* ("people"). In the Nazi era, *volk* wasn't merely a people—it was *the* people, superior and inviolable. *Volk* signified both

---

[*] They were referring, presumably, to the plot of the 2016 movie *Hidden Figures*, about black women who worked for NASA during the Space Race.

Aryan identity and collective ideology; someone couldn't really be part of the *volk* if they didn't support the Third Reich's mission to purify its empire.* With its blind nativism and hero worship, Trumpism had tapped into the notion that there was one people worthier than others—in this case, white Americans who supported the president. "Under Trumpism, no defense of the *volk* is a betrayal, even if it undermines the republic," Adam Serwer would write in *The Atlantic* in 2019, "and no attack on the *volk*'s hegemony can be legitimate, even if it is a defense of democracy."[9] Most Trump supporters proclaimed their identity with the MAGA imprimatur. The far right, though, went to the heart of the matter and sometimes called themselves "folk."

"Kangz" originated on the website 4chan. It sometimes took longer forms—"we wuz kangz" or "kangz and shiet." The word was slang for "kings," intended to mimic phonetic stereotypes of black Americans' speech patterns. Internet trolls used it to mock the notion that white power structures, from European colonialism to U.S. law enforcement, had suppressed black freedom. If it weren't for white people, the joke went, black people would be royalty. Kangz was bigotry cloaked as satire. One meme in the kangz universe was a photo of a black man dressed as a pharaoh with the caption "Claim he trace his lineage back to king tut doesn't even know his father." Another meme showed an image of an abandoned, dilapidated house in Detroit, with the words "We wuz kings of Egypt while whiteys were living in da caves."

Writing "kangz"—to say nothing of skipping over Discord users' slurs or agreeing to speak at Unite the Right—was incompatible with Ayla's claim that she wasn't racist. Yet she seemed to register no inconsistency. Ayla had established herself as one of the internet's most vocal proponents of tradlife, short for "traditional lifestyle," a

---

* "Everything is spiced with a soupçon of *Volk*," writer Victor Klemperer, who documented the Nazi period, noted in 1933. "*Volksfest* (festival of the people), *Volksgenosse* (comrade of the people), *Volksgemeinschaft* (community of the people), *volksnah* (one of the people), *volksfremd* (alien to the people), *volksentstammt* (descended from the people)."

movement advocating retrograde values and hierarchies between men and women, states and citizens, God and humankind. She believed that white, Christian, heterosexual people, who represented all that was natural and good in America, were under threat from immigrants, feminists, liberals, and LGBTQ people. "Tired," Ayla once typed in red letters over an Instagram image of two transgender women of color; "woke," she wrote over an adjoining photograph of a large white family.

Ayla always insisted that she loved all God's children and even prayed for the ones who didn't agree with her worldview. It wasn't racist, she said, to believe that people should stay in their cultural lanes and within their national borders. A few months before the Beyoncé controversy, just after Trump's victory, she had tweeted another photographic comparison—her favorite type of meme, it seemed—of a black woman and a white one. The black woman wore a turban and dress cut from a colorful wax print. The white woman's blond hair was twisted into a long, thick braid that poured over her peasant blouse. The images were supposed to represent pan-African and pan-European aesthetics. "You preserve your culture and people and I'll preserve mine," Ayla wrote beneath the images. "You're not racist and neither am I."

Ayla didn't hesitate to malign critics of tradlife—or, really, anyone who refused to embrace the culture. If they didn't model their lives on the values of the past, they were lazy, or worse. "None of this degenerate behavior should we accept as normal practice," Ayla once said. "When people speak out against it, we shouldn't label them phobics or try to shame them for speaking out in favor of normal, healthy standards." In her mind, people who agreed with her were courageous.

Ayla claimed that she knew what she was talking about. She'd been one of the degenerates, one of those "losers who don't try."[10] At thirty-eight, she was a nationalist and a traditionalist. At twenty-eight, she'd been a liberal and a feminist.

WHENEVER SHE TOLD the story of her life, Ayla described a gradual awakening—a realization that the media and America's raging liberal culture had taught her to hate herself, her femininity, and her race. The first time I heard this story, in 2017, I was watching tradlife videos on YouTube. There was Ayla on my laptop, telling me how her journey from left to right saved her soul. She'd filmed herself at home; the footage was a little grainy. Ayla's earnest face filled the center of the frame, making it seem as if her sole focus was the viewer. To her right was a sliding glass door leading to a yard where a yellow jogging stroller sat next to a wood fence—evidence of domestic contentment.

There was no doubt that, in some ways, Ayla had changed her mind. Whereas she'd once believed in LGBTQ rights, she now called for making same-sex relationships taboo. She'd previously listened to Amy Goodman host *Democracy Now!* but these days preferred reading far-right pundits with names like Vox Day and RamZPaul. Still, in the midst of so much that was different, there were familiar notes. Throughout her life, Ayla had been in zealous pursuit of meaning; tradlife was just her latest aspiration. And in the models of whiteness and Christianity that she promoted were echoes of other women who had weaponized normalcy to advance racist initiatives. "Dear Haters," Ayla wrote on Instagram, next to a photo of two of her children hugging. "The normalcy will increase, until your morale improves. Love Ayla."

In proudly showing off her life, Ayla demanded to know one thing: If all she wanted was safety, prosperity, and health for her family and nation, how could she be considered hateful? It was a disingenuous defensive trick, and she was far from the first woman to use it. Historian Elizabeth Gillespie McRae, whose research focuses on resistance to the civil rights movement, has described the profound impact of "politics that emphasized performing whiteness as synonymous with 'good' womanhood."[11] In the hate movement, many women have found agency and purpose in this role. As wives and mothers, they support loved ones while also serving a higher racial cause. When someone criticizes their politics, they express dismay. "I don't cuss," Ayla assured her online followers. "I don't attack people. Nothing."

By the time Unite the Right was on the horizon, Ayla was staging an increasingly exaggerated performance of good white womanhood. The same week that the controversy over the Beyoncé meme erupted, Ayla ruminated on ladylike behavior. What were the most important dos and don'ts? She compiled a ten-point list on her personal blog. Don't gossip, step lightly, dress modestly, speak softly—certainly don't use "urban accents," a prohibition that seemed to reference the same stereotypes that birthed "kangz." Also, ladies should learn "womanly arts" like cooking and sewing and biological conception.

Ayla tried to fit the mold she described. She wore long skirts and loose tops to avoid showing her curves and skin. She shared recipes for spelt biscuits. Her children were a testament to her ability to conceive. If she failed at anything on her list, it was perhaps the seventh count: "A lady does not argue or forcefully assert her opinions in an uncomfortable way when with her family and friends." Ayla spoke her mind all the time, demanding a restoration of old-fashioned values and deference to white culture. But maybe, in her mind, she got a pass? She mostly argued with people who didn't agree with her—losers and slanderers, enemies of whiteness. Maybe her adversaries were bad enough, and the topics she cared about consequential enough, to warrant unladylike exertions.

One way or the other, if being vocally nostalgic for the past was a sin, Ayla wasn't about to repent. Invoking ideals of femininity rooted in whiteness—Beyoncé need not apply—Ayla compared the America she yearned for to the world of Jessica and Elizabeth Wakefield, the twin teenage protagonists created by young-adult author Francine Pascal. "If things stay on track," Ayla warned on Instagram, "one day, Sweet Valley Twins books will be illegal for featuring two blond, straight, skinny, girls, whose parents were still married and live in a place called

Sweet Valley, where there were no mall shootings, no illegals, no homosexuals*, no transgenders, no Muslims, everyone spoke English and the internet, blissfully, didn't exist. A land where girls still baked cookies for the boys and mom's prioritized their homes.

"This was the America of my youth and there was nothing wrong with it," Ayla concluded. "It was a lovely culture just as valid as any other culture on earth."

---

* There are gay characters in the Sweet Valley High series, including the twins' brother, Steve, and Jake Farrell, a character in book number seventy-five.

2.

Her name wasn't always Ayla. She was born Erin Donnelly in a small town in Tennessee. For much of her life, she thought that she had roots in Europe and America. "A Mennonite boy from the Rheinland stepped off a boat, a Scottish sailor had a family in America as well as Scotland and members of the Powhatan nation shad fished in the waters near modern day Maryland," she wrote on a blog she started as an adult. "What do they all have in common? Me!" Later, she would claim that a DNA test revealed she had no Native American roots—she was "100% European."

In Ayla's telling, when she was two, she was baptized in the Episcopal church. The same year, her parents moved the family west. They relocated to Las Vegas and kept a second home in bucolic Beaver, Utah, where Butch Cassidy was born. More recently, Beaver's claim to fame is having America's "#1 water," as advertised on a billboard towering next to Interstate 15. Judged by the National Rural Water Association's Great American Water Taste Test,[1] the delicious stuff flows from the Tushar Mountains. When Ayla's family visited Beaver, she loved playing in that water, wading in a river that ran near their house.

She was an energetic kid who danced, did gymnastics, and ice-skated.

She went to a high school specializing in international studies and the arts. She studied German and spent time in Europe. It was cold and rainy when Ayla visited Paris with a school group. She posed for a photo next to Notre-Dame wearing an oversize black jacket and khaki-colored pants, her blond hair pulled into a low ponytail.

Ayla's teenage years were typical enough for a white American girl in the 1990s. A friend from back then, who asked to remain anonymous, described her to me as shy, bookish, and square—she didn't drink or smoke or get in trouble.[2] She danced to Tori Amos songs in her bedroom and loved U2 so much that she and her friends threw parties on the band members' birthdays. She had a "jones" for the undead, as she once described it, seeing *Interview with the Vampire* multiple times in theaters and later becoming a fan of *Buffy the Vampire Slayer*. She read fashion magazines and watched MTV. Images of models and actresses made her feel inadequate. Ayla was pretty, but she didn't think so. "I had curves, large hips, and short legs," she once wrote, "and my mind took that to a teenage extreme that saw myself as nothing short of the creature from the black lagoon." She became obsessed with diet and exercise, and she would later credit her high-school boyfriend with helping her overcome her negative thinking about her body. "He loved me and that gave me the external validation that allowed me to come back from the brink of self-destruction," she wrote.

Another development helped too: finishing high school and moving out of her house, away from her mother, a registered nurse who mostly stayed at home with her daughters. "She cooked every meal, she sewed Halloween costumes and went to our school functions," Ayla later said in a radio interview. "But she acted as though she hated it." Ayla also described her mother as abusive: "[She] took out her anger on her children physically. Beating her children was her release."[*]

As a young adult, she decided to call herself something other than

---

[*] According to an online obituary, Ayla's mother died in 2012.

the name her mother gave her. She chose Ayla, which is found in several languages, including Turkish, where it describes the halo of light around the moon. She eventually took a second, related name: Serenemoon. Various cultures associate the moon with motherhood—with the menstrual cycle, for instance, and with goddess figures. Ayla Serenemoon wanted to become a mother one day. A good one. The kind of mother other women would look up to.

First, though, she went to college. She was married by then, having tied the knot with her high-school boyfriend when she was nineteen. She studied German and anthropology at the University of Nevada, Las Vegas. Outside of the classroom, she practiced yoga and explored New Age culture. When she started suffering from panic attacks—she attributed them to stress and past abuse—she chose meditation and St. John's wort over Zoloft. She read extensively about astrology, the Wiccan faith, and pagan goddess worship. She dedicated herself to natural living, which included becoming a vegan, studying midwifery, and disavowing vaccines.

By the time she finished college, in 2002, she considered herself a feminist and was committed to radical autonomy—over her body, her lifestyle, and her family. She saw making unconventional choices about her circumstances as brave, even righteous. Ayla's mother wanted her to put her college degree to use by becoming a linguist. Instead, Ayla got pregnant. "I said, no, this is my dream," she later recalled. "This is what I want to do with my life. And she just really was very upset about that."

Ayla's first son was born in 2003, several weeks past his due date. Ayla had him at home, with a midwife, though she'd wanted to have an unassisted birth. "Every night before I went to sleep I dreamed of catching my own baby," she wrote of the weeks leading up to the birth. She claimed that her family had badgered her into having a midwife present, and even then some of them were judgmental. "My own sister didn't talk to me until a month after my son was born because she was convinced I was going to 'kill my baby' by having him at home," Ayla wrote. She regretted giving in. She felt that the midwife hadn't listened to her, insisting that she use a birthing chair and lie on her back instead of squatting when it was time to push. Ayla had wanted to be the first person her baby saw and to hold him before he was cleaned, but the midwife didn't honor those plans. "Most women have to use all their courage just to have a home birth in our society at all, let alone have any courage to birth alone," Ayla wrote in a personal essay, published in a niche magazine called *Birth Love* a few months after her son arrived. "My experience taught me that simply having a home birth was not enough for me, and that I have to fight harder to educate other women as well as myself."

Ayla wanted to share her beliefs and experiences. Indeed, she felt called to do so. She'd become what she'd always wanted to be— a mother—and relished the opportunity to raise a child and connect with other women. She took her infant son to yoga classes with her, where she "gently guided other moms toward vaccine and circumcision alternatives. It was a give and take of support, information and sisterhood." A friend from back then told me that Ayla emphasized health—her definition of it—above all else.[3]

Then her marriage collapsed. She told the old friend with whom I spoke that it was because her husband felt like she'd become a different person. In an interview, Ayla told me that her husband left her when their son was only a few months old, that he came from a line of men who'd done the same before him.[*] Suddenly, Ayla was a single mother in her midtwenties without a career. She bounced from Nevada to Utah to Northern California looking for someone, or something, to anchor her life. She didn't want an occupation; she wanted a family.

She found what she was looking for in the small town of Willits, California, situated in Mendocino County at the edge of the redwood forests. His name was Seth, and Ayla was "impressed with his quick

---

[*]   I reached out to her ex-husband online and didn't receive a reply.

wit, his calm and gentle nature and his broad shoulders." They dated for three months and often visited NorCal beaches together. "Even though the water was literally freezing, Seth would jump in and swim," Ayla once wrote on a blog, beneath a snapshot of Seth dripping wet in a black T-shirt and gym shorts, walking barefoot across the sand toward the camera with a wide grin on his long, lean face. They decided to spend the rest of their lives together. "It was a quick whirl-wind romance but the second we started dating we just knew we were a family, that we were meant to be together," Ayla wrote. Like her, Seth was liberal, committed to green living, and eager to have kids. When they had their first child together, no midwife was present. Seth helped Ayla deliver the baby in their living room. He understood, Ayla later wrote, "that motherhood was a unique and special calling."

That calling eventually led Ayla back to school. In 2005, she started a master's program in women's spirituality at New College of California. The San Francisco–based school had a decidedly progressive bent; its slogan was "education for a just, sacred, and sustainable world."* Ayla still lived in Mendocino County, so she commuted two and a half hours to attend classes. NCOC owned buildings around the Bay Area, including a former mortuary in the Mission District and the Roxie, a beloved art-house movie theater with a neon marquee that the college's administration had saved from demolition.

The women's spirituality degree stood at the intersection of feminism and faith. Participants studied the sacred feminine, a concept popularized in 1970s New Age circles that rejected the male-centric nature of Christianity and other monotheistic faiths. Advancing women's spirituality was about identifying the divine in female experiences across cultures and throughout history. It was about encouraging women to embrace their female energy, which acolytes believed was associated with empathy, justice, and nurturing. The sacred feminine

---

* NCOC lost accreditation in 2008, and the women's spirituality program relocated to another area college.

enjoyed a moment in the spotlight with Dan Brown's bestselling novel *The Da Vinci Code;* the plot revolves around Mary Magdalene giving birth to Jesus's child and the Catholic Church spending two millennia trying to erase proof of her vital—and sexual—contributions to Christianity.

In an interview, one of Ayla's professors at NCOC remembered her as smart, provocative, and defiant. She wanted "to be different" and "really, really radical about whatever she [was] doing," the professor told me.[4] That included unassisted birth, which Ayla championed in the program but which her cohort of students—roughly ten women, the professor recalled, most of them in their forties or fifties—found too extreme. They were looking for intellectual stimulation and spiritual fulfillment. "The other women were at a point where they were really focusing on seizing their lives," the professor told me. "They'd already been mothers. They'd already stayed at home in some sense, or been locked into something that they were finally breaking out of after midlife, and they were starting to take up the questions 'Who am I? And what am I doing here?'" In hindsight, the professor added, Ayla may have felt like an outsider.

For her thesis, Ayla chose to study home birth in traditional, conservative communities, including Mormons. She'd grown up around Mormons in Nevada and Utah, but her mother had warned her to stay away from them. "She said they wanted to convert everyone and that they thought the end of the world was coming and that only Mormons would be saved," Ayla once said. She became curious about the faith because she knew several midwives who practiced it, as did some members of Seth's family. Based on her reading of Mormon history, Ayla developed an argument that, because founder Joseph Smith's wife Emma had been integral to the church's genesis and spiritual underpinnings, Mormon women felt empowered to make relatively independent choices, including ones about how to be mothers. This was among the reasons, Ayla said, that home birth persisted in popularity among members of the Church of Jesus Christ of Latter-Day Saints, even as most American women delivered in hospitals.

It was a contrarian take on a notoriously patriarchal culture, which in its most fundamentalist form can be oppressive and exploitative of women and girls. Ayla's revisionism suggested that, thanks to motherhood, Mormon women had more agency than outside observers assumed—more, certainly, than women coerced into using the medical establishment, where male physicians took away their choices. Meanwhile, Ayla believed that the media pushed an unfair message on mothers-to-be: *You will fail miserably unless you're in the presence of a doctor.*

When she presented her thesis, Ayla donned sturdy hiking sandals and a floral dress with cap sleeves. Her shoulder-length hair, recently died a deep blue, was partially hidden by a white kerchief. Behind the podium, before her classmates and teachers, she wore her toddler son in a sling and nursed him. In a room full of women deeply in touch with their femininity, she seemed to savor standing out as the most maternal. She was, as she described herself on one of the many social networks she joined around this time, "a radical, primal mama."

AYLA WAS SKEPTICAL of the mainstream media. She once said that she didn't trust the *Washington Post* to tell "real news," nearly a decade before phrases like "fake news" and "lamestream media" became part of the vernacular. Her daily media diet ranged across the ideological spectrum, from a then-fledgling Infowars to *Angry Black Bitch,* a blog run by liberal activist Pamela Merritt.

Ayla launched a new personal blog midway through her master's degree program. This was near the height of blogging's popularity. By 2007, there were some seventy million blogs online, whereas in 1999, there had been fewer than fifty.[5] "Mommy blogging" was on the rise, and Ayla jumped on the trend. She called her site *Mother, Lover,*

Goddess. She wanted to share political opinions—support for immigration, opposition to the death penalty, defense of parental rights—alongside raw food recipes and photographs of family camping trips. She also wanted to be "a voice of solidarity and hope for all moms out there in internet world." Ayla believed that motherhood should be an unbreakable bond among women.

Some of her first blog posts were about being poor. Seth, who then worked as a day laborer, didn't make much money. "This month I have almost no spending cash, with school coming up I need to save where I can," Ayla wrote in December 2005. "But money is also about the flow of karma which is why I chose to spend what cash I could in...small mom and pop shops." Ayla struggled to figure out how the family could eat organic meals—often an expensive prospect—on food stamps. "I'm thinking of striking a compromise. Buying some local produce that is on sale each month at the local grocery store and then buying the rest organic at the co-op," she wrote. She was frustrated that the global economy and Americans' food preferences made it unaffordable to eat the way she wanted to. "What if we weren't feeding all that grain to cows and using all that land space to torture and slaughter animals? Would the ease and cost of real food come down???????" she wrote.

Criticizing institutions became a consistent theme on the blog. Ayla wrote about refusing to shop at Walmart and being disappointed when she discovered that most of the stock at a local toy shop was manufactured in China. She required financial aid, including student loans, which she found predatory. "College should be free in this country, or very cheap, like Europe," she wrote. In another post, she described what she did once after using the bathroom, when she realized that she was out of toilet paper: "So I....um...well...how do I say this? I wiped my ass with my student loan bill!!!! ROFL!"

Ayla avoided hospitals and took her kids to a naturopath. She preferred politicians like Dennis Kucinich and Cynthia McKinney to leaders of either major political party. She resented the raft of government bailouts in the aughts, decrying them as helping the "elites who screwed and screwed and screwed all the money out of the American people." She described herself as an "anarcho-syndicalist" who believed that all systems, from health care to agriculture to education, should be run by community cooperatives. She didn't believe in national borders and considered herself anticapitalism and antigovernment. "I do not recognize the police state however I have no need to currently violate any of their laws," she wrote. When her children were old enough, she planned to homeschool them.

Articulating her identity was a vital project. Ayla wanted to do it on her own terms, without parameters imposed by social convention. She even defined her own religious faith, choosing to convert to Mormonism on the heels of her thesis research, but imbuing her belief system with pagan goddess worship. She liked that the LDS Church encouraged big families and domesticity, including a home-spun parenting style. She liked the ritual and fellowship of attending services, and Mormons' willingness to buck cultural expectations. She didn't even mind the idea of polyamory. For a while, she and Seth tried it because they thought several adults raising children together might generate a kind of self-sustaining community. Plus, Ayla later claimed, it seemed culturally trendy and maybe even a way to prevent cheating. She didn't like dating a woman, however. "I felt like a failure for not making this hip lifestyle work," Ayla wrote. "I thought I was doing the 'right' thing, don't all men want an open marriage? That's what the media told me, but no, my husband told me he hated it too so we vowed to never do it again."

A sticking point on her path to formally joining the LDS Church was its rejection of same-sex relationships. Ayla began preparing for her Mormon baptism in 2008, the same year that Proposition 8, which defined marriage as being only between a man and a woman, was on the ballot in California. Her blog featured a picture of one of her sons looking sternly at the camera, overlaid with text that read "Hey, be nice! We practice Radical Tolerance." It troubled Ayla that the church was pouring money and man power into the high-profile campaign to pass a bill writing LGBTQ people's relationships out of legal existence.

Just as troubling to Ayla was another event that occurred in 2008. After a person claiming to be a teenage girl reported physical and sexual abuse at the Yearning for Zion (YFZ) Ranch, a fundamentalist LDS compound in Texas, law enforcement raided the property. The report was a hoax—it was called in by a thirty-three-year-old woman living in Colorado Springs—but abuse was happening. Law enforcement removed more than four hundred children from their families and placed them in foster care. Critics decried the incident as government overreach and the courts agreed, ruling that Texas had to return the children to their parents. Investigators subsequently determined that girls at the ranch as young as twelve had been forced to marry, and several underage brides had given birth. Eleven men were convicted of crimes pertaining to assault and bigamy.[6]

To Ayla, the raid was an abomination, "an imperialist assault on an ethnic and cultural minority" who practiced parenting not so different from her own. "I cannot imagine the grief of these women," she wrote on her blog, "separated from their children, their husbands (whom many of them love dearly despite your view point) and their sister wives who are their best friends." Ayla didn't deny that abuse might have happened at the ranch, but she believed that it could have been stopped without destroying families. She was dismayed that more people didn't agree. "I am outraged both at the US government for perpetrating this crime against these women and children and by the lack of response from the liberal, feminist and motherhood communities," she wrote. "Who will be next? Will they perhaps remove the children of polyamorus, transgender or homosexual families? Will they routinely be taking children from any teen mothers in our country from now on? Will CPS be investigating Irish Catholic families with eight children simply because they have a lot of children? What about the Amish with their style of dress, no electricity, young marriages and large families? Will families controlling their children's education either through home school or private school find themselves targeted next?"

Ayla was baptized into the Mormon church several weeks after the YFZ raid. On the day of her confirmation, her priest read aloud a letter from Mormon leadership encouraging followers to support Proposition 8.[7] Ayla was upset and exited the church during the reading—a small show of defiance. She returned to her pew when it was over and was confirmed as Sister Serenemoon. "Despite everything I managed to beam at the sound," Ayla wrote of hearing her LDS name spoken for the first time. Later, driving her sons home from the service, she explained "what it means to be gay and why it's absolutely fine to be so and how mommy doesn't agree with church about it and it made me so sad I felt sick."

Well, then, we should go to another church, her older son said.

It's not that simple, Ayla replied. *I really believe our church is the truest church on earth. I don't want to leave.*

She didn't leave, at least not spiritually. Proposition 8 passed that fall, and Ayla's attendance at church dwindled. Still, she told her blog readers that she tried "to live deep Mormonism in my home everyday." She was surprised at the backlash. Ayla was beginning to feel like the church and government weren't the only support systems that were letting her down. So were other women.

———

AYLA ASSURED FOLLOWERS of *Mother, Lover, Goddess* that converting to Mormonism didn't mean she was becoming a political conservative. Still, she received emails asking why she was letting herself be brainwashed and how she could join such a bigoted institution. "It seems a lot of my friends are scurrying away faster than the barn cats when the door bangs," she wrote in one post. She didn't understand why some of her fellow feminists and mothers were so mad;

she found it insulting to her intelligence. Wasn't it possible—maybe even better—to be an agent for change inside a system like the LDS Church? "I think I can be a voice of peace and love," Ayla wrote. "You all know me, and I don't sit around and complain, I get involved. . . . The younger Ayla might have gone and spray-painted a huge pink vagina on temple square to get my point across. The new Ayla feels like I make much more of an impact simply raising my hand."

She also felt unfairly judged—"shunned and ostracized and called down," she once said—by women who disagreed with her approach to marriage and family. She'd come to view Seth as the head of their home, the parent who was best at earning money, making big decisions, and dictating structure. "It's my choice to be led," Ayla wrote in 2008. She focused on the quotidian side of family life— the cooking, cleaning, teaching—because she was good at it. "I think nothing makes a family work better than honoring our authentic selves," she said. Ayla wasn't opposed to women working, but if they did, she thought their careers shouldn't interfere with mothering: "They should either have a job they can do with their children or NOT HAVE CHILDREN if they want to work. . . . When will we learn that pushing women into the work force at the expense of our kids is NOT feminist?"

In 2009, she had another son. She later claimed that on one of her first outings with all three boys, to a Whole Foods in Oakland, a woman berated her for having such a large family. *No one needs that many children,* Ayla recalled the woman saying. In another instance, she was in a thrift store when she heard a woman talking about how it was wrong to have children, period, given the state of the world. "I never have a clever response in the moment," Ayla wrote on her blog. "In fact I end up letting people get away with saying mean things or bullying me into some awful stuff in the moment because of my inability or lack of self esteem in standing up for myself or my beliefs."

If these encounters happened as Ayla remembered—or at all—there might have been any number of reasons why. Eventually, though, as a matter of personal history, Ayla concluded that the women who had criticized her were liberal. They were of the same mind as the people who emailed her or commented on her blog, telling her she was endorsing the patriarchy.

Ayla wondered if she was on the wrong side of the political divide. Maybe feminism wasn't the answer—maybe it was the problem.

3.

Among the most basic of social equations is this: Whenever and wherever there is a push for women's liberation, resistance follows. Mary Wollstonecraft's *A Vindication of the Rights of Woman* received some favorable reviews from Enlightenment thinkers when it was published in 1792, but public reactions ranged from dismissive to disdainful. Writer Horace Walpole famously called Wollstonecraft "a hyena in petticoats."[1] In an essay entitled "A Note on Men's Rights," a writer for *Putnam's Monthly Magazine* argued in 1856 that public opinion continued to hold a husband responsible for his wife's choices and actions, even as the means by which he could control her were diminishing: "The American husband has thus become a legal monster, a logical impossibility, required to fly without wings, and to run without feet."[2] The emergence of the suffrage movement was met with ridicule, punishment, and panic, and more than seventy years passed between the Seneca Falls Convention and the adoption of the Nineteenth Amendment. Six decades later, second-wave feminists lost the protracted battle over the Equal Rights Amendment (ERA); the deadline for state ratification came and went, taking with it the dream of the Constitution stating, "Equality of rights under the law shall not be denied or abridged by the United States or by any state on account of sex."

Throughout this turbulent history, women were often at the forefront of the charge to stymie gender equality. Most famously, conservative activist Phyllis Schlafly used her uncommon political-organizing skills to rally millions of women and defeat the ERA, knocking second-wave feminists back on their heels. Before Schlafly, there were others—Josephine Jewell Dodge, for instance, the president of the National Association Opposed to Woman Suffrage, who in 1913 said that women clamoring to cast ballots were "straining after artificial happiness and unnatural enjoyment" and putting faith in "the mirage that good morals and good manners can be legislated."[3]

The obvious question—why do women organize against their own freedom—is thorny.[4] In her 1983 book *Right-Wing Women,* radical feminist author Andrea Dworkin tried to answer it. She described three types of antifeminism. "Man dominant" was the crudest form, resting on the principle that men should subjugate women because male dominance is natural, necessary, and rooted in love. "Woman superior" held that female power resided in women's lofty moral sensibility and sexual desirability—not to be confused with their sexual desire. Women's authority was innate yet limited, physical yet passive. ("She's ethereal," Dworkin wrote, "she floats.") The last type, "separate but equal," emphasized that the sexes were destined for different spheres of existence, neither of which was better than the other. Women bearing and nurturing children was just as important as men providing for them financially or fighting wars to protect them.

Dworkin theorized that some women embraced antifeminism, in one form or a combination, as a means of self-preservation in the face of male oppression. "Feminists, from a base of powerlessness, want to destroy that power," she said. "Right-wing women, from a base of powerlessness, the same base, accommodate to that power because quite simply they see no way out from under." Dworkin also argued that any disdain antifeminist women felt toward an "other" on the basis of race or another identity marker was really displaced rage they felt toward men. "They are easily controlled and manipulated haters," she said of these women. "Having good reason to hate, but not the courage to rebel, women require symbols of danger that justify their fear."[5]

Dworkin's interpretation was compelling, but it contained two monolithic assumptions: that the patriarchy is an absolute negative for all women, and that women act largely on the basis of their woman-hood. In fact, the overlapping lines of race, class, and culture complicate both ideas. What about women who benefit—or want to benefit—from existing structures of dominance? We risk stripping them of responsibility when we suggest that the harm they do is merely a way of coping with their own oppression, whether real or presumed. As Adrienne Rich wrote in *Of Woman Born,* "Theories of female power and female ascendancy must reckon fully with the ambiguities of our being, with the continuum of our consciousness, the potentialities for both creative and destructive energy in each of us."[6]

Neither side in the battle over feminism has ever held pure intentions. Many prominent early feminists wanted equal rights for disenfranchised groups, so long as white women got them first. Susan B. Anthony opposed the Fifteenth Amendment, which granted black men the right to vote in 1870, because it did nothing for women's suffrage. According to Anthony's biographer, a fellow suffragist named Ida Husted Harper, the amendment "recognized as the political superiors of all the noble women of the nation the negro men just emerged from slavery, and not only totally illiterate, but also densely ignorant of every public question."[7] Meanwhile, women who opposed suffrage tended to be married, wealthy, and white. In the north, these women were often located in cities and already engaged in civic or charitable activities; they viewed voting as unnecessary for their ambitions and well-being. In the south, female opponents tended to be upper-class women who, in the wake of the Civil War, were anxious about further disruption to the racial and social order that might diminish their position.[8]

After the passage of the Nineteenth Amendment, some women used their votes to resist racial equality. The 1920s were the heyday of the Ku Klux Klan, and women were among its most important participants. The women's Klan, or WKKK, had up to three million members spread across the country; Indiana and Oregon were hotbeds. Imperial commander Robbie Gill Comer of Little Rock, Arkansas, was a vocal advocate of women's rights who once declared, "It has never been the purpose of God that women should be the slave of man."[9] Women had duties to their families, but they also had a responsibility to their nation—their *white* nation. As political actors, America needed them. "We can prove a power in the preservation of America for Americans in our home life and in the development of the ballot now," Comer declared in a pamphlet entitled *The Equality of Women.*[10]

WKKK members registered voters, transported them to the polls, and watched one another's children so that they could all cast ballots.[11] The Washington State chapter recruited members with a poster appealing to a sense of duty: "As an enfranchised woman are you interested in Better Government?...IT IS POSSIBLE FOR ORGANIZED PATRIOTIC WOMEN TO AID IN STAMPING OUT THE CRIME AND VICE THAT ARE UNDERMINING THE MORALS OF OUR YOUTH."[12] As the poster's call indicated, the WKKK was closely aligned with Progressive Era activism that promoted family values, temperance, and anticorruption measures intended to cleanse America of perceived ills—everything from violence to divorce to Marxism. Racial segregation was another important Progressive idea, premised on Social Darwinism and eugenic science and goaded by popular depictions of white superiority (most famously in *The Birth of a Nation*).[13] The Klan crystallized and amplified beliefs held by many white people. Male and female members alike supported President Warren Harding's "return to normalcy," the loaded slogan of his front-porch campaign that, inadvertently or not, spoke to the Klan's own promise to protect and elevate white Protestants. In the

KKK's telling, those people were "100 percent American." No one else could make that claim.[14]

Female pioneers in various spheres of American life linked their pro-woman agendas with bigoted ones. Among the most extreme was Alma Bridwell White, the country's first female bishop. In addition to leading a Methodist sect—Pillar of Fire, based in New Jersey—she was a prolific writer. In *Women's Chains,* a periodical that she launched in 1924, White demanded that women have better access to opportunities and representation. "We hear much of woman's equality with man," she once said, "but where are our women senators, where are our women judges, where are our women jurors?" White supported the ERA, first drafted in 1923, and historians believe that Pillar of Fire was the only religious denomination in the country to formally endorse the amendment.[15] But the church also openly associated with the KKK, and White wrote several books defending the Klan. She believed that racial segregation was a matter of biblical law and that women's suffrage was vital to sustaining white supremacy.[16]

Much changed over the next fifty years. The Klan's power declined, civil rights advanced, and second-wave feminism emerged. But Alma White was correct: Women's political participation was crucial to the perpetuation of white supremacy. During the peak years of the ERA debate, surveys found that opponents of the amendment were significantly influenced by their religious and cultural networks—regular attendance at church, for instance, exposed them to "traditional images of women and the family" and also made "them especially available for mobilization." Given the ascendance of the Christian right, this dynamic made sense: Conservative women's activism derived from their faith, their community, and their fear that change might compromise their interests. Race was also a source of division. Research showed that black women tended to favor the amendment,[17] while its adversaries drew strength from the memberships of racist organizations like the Klan, the John Birch Society, and Women for Constitutional Government, which described its female-led opposition to civil rights as a matter of "racial self-respect."[18] This too made sense: If feminism was, in Andrea Dworkin's words, "a revolutionary advocacy of a single standard of human freedom,"[19] its successes could disrupt more than traditional gender roles and relations. White supremacists, including female ones, saw a complex threat that they intended to stop.

Since the demise of the ERA, white women have often challenged egalitarianism or opposed its champions. A majority of white women haven't voted for a Democratic presidential nominee since 1996—and before that, the last time they had done so was 1964.[20] The most high-profile legal cases against affirmative action have been headlined by white women, and a 2014 Harvard study found that nearly 70 percent of white female respondents somewhat or strongly opposed the policy.[21] In the South, research shows that white women have played a critical role in moving politics to the right. They've been instrumental, for example, in getting states to restrict reproductive rights, which disproportionately affects poor women of color.[22] In 2017, more than 60 percent of white women in Alabama voted for Roy Moore for the U.S. Senate, despite the Republican candidate being accused of sexual assault and misconduct with teenage girls.[23] And that was just one year after exit polls showed that Trump won roughly 53 percent of votes cast by white women.

These numbers aren't included here to suggest that all or most or even many white women are part of the hate movement. Rather, the data point to motivations and consequences that muddle easy assumptions about women's political behavior. They reveal, as political analyst Alexis Grenell wrote in a 2018 *New York Times* op-ed, that "the gender gap in politics is really a color line."[24]

⸻

WHEN AYLA'S THIRD son was still a baby, a Mormon friend who also came from a liberal background gave her a book to read. It was *Fascinating Womanhood,* written by Helen Andelin, an LDS mother of eight. Published in 1963, the same year as *The Feminine Mystique,* Andelin's book had spawned a movement promoting traditional marriage and gender roles. The text promised to teach women "how to cause a man to protect you," "how to bring out the best in your husband without pushing or persuasion," and "how to be attractive, even adorable, when you are angry."[25] Ayla found comfort in Andelin's assertions that men and women have different needs. The book helped her see her first marriage in a new light: One reason it failed, she told me, was that she didn't provide her husband with the respect he required.

Ayla kept doing research on traditional lifestyles and gender roles. She read books like *Passionate Housewives Desperate for God,* endorsed by Michelle Duggar of TLC reality-show fame.[26] By 2010, Ayla's blogging tone had morphed. That year, she wrote a four-part instructional guide for female readers on how to treat their husbands and raise their sons "in a society where feminism has gone so off track that women proudly call themselves 'bitches' and behave thusly. A community where it is completely acceptable to degrade men in favor of holding women up to be the nobler and smarter half of the human race." Whereas when her first son was a baby she'd dressed him in a T-shirt that read "I love my feminist Momma," now she said that she would never show her three boys a pro-woman movie, just as she wouldn't let them watch a violent one. She recommended, however, that women "read at least one book per year aimed at gaining a deeper insight into men and boys."

In other posts, Ayla warned of the ways in which she thought feminism undermined families. She observed that working women often filled caretaking roles—teachers, nurses, secretaries—for clients, bosses, and customers, when they should have been filling them at home. "What a backwards world we live in where Mom doesn't simply serve her own family in this function," Ayla wrote. Meanwhile, she believed that a liberal arts education taught young people how to speak foreign languages and talk about philosophy but not how to live everyday lives: to cook healthy meals, sew their own clothes, or change a flat tire.

In August 2010, Ayla decided to leave *Mother, Lover, Goddess* behind. "Back when I started...I was a 25 year old polyamorous, raw foodist-vegan, feminist, pagan. I am now a monogamous help-meet to my husband, a Mormon, and a traditional foodist. This blog just no longer seemed to fit me after my heart had changed on so many issues," she wrote in her final post. "This is a museum of the old me." People could peruse the glass cases if they liked, viewing the dioramas of her bygone existence. When they came to the end she'd be waiting on a new blog—she provided a link—where she would illuminate the path to a good life. A life where family was paramount, men were men, women were women, and feminism had no place.

Ayla's instinct and faith told her that "being a homemaker was sacred," as she once said in a video. But she "had not felt the truth of that in the progressive perspective, in the feminist perspective." Instead, she felt betrayed.

Betrayal was a sentiment that the crusade against the ERA channeled with remarkable success—along with fear, frustration, and intolerance. Phyllis Schlafly's campaign was dubbed STOP, the acronym for Stop Taking Our Privileges.[27] The slogan referred to the privileges of being a wife and mother, protected by men, unsullied by the unladylike muck of feminism. Schlafly argued that women benefited from "being put on a pedestal," not from "straggly-haired women on television talk shows...yapping about how mistreated American women are, suggesting that marriage has put us in some kind of 'slavery.'"[28] STOP also alluded to the particular privileges of being a *white* woman, situated in the social hierarchy above racial minorities and within favorable distance of white men. Anti-ERA activism was an ameliorative movement, which sociologists have described as "not challeng[ing] the privileged status of males in the society" but intending "to make more effective the female's pivotal roles as wife and mother."[29] STOP was both a battle cry hurled at feminists and a clarion call to white men—

a bid to maintain social status by simultaneously fending off upstart forces and demonstrating solidarity with more powerful ones.

STOP didn't invent all the tropes it used, but it flooded the cultural discourse with them. They've proven resilient. In her 2004 book *How to Talk to a Liberal (If You Must)*, right-wing pundit Ann Coulter argued that feminists tend to "have been at the forefront of tearing down the very institutions that protect women: monogamy, marriage, chastity, and chivalry."[30] Christina Hoff Sommers wrote a bestselling book lamenting a purported war against American boys and delivered lectures criticizing feminism's "irrational hostility to men."[31] Some antifeminists have found fame on social media. Blogger Janet Bloomfield, who started the popular blog *Judgy Bitch* in 2012, has criticized famous figures from Simone de Beauvoir ("slag") to Jessica Valenti ("hypocritical bitch"), as well as single mothers ("bona fide idiots") and nameless women she deems representative of feminism:

> Feminists throw their OWN children under the bus by choosing a career over family. And what do they spend that money on? Walk into any supermarket and look at the products. Look at them carefully. 95% of the shit you can buy at any WalMart or Tesco is fucking rubbish aimed at assuaging the guilty consciences of women who get up every day and leave the baby at the day orphanage while they go off to their 'job' which is incredibly unlikely to involve A) curing cancer, B) creating technologies that improve the world or C) anything useful at all.... The truth is that women don't give a fuck about other women. There are no women rallying around me.... It's the men in our lives who care. Who value us. Who pay the bills. Who love us for what we CREATE and PRODUCE and who are prepared to pay for that.[32]

Recent polls show that fewer than half of American women, including millennials,[33] identify as feminist.[34] Viral campaigns like

#WomenAgainstFeminism invite anyone who opposes the movement to say so publicly. One reason for this opposition, surely, is the prevalent caricaturing of women's rights advocates as obnoxious and undesirable. Unflattering depictions serve to warn other women: Do you *really* want to risk being described like that?

Another reason seems to be a more positive depiction of feminism—one promoted in entertainment, fashion, and popular culture. "Choice feminism" is liberation in the eye of the beholder, celebrating the fulfillment of women's personal desires over the dismantling of harmful hierarchies and ideologies. Author bell hooks once described feminism as "a movement to end sexism, sexist exploitation, and oppression." Choice feminism isn't that: It's the belief that every decision has equal value so long as a woman makes it. If a woman decides to do something, it must be feminist.

Choice feminism flattens or obscures the complex factors that curate and curtail women's existences: sexism, racism, occupational segregation, late-stage capitalism, economic inequality, and more. It seeks instead to make women feel empowered by will alone, a simple and intoxicating notion. In practice, choice feminism is too often about safeguarding privilege under the guise of individual liberty. As journalist Lauren McKeon writes in her book *F-Bomb: Dispatches from the War on Feminism,* the idea is "soft on critical analysis but big on empowerment," and it makes women's advancement that "requires political action, tough reflection, and constant work passé."[35] More to the point, in the words of critic Linda Hirshman,* "a movement that stands for everything ultimately stands for nothing."[36]

It is easier to be the kind of feminist you want to be than it is to question how that identity might be harmful to other women. Choice feminism claims to value civility and crams a big tent with clashing opinions. You can be a choice feminist if you buy into systems of

---

* Hirshman is credited with coining the phrase "choice feminism."

oppression or oppose them—if you want to expand social benefits or slash them, if you're a protester outside an abortion clinic or a volunteer ushering patients in the door, if you're building a corporate empire on the backs of underpaid employees or an advocate for a fifteen-dollar-an-hour minimum wage. Disagreement inevitably happens, and too many people in the teeming tent "focus their ire...on the tsk-tsking of other feminists," according to political scientist Jennet Kirkpatrick.[37] This dynamic limits collective, meaningful progress. It can stoke conflict that pushes some women toward the tent's exit and prompts others to waffle about entering in the first place.

The diffuse nature of choice feminism also plays into the hands of forces keen to demonize women's liberation as overly sensitive, aggressive, and hysterical. Antifeminists have always cherry-picked examples to fit their arguments, and they always will. But when the definition of feminism is so blatantly up for grabs, the job of critics is only made easier. They too can use feminism as a screen, projecting blame for a woman's frustrations or ambivalence onto whatever definition of the movement suits them. Adversaries find ways to bridge the distance between the belief that any woman can be a feminist and the assertion that feminism is every woman's problem.

Antifeminist women boast the fact of their sex as proof of their authority. Consciously or not, they exploit choice feminism's inherent limitations. They argue that today's feminists are spoiled brats and selfish hypocrites, jockeying for cultural sympathy while looking down their noses at women whose lifestyles and politics they disagree with. A young Florida woman named Erica Alduino was quoted in the *International Business Times* in 2016 defending the hashtag #feminismiscancer. "The biggest problem I have with third-wave feminists is that 21st Century American women are possibly the most privileged and well treated women since the beginning of human existence," Alduino said, "and they act like they are simply victims."[38]

SOME OF WHAT Ayla found in the antifeminist space was likely too strident or crass for her taste. Still, there was plenty of common ground and inspiration—Ayla once described Ann Coulter as an "all around great lady." There were women who waxed nostalgic for a Rockwellian idyll: white fences, happy kids, stocked kitchens, husbands with careers. Antifeminists claimed to be free of the heavy chains of political correctness. They didn't hate men, and men didn't hate them. Wasn't that for the best? They even had allies across the sex divide in the manosphere, a loose network of blogs, message boards, and other digital platforms that decried feminism as a threat to male well-being. As evidence, the manosphere cited fathers' struggles to win parental rights in divorce cases, false rape accusations, unfaithful wives, and even circumcision.[39]

Ayla decided that feminism had made her unhappy. "It didn't support me as a traditional mother," she later told me. "It didn't consider my needs valuable." There seemed to be proof that she wasn't alone: A widely covered 2009 study by economists Betsey Stevenson and Justin Wolfers found that over the previous thirty-five years, as their rights had expanded, women's happiness had declined. Stevenson and Wolfers were careful to posit that the trend they'd identified didn't necessarily point to a causal relationship—that is, their findings didn't prove that feminism made women miserable. "Greater equality may have led more women to compare their outcomes to those of the men around them," resulting in disappointment when women found their relative positions lacking. Or, the researchers continued, "if the women's movement raised women's expectations faster than society was able to meet them, they would be more likely to be disappointed by their actual experienced lives." Perhaps rising income inequality disproportionately affected women's well-being; perhaps the documented reduction of social cohesion did too. There were no easy answers, Stevenson and Wolfers cautioned.[40]

Antifeminists ignored the study's nuances and ambiguities. Although the research showed happiness falling among women whether they worked or stayed at home, and whether they had children or didn't, antifeminists interpreted it as proving that they'd been right all along. Even Schlafly, by then eighty-four, jumped on the bandwagon. "The feminist movement taught women to see themselves as victims of an oppressive patriarchy in which their true worth will never be recognized and any success is beyond their reach," she wrote for *Human Events*. "Grievances are like flowers—if you water them, they will grow, and self-imposed victimhood is not a recipe for happiness."[41]

This sort of reaction was confirmation bias in action[42] and well suited for digital platforms that thrive on bites of opinion, simplistic generalizations, and conspiracy theories. Content questioning the virtues of feminism was a slippery slope to darker fare. In some corners of the manosphere, bloggers like Matt Forney, active since at least 2009, suggested that America's real gender problem was the decline of the patriarchy. "Inside every Strong, Independent Woman™ is a suppliant girl yearning to break free," Forney once wrote.[43] Liberation made women miserable, he said, by denying them access to the submission they craved, and it harmed men by sapping them of their ability to control women. Order could be restored only by rebuilding the patriarchy. Forney wrote posts with headlines like "How to Beat Your Girlfriend and Get Away with It."

Even murkier digital corners, frequented by men bitter about their lack of romantic partners, encouraged the killing of women. Some men did commit murder, in Isla Vista, California (2014); Roseburg, Oregon (2015); Toronto (2018); and Tallahassee (2018). More than twenty people died as a result of just those four incidents, and many more were injured. Antifeminist women justified their proximity to dangerous cohorts by calling them provocateurs or extremists and their language the stuff of locker-room banter.[44] Much like defenders of expansive gun rights, they said the thing was never a problem—not the semiautomatic weapon, not the toxic ideology. The problem was the way people used it.

The manosphere's arguments seeped into those of internet pundits anxious about the fate of the white race. In their view, science determined gender and race, so preserving both went hand in hand. "If you're fighting a) your own biology, b) history, and c) Mother Nature, you should not be terribly surprised when the results are less than entirely triumphant," blogger Vox Day, whose real name is Theodore Beale, wrote in a post titled "Feminism is a loser's game."[45] Beale also argued that feminism begot lax immigration policies: When white women secured rights and opportunities, birth rates declined and the demand for certain jobs—cleaning houses, for instance—surged. Liberals jumped at the chance to fill population and labor gaps with people of color and opened borders accordingly. Feminism, Beale concluded, was a tool used by liberals and globalists to "weaken national sovereignty."

In making his case, Beale cited Janet Bloomfield, a.k.a. Judgy Bitch, who had written that women "with their fancy college degrees in reading and feeling . . . need an exploitable class of individuals to provide domestic services at wages that won't eat up their own wages."[46] Ayla described Beale as an influence on her political transformation—she told me that he was a thinker she "trusted and respected," a man "of good character."

Ayla's journey from one resentment and pundit to another proved remarkably easy with the internet's ubiquitous shortcuts: algorithms recommending what to watch or read next, feedback loops reinforcing certain viewpoints, talking heads making specious connections, memes reducing complex ideas to logical fallacies. Proponents of the far right saw even the most outrageous leaps as part of a coveted path to enlightenment. At the end of it lay the truth that the world had grown hostile to white people, especially white men.

"It suddenly dawned on me that I'd been incredibly sexist," Ayla told me. She'd been pro-woman at the expense of white men, simply because they traditionally held so much power. She'd been taught by schools, her family, her friends, and the media to question why men were in charge, with the predetermined goal of showing that it wasn't fair. But maybe there was a good reason for the old way of doing things. Maybe white men deserved their power, Ayla thought, because society required it. And maybe white women had plenty of power already, if only society would recognize it.

4.

Her new blog's name came from a quote: "For a wise and glorious purpose, Thou hast placed me here on earth." It was attributed to Eliza R. Snow, a Mormon poet who was also one of Joseph Smith's wives. To Ayla, purpose meant serving her family and God—and blogging about it to show women how they could do the same. "I try to keep it sweet, simple and inspirational," she once wrote. "I try not to rant (too much lol) I want to present things to uplift so that you might be inspired in your home making, your home schooling and in your walk with the Lord."

A Wise and Glorious Purpose was populated with recipes, housekeeping tips, and religious imagery, alongside pictures of Ayla's children eating ice cream sundaes, helping their dad tend to their yard, and doing craft projects. Ayla explained how she homeschooled her kids and decided which pop culture they could consume. She graded movies according to what she dubbed "SUD" criteria—sass and selfishness, ungodliness, disrespect—and included the Disney blockbuster *Frozen* on the no-watch list because its "main theme is about 'being who you are' without exception or compromise even if it harms, confuses or hurts your community. That's selfishness." She linked to Christian mommy blogs and personal websites of other redeemed women; one was *The Time-Warp Wife,* run by evangelical writer Darlene Schacht, who had committed to becoming a better, more obedient spouse after cheating on her husband. In a Valentine's Day post, Ayla encouraged female readers to always say yes to their husbands when they wanted to have sex.

Her past self often mixed with her new one. Still a devotee of natural living, she once suggested that sunscreen didn't protect people from skin cancer. She toggled between contradictions, first criticizing chemical-filled lotions for not working against the sun's UV rays and then asserting that the sun wasn't actually dangerous. "Why would God create a sun that gives us cancer yet then not allow us to develop sunblock for thousands of years? It makes no sense. God created the sun to help people not to harm them," she said. Sometimes she wrote book reviews, including one of *Unplanned* by Abby Johnson, a woman who was employed by Planned Parenthood until she had a purported change of heart. Johnson defected to join the antichoice group Coalition for Life, which protested outside the same clinic where she'd once worked. Ayla related to the book. Like Johnson, she believed that she'd been seduced by liberal thought in her twenties, before realizing that Christianity was the only guide she needed. Ayla's sole criticism of the text was that it seemed like Johnson didn't spend enough time at home with her husband and daughter. Ayla quoted the Bible, adding her own emphasis: "Train the younger women to love their husbands and children, to be selfcontrolled and pure, to be *busy at home,* to be kind, and to be subject to their husbands so that no one will malign the Word of God."

One day, while checking the latest posts in the "bloggernacle," the name for the Mormon blogosphere, Ayla came across a post by a woman who, like her, was raising three boys. The woman had written a post criticizing teenage girls who posted immodest photos—selfies in pajamas, say—on social media, where her sons could see them whenever they scrolled through their feeds. In response, some readers were accusing the blogger of slut-shaming.

Ayla was furious. Panicked, even. She worried that she was raising her boys in a world gone mad, where feminism taught women to never take responsibility for anything. She remembered what she'd once been like, when she dressed "like a hooker" and "did violate the laws of chastity in a big way." She would have been a terrible influence on a boy raised by a nice Christian mother, the kind she'd finally become. Ayla sat down at her computer and, in unusually angry prose, shared her thoughts: Young women, she wrote on her blog, knew exactly what they were doing when they posted sexy photos.

"God gave girls a *desire* to be *desirable* and He gave boys a *desire* to *desire* that girl," she said. "And yes, boys can misdirect or refuse to control that natural desire but a woman can also unrighteously stir that desire up and BOTH *are wrong*." To emphasize the point, she wrote it again, this time in bold lettering. More bolding followed. "If **your profile picture shows your breasts** on a platter and your back arched like a $10 call girl **we all know what's important to you.** It's no secret and you're not getting anywhere near my boys either as long as I draw breath," Ayla declared. "Children don't have the mental maturity to handle influences like that and it is literally our job as parents to protect them."

Ayla seemed to be saying that young men couldn't necessarily control their sexuality, but young women knew exactly how to use theirs. They were all Eve tempting Adam to sin in the Garden of Eden. Ayla's words also reflected a rote narrative in the manosphere and other antifeminist spaces—that of the blameless woman, forever shirking responsibility for her errors and wrongs, instead pointing the finger at men.

Was it possible that history was replete with men castigated for things they didn't actually do? Ayla read Christopher Columbus's logbook, his journal from his 1492 voyage to Hispaniola, and decided that he wasn't the terrible figure that liberals always made him out to be. "I can honestly say he truly was a very brave, smart and faithful man," Ayla wrote on her blog. "I would even venture to call him a 'hero.'" Preemptively rebutting critics, she said that she didn't dispute the fact that millions of Native people died at the hands of Europeans or from diseases imported into the New World. Still, she thought Columbus—just one man—bore too much blame. She cited quotes from his personal papers in which he praised Natives and described instructing his men to treat them with respect. Ayla judged Columbus's intentions and found them godly. "He wanted to convert them, not kill them," she insisted. All in all, then, Columbus was misunderstood. He was "the perfect fall guy for the current social trend to hate all things Christian, white and male," Ayla said. She pledged to have her sons read his logbook as part of their homeschooling curriculum. He was the kind of role model she wanted in their imaginations, and part of the cultural history she wanted them to cherish.

Ayla wasn't alone in admiring Columbus. Protecting his legacy had become a pet cause of white nationalists. Some far-right groups had even petitioned the U.S. government to make October European American Heritage Month because it was when Columbus Day was celebrated.[1] Given the trajectory of her politics, it was hard not to read Ayla's reevaluation of Columbus in a racist, revisionist context.

Ayla kept *A Wise and Glorious Purpose* going through several major life events. She had two more children—both girls, both born at home. She called them her "homemakers," while the boys were her "heroes." (Eventually, she would have a sixth child.) She and Seth moved their family from California to Utah because, as Ayla wrote cryptically, they had "witnessed first hand the illegal arms of the police state ripping our freedoms apart." In 2015, she traded in the blog for a new one, which she called *Nordic Sunrise*, a clear nod toward her deepening interest in whiteness and European culture. She would eventually change the name to *Wife with a Purpose*.

She supplemented the blog with a Twitter account (@apurposeful-wife) and a YouTube channel. In an early video, filmed in her kitchen,

Ayla wore a red blouse with short puffy sleeves and her hair coiled into a bun.[2] She sorted and sliced peaches on a table—there'd just been a big harvest, she explained. Her children scooted around the room, coming in and out of the camera's view. One of her sons began to shimmy down his pants as he went into the bathroom, and Ayla ordered him to shut the door.

"This is real life," she said, looking at the camera and laughing. "This is raw."

By way of introduction, Ayla described herself to viewers as sarcastic but loving, and "not some Molly Mormon who's never been outside of Utah." After making quick work of her personal story, she discussed the Boy Scouts, which had a few days prior announced that it would allow gay men to be troop leaders. In explaining why she disagreed with the policy, she revealed how deep her antifeminist beliefs now ran. "Up until recently the Boy Scouts have been one of the last bastions of masculinity in our culture," she said. "Men have been pushed and pushed and pushed out of spaces where they can and do express themselves as men, that they can honor those callings they have to guard, protect, and provide."

Why, she wanted to know, did gay men *have* to be part of the Boy Scouts? She believed that people chose to have a "gay lifestyle," and "some of the consequences are that maybe they don't get to participate in certain organizations." Ayla posed a comparison: Because she homeschooled, she couldn't participate in a public school's parent-teacher association, which made it hard for her to make mom friends and arrange playdates. She accepted those circumstances, however, because she'd made the decision that created them. Gay men should do the same.

"You can call me bigoted and hateful all you want, that's fine, that's your opinion," Ayla continued. "I haven't said anything hateful."

She said that she was worried about her sons continuing their involvement with the Boy Scouts because homosexuals, despite comprising less than 10 percent of the U.S. population, were responsible for one-third of pedophilia cases. "I like statistics, I like facts, I like science, I like trying to think things through logically and get my emotions out of the situation and say, where are the safest places for my children to be? That's me, as a mom," Ayla said. But what she claimed as truth was not—studies and scholars had widely discredited the statistics she cited. The institutions still propagating them were conservative Christian media and right-wing "think tanks" like the Family Research Council.

Ayla was sketching a persona that she would nurture in the coming years: the good white mother castigated as a hate-monger simply for trying to protect her children from harm. Ayla didn't identify as a white nationalist when she shot the video, which logged a few hundred views. But it wasn't long before she did.

Two MONTHS LATER, in September 2015, she recorded a new monologue titled "Welcome Refugees?? I blame feminism, here's why." For a half hour, Ayla argued that allowing a "mass influx of migrants/refugees/Islamic invaders" into Europe was an emotional choice made by societies that had become feminized—that is, weak because of women's political influence—and riddled with the impossible demands of equality. "It's based on white guilt. It's based on this notion that white countries should be guilty for colonialism, and that we should feel guilty about the resources we have," she said. She talked about how by nature women want to be caretakers, but they can't "nurture the world" without devastating results. "You can't give what the West has to all of them," Ayla said, insisting that recent arrivals in Europe were bringing "diseases; they're trashing places; they're causing crime, riot; they're spitting; they're throwing rocks." She begged European men to "shut the door" of their countries and to tell women *no* more often. "Please. We need it," she said, comparing grown women to little girls at carnivals who, once you give them treats, won't stop demanding more.

The video showed the extent to which Ayla had journeyed into the far right's landscape of disinformation. Ayla took the prevailing tenets of antifeminism and roped them together with those of white nationalism, even though she didn't endorse the latter outright. She cited no real evidence for her claims, referring instead to "a lot of people who've done amazing videos, blog posts, tweets, lots of journalists who are going after the real story." She also described a Netflix series about a fictional pandemic in which a father slams the door on his teenage daughter after she's exposed to a virus that's wiping out humankind. "I would let her in. And I think most women would," Ayla said. It was a confession, not a boast. "Men do the hard thing," Ayla explained.

She lamented that Sweden had "become the garbage can of Europe," where because of immigrants, "rape has gone up 1,400 percent." That statistic was making the rounds on the right-wing internet in 2015, fueled by a report from the Gatestone Institute, an organization that counted among its leadership Trump donor Rebekah Mercer and neoconservative John Bolton; before the year was out, the Daily Caller and Ann Coulter would be calling Sweden the rape capital of Europe.[3] But the roots of the idea that immigrants were raping Swedish women en masse and with impunity went further back. In 2012, for instance, a Stormfront user[4] shared an article from the xenophobic website Bare Naked Islam, which claimed that Muslims were almost never convicted of rape in Sweden and that "politicians continue to insist that more of these uneducated, uncivilized refugees are needed."

While it was true that the number of reported rapes in Sweden had increased dramatically in the last quarter century, the reasons why weren't clear. Perhaps it was decreasing stigma among survivors, who now felt safer reporting. Maybe it was Sweden's legal definition of rape, which lawmakers had broadened. A 2019 study released by the country's National Council for Crime Prevention could not establish a connection between the surge in foreign-born residents and an increase in sexual violence; the municipalities that took in the most asylum seekers, for instance, were not where crime reports were the highest.[5] The far-right internet, however, vigorously peddled its interpretation that immigrants of color were a sexual menace—and Ayla got on the bandwagon. "Some people say, 'But multiculturalism and diversity, it makes us strong,'" Ayla said in her video. "But that's been proven bunk, that's complete and total bunk." She was sick of the media and politicians talking about the plight of migrants—what about the women and girls victimized by all the men being let into *their* countries?

White supremacists quickly noticed the video, which would become Ayla's most popular to date. Someone shared it on Stormfront. "This video is excellent and gives me hope," the user said. "Please give her some likes and subscribers. We need to stick together." Other commenters suggested that Ayla had the potential to become a true believer once she realized the full scale of the war being waged against whiteness. One described her as "a half-awakened white woman, and people like her should be the ones we spend the most time 'recruiting.'" Another chimed in, "She seems like someone who might be open to WN. I hope someone who is both knowledgeable and patient introduces her to it."[6]

That person, ultimately, was a woman: Lana Lokteff, host of the far-right podcast *Radio 3Fourteen,* contacted Ayla and invited her to be a guest on the show. Ayla later described Lana as "a bit of a mentor," someone who was "public and professional." Lana was Ayla's introduction to full-blown white nationalism, which had recently adopted a new moniker: the alt-right. "I wasn't yet familiar with the alt-right, but I had incredibly similar views to them," Ayla told me. "I just didn't know anybody had collected these all together and labeled them, and started a movement about them." She described Lana as someone "in the movement already, that I could turn to and say, 'Oh, okay. This is happening. What do I do?'"

After more than a decade of maintaining personal blogs, *Radio 3Fourteen* was likely the largest platform Ayla had ever had. Launched in 2012, the online radio show was steadily gaining listeners and viewers, thanks to a membership program and strong presence on social media. If Ayla was nervous, it wasn't obvious. The conversation was audio-only, so users on YouTube—where the conversation racked up more than fourteen thousand views—saw a static collage. In the center was a photo of Ayla, smiling demurely with her left hand supporting her chin; her blond hair was down, her wedding ring clearly visible. Her image divided the opposing sides of the collage—one had a 1950s-style illustration of a rosy-cheeked woman and her children peering out a front door, preparing to greet the suit-clad father coming up the front walkway, while the other had photographs of feminist rallies where naked or barely clad women held signs with slogans like "Smash the patriarchy."[7]

The episode began with a rousing introduction from Lana—"this is gonna be a great show," she told listeners—followed by a blunt question that she often posed to guests: "What's your ethnic background?"

"I just typically consider myself extremely northern European," Ayla replied.

"Not a bad thing!" Lana said. Ayla laughed ebulliently. It was the first of many affirmations.

Their conversation lasted more than an hour and covered an array of topics, which taken together boiled down to a warning: If white people didn't protect themselves by halting immigration and reversing demographic decline, the race was doomed. In fact, the whole world was doomed because white people were its most civilizing force. The pitch of her voice rising the more she spoke, Ayla described a future without quality scientific research or health care, where people would be living in "mud huts." She continued: "It's a frightening prospect to think that there won't be a white culture anymore. Penicillin, painkillers, cancer research. This is all coming from white people and white civilization, and for whatever reason it doesn't come from other races and cultures"—a pristine articulation of white supremacy. Lana agreed, as she did with everything Ayla said, and described the uncertainty of the future weighing heavily on her. "I feel the spirit of what's to come," Lana said. "If there's less and less white people, and we're not around and we don't have countries, exactly, it could go back into some real dark times. And I just worry what kind of future that's going to be for our children. Is it going to be violent?"

The women were touching on several of white nationalism's enduring myths and stereotypes: white genocide, the 14 Words, race war, vanishing homelands. "I remember in France in the late 1990s, you know, they had a Muslim population, obviously. But it was mostly domestic servants, you know, maids in your hotel or whatever. And over where I was living in the Southwest of America, we had a similar situation where we had Latino immigration, but again, it was fairly small, even still at that point. And they were mostly domestic servants working as maids in hotels, et cetera," Ayla said. "Flash-forward fifteen years later and look at how both those populations in both of our countries have absolutely exploded and taken over." Meanwhile, she added, white people had no cultural identity, save that of the "social justice warrior," or SJW, a far-right insult for liberals. "The social justice warrior philosophy is really what crawls inside the dead husk of white identity. When we took away the ability for white middle-class people to have a strong sense of identity and pride in their culture, their heritage, their religion, et cetera, we created a vacuum," Ayla lamented.

The most prominent "politically correct" identities that people could inhabit, she continued, were that of the feminist and the homosexual. "They have their own history and background. They have their own heroes of their movement. They have their own flags, they have their own terminology, their own communities both locally, especially if you're in a larger city, and of course online," she said. "That gives people a purpose and an identity." As for why many people of color were committed to social justice, she said, "It's a way of taking no responsibility for your own life. It's really an easy way out. They get to blame, you know, the whites or Christians or men or patriarchy or whatever." Ayla compared SJWs of color to women who go to the hospital for a prescheduled caesarean. "They don't have to push, they don't have to risk anything, they don't have to break a nail," she said. "If something goes wrong, because life is life and things go wrong, no matter who you are, where you're at, they can absolve themselves from guilt." Women who gave birth at home, by comparison, were brave and willing to be accountable.

It was a telling moment, when so many facets of Ayla's life seemed to converge: her disappointment in feminism, her valorization of natural birth, her commitment to motherhood, her alienation from previous identities, her anxiety about social conditions, her desire to be seen and heard. The *Radio 3Fourteen* conversation validated Ayla's choices and offered her a worldview that celebrated them. Lana lamented the declining birth rate among Europeans and white American women. She described watching people snicker disdainfully at large white families in public and said that she made a point of stopping to smile and compliment mothers herding lots of children around. "They're always shocked," she said. In an emotional rush, Ayla told the story about being accosted in a Whole Foods parking lot in California by a "social justice warrior woman" who yelled at her because she "had too many children." Lana gasped in horror—another affirmation, a balm. What an "awful lady," Lana said, adding that she hoped the woman didn't have any children of her own. Lana asked Ayla if she thought anyone would ever be unkind to a large black or Mexican family. "Probably not," Ayla said. "I can't imagine it."

The conversation went on—and on—applauding white motherhood. Having babies was good science and good politics. It was a celebration of heritage and a commitment to the future. It made women happy. Any mother knew that. Ayla knew.

On YouTube, viewers who identified as men seemed to take as a given that they could, even should, judge Ayla on both physical and philosophical merits. Some commenters were skeptical. "I like her, but she will bounce around in ideologies," one wrote. "She's an endless seeker." Most reactions, though, were positive. "This is my dream woman," one person said—a woman dedicated to her femininity, her husband, and her blood.[8]

———

AMERICA LOVES MOTHERS. Or so it claims. In reality, it loves wielding mothers as symbols more than it does the actual women who bear and (or) raise children. Motherhood is used for all manner of political ends as economic conditions, public policy, and social mores make the practical realities of mothering confounding and crushing. Mothers are at once venerated and subjugated, cherished and expended. Navigating the divide between the cultural meaning of motherhood and the messy experience of living it is a Sisyphean project.

White nationalism promises clarity, treating motherhood as a cornerstone of its racial project. Sociologists JoAnn Rogers and Jacquelyn S. Litt have described the movement as "tap[ping] into a profound sense of alienation and uncertainty regarding gender and motherhood" shared by many American women, particularly around issues like "reproductive politics, work-family conflict, inadequate schools, and environmental danger."[9] White nationalism pledges to esteem mothers and treat the issues they care about with the utmost concern.

The movement has always considered having children to be white women's destiny—what nature intends for them and what will bring them personal fulfillment. Motherhood is also a necessary racial contribution, without which white people would falter and vanish from the earth. Raising children might keep women busy at home, but white nationalists argue that this seems limiting only to someone who underestimates the political importance of the domestic sphere. Home is the microcosm of the nation; mothers are its teachers, keepers, and defenders. In nurturing children and warding off polluting influences, mothers are modeling a better world. In the words of Women's Frontier, a racist website operational in the late 1990s:

> When we women take care of our household tasks, we must respect that intrinsic value of this work. It is not demeaning. Done properly, it results in a beautiful, clean, inviting, peaceful environment for our families, our husbands, and our children. . . . We regard such work a noble pursuit.

Across time, white-nationalist propaganda has been littered with images of women holding infants or surrounded by broods of children. The women appear joyful and stalwart. They are always beautiful. Some images depict mothers as goddesses or warriors, ready to rise in righteous defense of their progeny if necessary. The language used to describe motherhood is equally glorifying. The director of the second Ku Klux Klan's department of propagation once wrote:

> She knows how to kiss away the sorrow of the heart, her hand knows just when and how to stroke a weary brow. Her sweet, soft voice gives the loving word of counsel and sympathy needed but—oh, how we miss her when she is gone. She has waded into the jaws of her death for her offspring and is willing to lay down her life again if need be that their lives might be spared. She has spent the long weary night in taking care of the babes, watching over them during their growing school days, planning the meals, mending the clothes, bandaging the hurts, following them closely up to young manhood and young womanhood, and then she gives them to some one else to have and to hold. THAT'S A MOTHER'S LOVE.[10]

By the late twentieth century, amid fretful national dialogue about women's liberation, civil rights, and population control, white supremacists seized on the cause of pronatalism with renewed vigor. David Lane coined the 14 Words, and *The Turner Diaries* depicted women as racial soldiers charged with replenishing the world. If they violated that duty, they were turncoats of the worst kind. The novel describes the lynching of characters in interracial relationships, including white women who've been marked with the phrase "race traitor."[11]

Hate groups initiated outreach to train and reward mothers for their service. The Aryan Women's League (AWL), run by Kathleen Metzger—wife of Tom Metzger, former Klan leader and founder of the organization White Aryan Resistance—offered rules and tips for being a good white mom. Homeschooling, for starters, was critical. The AWL celebrated the birth of followers' children by sending out announcements and requesting donations to support new mothers.[12] According to Kathleen Blee, "Maternal responsibility is made explicit in the recruiting effort of some groups that seek to win the 'birth-rate war' by enlisting race-conscious Aryan women who will give birth to a large number of children."[13] Hence a poster created by Resistance Records—producer of Prussian Blue's albums and other racist music—featuring an illustration of a blond woman beneath the words "Blessed are the sires of Noble Maidens, For theirs is the Blood of the Gods."[14]

This messaging has persisted. In a 2017 issue of *Homefront,* published by Women for Aryan Unity (WAU), a commentary notes, "If not for the white women where would the proud white men plant his seed?"[15] WAU's motto, "Securing our future one child at a time," is a play on the 14 Words, emphasizing women's agency as mothers. Victoria Garland, the name used by a nationalist writer and aspiring home-maker, penned a 2017 article for the website of *American Renaissance* that described mothers' power and valor:

> Aside from our most valuable role as the vessels that literally carry
> our people into the future, women have also been leaders of

the household, responsible for creating safe, stable environments for nurturing greatness. We have been providers in our own right, tending gardens, helping in the harvest, and preserving food for the lean season. We have been governesses and teachers; our schoolrooms were places where raw talents were cultivated into staggering accomplishments and discoveries that changed the course of history. We have held the home front when our men were called to defend us from invaders. We have held our communities together during times of crisis.[16]

White nationalists also deploy the theme of motherhood in their fearmongering. They suggest that the capacity to give birth is so vital as to be a vulnerability. That's why white women should fear men of color with animalistic sexual appetites—one of the oldest of racist stereotypes—as well as feminists, Jews, and other leftist enemies canny enough to recognize the political potential of undermining white motherhood. By discouraging white women from having large families, pushing them into careers, and celebrating same-sex and mixed-race unions, the enemies of the white race hope to doom it. "Whom do the purveyors and accelerators of cultural genocide target first?" a writer on the website National Vanguard once asked. "Our women, always the women—as they are the ones who bring forth new life into this world and instill the foundation and framework for new generations."[17]

A no-less-critical function of motherhood in the hate movement is normalization—plastering a veneer of social acceptability, even banality, on the whole enterprise. Blee has described the women she encountered in studying racist groups as "disturbingly ordinary, especially their evocation of community, family, and social ties." Many were educated and held good jobs, while simultaneously "socializing their children into racial and religious bigotry....Homes are strewn with drawings, photos, flyers, videos and pamphlets with vicious lies and threats against racial and religious enemies." The women interacted with outsiders in the most mundane of activities—grocery shopping, community picnics, Bible studies, crafting—and popular social causes, like environmental protection and animal rights. Any of these spaces and pursuits could double as a recruitment venue. Discussions of the chemicals poisoning their children's food and water could segue into talk of other noxious influences—ideological ones, perhaps, or racial ones. One racist activist described her standard invitation to outsiders: "Come over. We'll get together, we'll talk, we'll have some fun."

Some white nationalists hold particular mothers up as proof of their cause's normalcy—women like Rachel Pendergraft, the daughter of a Klan leader in Arkansas who is now a KKK spokeswoman. Blee has described Pendergraft as a one-time high-school cheerleader, pageant contestant, and member of Future Homemakers of America. Pendergraft's father put it more succinctly and in more Trumpian terms: She's just "average American people."[18] On a blog she kept between 2008 and 2012, Pendergraft wrote about issues on the minds of many American parents. School security was one, but rather than focusing on mass shootings, Pendergraft described threats to children's racial identity posed by teachers and curricula that promoted white guilt. The best course of action, she said, was to homeschool white kids. If that wasn't economically possible for a family, the matriarch had to stay vigilant about the notions her children brought home from school. "Guard the heart and mind of your children just as you would their physical bodies," Pendergraft wrote. "We warn about not texting and driving or drinking and driving. We caution to wear seat belts, and to be kind and considerate.... Guarding our god given genetic legacy from the on going global genocide is no less important."[19]

ANALYSES OF THE far right often dismiss the elevation of motherhood as a way of keeping women subservient to men by convincing them that they have more power than they actually do. As Corinna's story shows, the hate movement can sideline women who aren't dedicated to having and raising children. Yet it's possible to acknowledge the rampant, persistent sexism of the far right while also giving women the credit they deserve. They aren't being duped or forced into hate. They have agency, they make choices, and they locate power in places other than standard political authority. Whether they're in a dominant order or a fringe crusade, women are getting something they want out of their position as mothers: validation, security, solidarity, visibility, purpose, bragging rights.

The exploitation of motherhood exposes a clear line connecting the American far right and insidious regimes of the past. The Nazis fostered a cult of motherhood and undertook what historian Claudia Koonz calls "the world's most ambitious fertility drive." It even gave mothers medals: gold, silver, or bronze, depending on the number of children they had. "Whenever a member of the Hitler Youth met a decorated mother," Koonz writes, "he had to snap to attention with a brisk 'Heil Hitler!'"[20] Gertrud Scholtz-Klink, the leader of the National Socialist Women's League, achieved gold-medal status. Hitler once described her as "the perfect Nazi woman." Scholtz-Klink, who appeared on a 1937 cover of the magazine *Mutter und Volk* ("Mother and People") with her long hair wrapped in a tight braid around her head,[21] ran an organization that taught millions of women how to be good Nazi wives and mothers—industrious, fecund, and contemptuous of non-Aryans. "The National Socialist movement sees the man and the woman as equal bearers of Germany's future," she said in a speech. "The calling to motherhood [is] the way through which the German woman will see her calling to be mother of the nation. She will then not live her life selfishly, but rather in service to her people."[22]

Koonz explains that, in following Scholtz-Klink's example and direction, Nazi women "made the world a more pleasant place in which to live for the members of their community. And they simultaneously made life first unbearable and later impossible for 'racially unworthy' citizens."[23] More to the point, "they made possible a murderous state in the name of concerns they defined as motherly."

Motherhood is also a link between the contemporary hate move-ment and what, before the Trump era, was perhaps white nationalism's last overt mainstream stand. White women were at the forefront of grassroots opposition to the civil rights movement. "Massive resis-tance," as the crusade was called, wasn't a genocidal regime like the Third Reich, but it took as gospel that the intermingling of races was undesirable, a concept that once undergirded Nazi law (and, before that, the eugenics movement in America). Massive resistance used motherhood as a unifying political tool, bringing together women of various backgrounds—far right and not—under the guise of protect-ing their families. Historian Elizabeth Gillespie McRae details how "segregation's female activists imbued women's civic duties, woman-hood, and motherhood with particular racist prescriptions. For many, being a good white mother or a good white woman meant teaching and enforcing racial distance in their homes and in the larger public sphere." Women who policed the color line did so in the name of decency and virtue, patriotism and pride, science and God. They justi-fied their white supremacy as maternal responsibility. White women penned letters to the editor and produced reports claiming that class-room integration was deleterious to their children's education, and possibly to their health. They also insisted that integration violated natural law. "Next to the mother instinct, the instinct of race is the strongest in nature," wrote Florence Sillers Ogden, a prominent Mississippi newspaper columnist and founder of Women for Consti-tutional Government.[24]

Schoolyards and municipal halls became mothers' battlegrounds. In New Orleans, white mothers gathered daily for the better part of a year at William Frantz Elementary School to harass black first-grader Ruby Bridges. The Mother's League in Little Rock, Arkansas, was formed in 1957 to oppose the integration of Central High School. The group filed a lawsuit; when that failed, the mothers circulated petitions, organized rallies, and campaigned to oust prointegration politicians from the school board. They triumphed when local residents voted to close public schools in 1958 rather than continue the integration process. As McRae points out, perhaps the women's biggest impact was teaching their children "that preserving whiteness and racial segregation mattered more than a high school diploma, a college scholarship, or even Friday night football."[25]

Lest women below the Mason-Dixon Line bear the full weight of criticism for massive resistance, mothers in the North led their own campaigns. Among them were councilwoman Louise Day Hicks and other "militant mothers" who opposed busing in Boston. They tended not to employ slurs or racist science in their public campaigns—they focused instead on couching integration enforcement as a violation of parental rights by government overreach. It was a soft shell, easily penetrated. McRae quotes a woman affiliated with the Concerned Parents League, a Boston anti-integration group, as "being startled 'by the virulent racism which was expressed'" behind the scenes.[26]

At the time, some mothers conflated federal regulations, Marxism, and the emerging global order—namely, the United Nations—with civil rights activism, exploiting Americans' ever-present fear of institutional intrusion into their lives. This was especially effective where Reconstruction loomed in recent memory as an imposition. Addressing Southern white women in one of her columns, Sillers Ogden warned that the U.N. Genocide Treaty would mandate that white husbands be tried in an international court for defending their wives' and daughters' honor by shooting or even just cursing at a black man who offended or harmed them. "It would also make it a crime to prevent racial intermarriage and intermarriage would destroy the white race which has brought Christianity to the world," Sillers Ogden added.[27] *

Women's strategic mixing of domestic and international politics in the service of prejudice wasn't a new approach. A group of American

---

* The United States has never ratified the treaty.

mothers had done the same in response to World War II. While many people who protested U.S. involvement did so in the name of peace, the ranks of isolationists were also littered with bigots who saw the war as a folly for white Americans. Most famous were figures like Father Charles Coughlin and Charles Lindbergh. Elizabeth Dilling was another key player.

A wealthy Chicago woman, Dilling believed that Marxism promoted evils like sexual promiscuity, interracial marriage, and the persecution of Christians, so she made it her mission to catalog Marxist organizations and sympathizers in America more than fifteen years before Joseph McCarthy's crusade. She published a regular "patriotic" bulletin and several nonfiction books.[28] When the war broke out, Dilling spearheaded a movement of mothers who, in petitions, rallies, and congressional testimony, demanded that their sons and husbands not be sent to fight. There may have been as many as five to six million women involved, though insufficient records survive to say for sure. While some were brazen Nazi sympathizers, others coalesced around the idea that, as mothers, they were charged with protecting their families, country, and race—the nationalist trinity—from conflict fought on behalf of "Jew-Communists," as Dilling called them. Agnes Waters, a Dilling ally, declared at a Philadelphia mothers' event in 1941, "The Jews have every key position in Washington, and if you mothers come down to Washington when you want something done, you will have to talk to some kike in order to have it done." Waters also blamed Jews for inciting "niggers" in the South to rebel against the white population.[29] According to historian Glen Jeansonne, "a complex, ironic mixture of maternal love and fanatical prejudice" fueled the mothers' movement. Its most fervent acolytes never believed U.S. involvement in World War II was justified, "even after the Allied victory and the revelation of the Holocaust."[30]

The isolationist mothers failed in their mission. So did Nazi mothers, given Germany's defeat. Eventually, so did the mothers of massive resistance, insofar as civil rights advanced to the point that politicians started talking about a postracial America—some as a matter of pride, others as a strategy for turning attention away from systemic white supremacy. Yet these women's ideas found devotees in new generations, including among women of the contemporary hate movement. Even the most nontraditional spaces in white nationalism, populated by punks, prisoners, and misfits, canonize motherhood and family, a facade behind which abuse and violence often lurk. In an interview with the SPLC, former skinhead Julie Widner described how, when her husband was killed in a car accident, the National Alliance supported her. "I was alone with the kids and they took me in as family," Widner said. She eventually exited the movement after seeing women, including young mothers, being used as sexual objects, and discovering that male leaders preferred exotic dancers and pornography to respectable marriages. Widner's new husband, also a former white nationalist, described having a similar realization. "What hypocrites! I mean, nobody cared about their kids, or their family," he said.[31]

Chasms between the movement's creed and lifestyle aren't always apparent to outsiders. Maybe some don't want to see them. In 2002, Kathleen Blee identified invocations of normalcy and solidarity as "perhaps the greatest threat posed by modern organized racism," more so than "highly visible parades" or other public spectacles dominated by men.[32] Overt displays of hate could be countered, prevented, or ignored. Diminishing white nationalism's quotidian allure and unfastening its hold on followers would be much harder tasks.

Ayla entered white nationalism more than a decade after Blee issued her warning. By then, it would sound unnervingly prescient.

5.

Ayla was angry. She was done talking only about "pleasant things" and being afraid that her friends and family might think she was racist. She was ready to speak out anywhere and everywhere about the Muslim invasion of Europe. A "beloved city was burning"—Paris, she meant—and she had a duty to tell "the truth" about why.

In the wake of the terrorist bombings and mass shootings that occurred on November 13, 2015, Ayla sat on her couch, stunned. She looked at the photo album containing pictures taken of her in France when she was a teenager. Would her daughters ever be able to take such a trip without fear? She cried. She texted a friend in Paris, who was safe from harm. Then Ayla wrote a blog post about how she felt. She said that she was heartened to find other people online recognizing, finally, that the white race was under assault. "I watched in amazement as people who were on the fence or people uncomfortable with the idea of white genocide started to rise up on Twitter, fences were abandoned and rapidly nationalists gained allies, Trump rose further in the poles," she wrote. "This is the issue of our times. We will not be gunned down, we will not be bombed, we will not be displaced. We are strong, we are white, we are proud, and we will rise again."[1]

The statement was emotional, and not wrongly so: The Paris attacks were horrific. Yet Ayla was also newly attuned to white nationalism's rhetoric and myths. She knew how to sound the alarm about perceived threats, and she knew how to speak from a place of pride rather than disdain. She used the language of "heritage not hate," a phrase first popularized by white Southerners after the Civil War in an effort to make the sins of the Confederacy seem less horrible and its symbols like mere vessels of history. Over time, white nationalists of many stripes have adopted similar language, deploying it as a disingenuous defense: By claiming to be focused inward, they deflect accusations of prejudice. To speak for one's own isn't to speak against anyone else. They parrot the language of the civil rights movement, second-wave feminism, and other causes that have demanded a more egalitarian society.

White nationalists are posing a challenge: If other groups can rally around their history, why not white people? This is a false equivalence, shorn of context, nuance, and power disparities. In theory, though, it's more effective from a PR standpoint than lynchings, cross burnings, and slur-filled pamphlets. A flair for polite language and penchant for glossing over history's rough edges give the illusion of distance between purportedly upstanding racists and what they might call the riffraff: violent criminals, say, and hard-core neo-Nazis. In fact, both cohorts draw from the same pool of beliefs. No figure makes this clearer than David Duke. The one-time KKK leader, convicted in 1976 for inciting a riot in Louisiana while wearing his Klan robes, went on to form the National Association for the Advancement of White People and, later, the European-American Unity and Rights Organization. At a 2004 gathering of white nationalists, Duke encouraged people to sign a document pledging nonviolence, "honorable and ethical behavior," and a "high tone" in public appearances.[2] In a 2010 article, Duke lamented, "It's considered noble to concern yourself with the well being of minorities even at the farthest ends of the earth. But if you're white, and you concern yourself with the well being of your own people, even of your own children, you're deemed racist."[3]

After the Paris attacks, Ayla continued to deliver political rants online, seeking to cast white nationalism as righteous. In March 2016, after terrorist attacks occurred in Brussels, Ayla recorded herself crying. "I don't want to make videos," she said, brushing tears from her cheeks. "There's no reason these people should be in our countries. The second greatest commandment is to love thy neighbor as thyself, and we've become so obsessed with loving our neighbor halfway around the world that we've forgotten our literal neighbor next door."

Ayla's videos were usually only a few minutes long and filmed with minimal staging or scripting. They conveyed the same intensity of faith that had once made her a disciple of goddess worship, unassisted home birth, and Dennis Kucinich. They also projected a familiar desire for admiration. Ayla never missed an opportunity to encourage people to follow her or like her content. She marketed herself as an authority on whatever she was talking about, particularly womanhood. And she regularly offered advice to other women. Sometimes it was mocking; she once said that women protesting Trump should move back in with their fathers or get married so that men would tell them *no* when they wanted to shave their heads and go to feminist marches. She delivered those particular pointers with a saccharine smile. It was unlikely, after all, that a Trump opponent would watch her videos or take her seriously if they did. The advice was mostly an inside joke with her viewers.

More often, Ayla offered unsolicited inspiration to sympathetic followers. "Your daily motivation to create something wonderful—a baby!" she wrote in a blog post. It featured a minute-long video of one of her children in a knitted hat, toddling around a garden. The video was tagged #tradlife.

As a HASHTAG, tradlife dates back to at least 2015. It anchors an archive of images, videos, and other online content produced mostly by women who call themselves tradwives. As a culture, tradlife is a mode of existing both online and off. To be trad is to seek a wholesale return to the social norms and gender roles of the past, when life for women was supposedly better, safer, and stronger.

What qualifies as traditional isn't precise—the only requirement is that it derive from a mythical, unspoiled version of history and celebrate clearly defined masculine and feminine archetypes. For some acolytes, that means life in suburbia, reclaiming "Stepford wife" as a badge of honor. For others, it's life on the frontier, à la *Little House on the Prairie*. Some people reach as far back in time as pre-Christian societies in northern Europe. Tradlife can be about getting back to nature, living in a house with a white picket fence, or some combination of both. The appeal is intentionally broad, attracting women like Lacey Lauren Clark (a.k.a. Lacey Lynn), a homemaker and vlogger who idolizes June Cleaver, and Sarah Dye (a.k.a. Volkmom), who lives on an organic farm in Indiana and posts YouTube videos about the medicinal uses of herbs.[4]

Tradlife champions the family unit, common sense, and self-reliance. Home is a woman's domain, and she manages it with the same eye toward efficiency and success that her husband applies to his career. Tradwives share tips for setting weekly chore schedules, baking the perfect pie, and saving money. The creator of the tradlife Facebook page "The Truly Vintage Housewife" once told followers, "Less waste means more money in your pocket, and more money in your pocket means more security. In today's world we are pushed to buy, buy, buy and never ask why, why, why."[5] Tradwives applaud one another's daily achievements and pleasures, constantly reinforcing a shared sense of purpose and belonging.

Tradlife is also an aesthetic ideal, ready-made for social media. Memes abound, repurposing midcentury illustrations of smiling wives handling household appliances and photographs of blond women in fields of flowers, wheat, or grass. "Maybe you're a sandwich away from happiness," reads one meme featuring an image of a handsome man hugging a woman who bears a striking resemblance to Grace Kelly. (The implication: Keep your man fed and you'll be better off for it.) Many tradwives curate their outfits—pearls and full skirts for some, bonnets and aprons for others—or stage vignettes of happy homelife, all to share with online followers. On Instagram, Facebook, and Pinterest, they show off baby clothes, watercolor paintings, and floral arrangements created by hand. Lacey Clark once posted an image of herself standing behind jam jars arrayed on a countertop. "Am I prouder of my canning or birthing two babies?" she asked. "The babies, but it's close."[6]

Like many digital influencers, tradwives present themselves as both aspirational and relatable. The message is simple enough: *You know you want to be like us, and you can if you try.* Unlike better-known social media mavens, however, they promote domestic fulfillment, physical modesty, and conservative values as sources of prosperity and joy. Whereas #blessed in internet parlance might mean partying in a bikini on a yacht in Mykonos, #tradlife means sitting down in a sensible dress to a family dinner you put on the table at six sharp.

Tradwives trumpet their bliss, but they often pepper it with truth telling about personal obstacles. Maybe they didn't get all the tasks done in a day that they'd hoped to. Maybe one of their kids is being a brat. Tradlife isn't always easy, they remind one another, but it's better than being a wage slave or, worse, single and childless. Every woman holds the power to be happy if she does what's natural to her feminine existence. "Amazing things will happen today if you choose not to be a miserable cow,"[7] a tradwife in Texas wrote in an Instagram post.

Generous interpretations of tradlife are that it's a subculture of mommy blogging or even the apotheosis of choice feminism: women taking enthusiastic ownership of the decision to lead traditional lives. "I think we, as women, should support each other. If a woman says she wants to be a homemaker, we should not say that's not right," a tradwife named Katrina Holte told the *New York Post*.[8] "What's right for me might not be right for someone else. We all have to do what's right for ourselves." Yet it's impossible to ignore that tradlife isn't just about women choosing to stay at home. It's propped up by the twin pillars of disillusionment and antipathy. Scholar Annie Kelly, who studies tradlife discourse, points out that it derives from "a frustrated yearning for a mythic past of material abundance, at a time when it is becoming increasingly difficult for young people to build careers and achieve financial security."[9] Tradlife offers up scapegoats while promising to give women a new calling and community.

Many tradwives are against as much as they are for. They deplore feminism, which they view as a vicious scam that has cheated women out of the happiness once gifted by the patriarchy. They wonder what empowerment has done other than leave women vulnerable to exploitation and abuse because they lack men's protection. They encourage the adoration of men as a corrective to modernity: It was men who built the noble societies of the past, and with the support of feminine women, the yin to their yang, men can reconstruct what's been lost. In tradlife culture, that mission isn't boring or fusty; it's revolutionary. The Facebook page "Feminine, Not Feminist"—fifty thousand followers and counting—encourages women to "restore, rebuild, revolt" and calls traditionalism the "new counter-culture."

Tradwives project fear of or distaste for change and play-act an existence in which they don't have to grapple with it. "No decade is perfect, definitely we had big social problems in the '50s, but the people I talk to who lived through the era say it was a time when you could leave your door unlocked and you didn't need to worry about people breaking in," Holte said. "People today have forgotten how to talk to people they don't agree with, and they have lost all their manners."

The postwar era's "big social problems" included racial segregation and oppression. This is where bigotry enters the tradlife picture: Most tradwives are white, and they embrace a dream of comfort, contentment, and affluence specific to lived white experiences. It's a reverie in which the diversifying of culture—from fashion to music, social perspectives to religious beliefs—never happened. To be sure, not every tradwife is a white supremacist, but the community's hunger for the distinct boundaries of the past makes it vulnerable to far-right messaging. Tradwives and white nationalists share core objectives (more babies), myths (America's moral decline), and iconography (happy heterosexual families). Such close proximity, particularly on social media, makes the exchange of ideas a straightforward prospect. When a tradwife mentions threats to "European culture" and "Western civilization," she's borrowing euphemistic language from white nationalists. When she talks about protecting her children from multiculturalism and black-on-white crime, she's all but reading from the hate movement's proverbial handbook.

Ayla became a symbol of this overlap when, in 2015, she appointed herself as a spokeswoman for tradlife culture. She already lived it, and she wanted other people to do the same. Only then could America be truly great again—for white people, at least.

Some of the content Ayla created was familiar: organic recipes, gardening tips, homeschooling materials, how-to holiday decoration guides. Sometimes she recorded herself in her car, while ferrying her kids around, because she said it was the only time as a busy mom that she had to talk to her followers. But much of what she produced was now layered with explicit mentions of white pride. In October 2015, a few days after she appeared on *Radio 3Fourteen* to talk about the dangers of immigration and shortly before the Paris attacks, Ayla suggested that her tradlife readers try making European dishes at home—schnitzel, perhaps, or creamed carrots. She knew how hard it could be to get those foods onto kids' plates. She lived in Utah, where there was a Mexican restaurant on every corner and avocados and tortillas on endless offer at grocery stores. Plus, she lamented, liberal culture had served white America a big dish of "propaganda," telling them that European food was boring and flavorless. "It's quite the opposite!" Ayla promised. "It's simply bursting with flavor and charm."

The same month, Ayla snapped a photo of her elder daughter after a dance class; the little girl wore a pale pink leotard and tutu. Ayla posted the photo on her blog. "Are your little girls in dance class?"

Ayla wrote beneath it. "Have you ever thought of this decision from a European, or white cultural perspective?" As ever, Ayla had advice, and she targeted white mothers: "Choose a European or White American Form of Dance." Among the examples she listed were ballet, waltz, polka, and country and western. "Every choice we make for our child can either strengthen or weaken their sense of cultural pride and heritage," Ayla wrote. "Choose wisely traditional momma."

Ayla positioned white culture as American culture, the most decent of tradlife options and also the most endangered. She claimed that people caricatured it unfairly—getting drunk on Saint Patrick's Day, wearing lederhosen on Halloween—and made white children feel shame about their ancestors. "Slavery is being taught in a polarizing narrative," Ayla once said, referring to public school curricula. Any good mother, she went on, knew that her children should learn about color blindness, not conflict. And wasn't schools' lack of instruction about white culture worrying? What about liberals telling young people that the mass incarceration of black men existed for any reason other than "because they commit more crime"? Not, say, because of what journalist Nikole Hannah-Jones has described as the "utterly predictable" conditions of "a country built on a racial caste system."[10] Ayla told white women to protect their children from revisionist history and antiwhite nonsense, and she told their husbands to do their own traditional duty. "You love your wife as though she were your own body. You would do anything to keep her safe," she said. "But are you really keeping her safe if you allow hordes of violent third-world immigrants into your nation?"

Ayla eventually monetized her content, setting up PayPal and Patreon accounts. She opened an Etsy store, where she sold items like tea towels with "tradlife" stitched on them. On her Instagram account, she shared carefully angled selfies in which she donned caps or capes that she'd crocheted at home. Down the road, in early 2019, she would dedicate a whole month of Instagram content to images of herself wearing outfits and hairstyles from the 1940s.

Ayla supported other racist tradwives' businesses. She bought her children an illustrated book called *Walls and Fences,* self-published by a woman with the pseudonym Mary Grey. "Why do we build walls? We have walls for protection," the text reads, set against a colorful image of the biblical city of Jericho as its walls tumble down at God's behest. Grey, a tradwife who hosted the now-defunct podcast *Good Morning White America,* told me in an email that she wrote the book "to help explain to my children why having a wall around our country is justified and a good and normal thing." One of the illustrations shows a cartoon Trump in overalls and a red baseball hat whistling while he lays bricks one atop the other.[11]

AYLA'S EMBRACE OF tradlife marked her utter immersion in the hate movement. She used her platform to interact with other far-right pundits and make a new name for herself. She endorsed Trump for president, describing her support as a matter of saving what was left of the America that honorable white people had built. She joined Gab, a social media site created in response to perceived censorship of conservative voices on Twitter. On Instagram, she posted a drawing of Pepe the Frog, a favorite subject of alt-right memes, that one of her sons had done in green-colored pencil. She made guest appearances on white-nationalist programming, including the podcast *Radical Agenda,* hosted by Christopher Cantwell, a racist shock jock later arrested for his participation in Unite the Right.* "You see these fucking hordes of

---

*   In July 2018, Cantwell pleaded guilty to assault and battery and was barred from entering the state of Virginia for five years. In early 2020, he was arrested again, this time on charges of sending threatening communications. According to the indictment, in an effort to "extort...a thing of value, namely, personal identifying information," Cantwell sent a message on the app Telegram, instructing the recipient to do what he said "if you don't want me to come and f*ck your wife in front of your kids."

unwashed religious fanatics pouring across borders with no resources just thinking that they're going to collect welfare and fuck our women and fucking breed us out of existence," Cantwell said in an episode prior to Ayla's appearance on the show. "That makes me want to bash people's skulls open."[12] With her talk of homemaking and child-rearing and making America safe for future generations, Ayla leavened Cantwell's rhetoric; in sounding more moderate, she was expanding white nationalism's appeal.

Sometimes Ayla experimented with her own tone, deviating from her demure comfort zone. When Trump won the South Carolina primary, and again when he performed well on Super Tuesday, Ayla recorded short videos of herself doing a frenetic "happy dance"—stomping her bare feet on the carpet and waving her hands in the air.[13] When she found out that the Anti-Defamation League didn't include her on a list of notable alt-right figures, she joked that maybe she'd have better luck next time: "My application is strong this year, I have a lot of condemnation from black Twitter. That's gonna have some weight. Fingers crossed."[14] When the Anne Frank Center for Mutual Respect made a statement in support of adding sexual orientation and gender identity to the Civil Rights Act of 1964, Ayla tweeted, "What if some-one's pronouns are Nazi, Führer and Seig Heil? Your move . . ."

Sarcasm was the closest she came to trolling, the modus operandi of the alt-right's self-proclaimed "shit posters," who used base humor as a Trojan horse for racist ideas. Many of the worst offenders hid behind pseudonyms, including women. For a while, "Wolfie James" was the avatar of Anna Vuckovic Gebert, a midthirties wife and mother whose husband, also a white nationalist, worked at the State Department until the SPLC exposed his politics.[15] Starting in late 2016, along with a white nationalist using the name "Cecilia Davenport," Gebert wrote an online advice column that told readers, "Ask your mom for cooking advice. Ask us about ovens." It was a reference to Holocaust crema-toria. The column was "Dear Abby" for bigots. Its first installment offered advice to a purported reader—"Horrified Uncle"—hoping to save his niece from an interracial relationship. "My instinct is to scream 'You're taking part in the genocide of your own people!'" he wrote, "but I suspect that won't gain much traction." Gebert replied, "What's in order is to step into a Jew's shoes and play a long game of emotional manipulation.... *Prey on your niece's natural insecurities and vanity.* Doesn't she notice the looks she gets when out with him?"[16]

Ayla, meanwhile, made mainstream headlines with her "white baby challenge." Responding to a March 2017 tweet from right-wing U.S. representative Steve King, who'd said it was impossible to restore "our civilization" with "somebody else's babies," Ayla issued the challenge across her social media channels. "I've made 6, match or beat me!" she wrote on Twitter, attaching photos of her children playing together. "Americans of original pioneer stock aren't having enough babies," she said in a concurrent YouTube video. "We've been told we have to bring in massive third-world immigration to make up for the slack of procreation. But if we bring in immigrants from another country and repopulate our country we simply create their country again. We don't have our country anymore." Her remarks spawned headlines like "This Young Mom Is the Face of Mormonism's Hateful Alt-Right" (*New York Post*) and "This Alt-Right Mormon Blogger Represents All That Is Bad About the Internet" (*Bust*). BuzzFeed also wrote about her, as did *The Atlantic*.

Red Ice invited Ayla on its programming to defend herself. The message of the segment was abundantly clear: Liberals were hypocrites who whined about right-wing trolls' mean jokes while assassinating the character of a nice white housewife—for shame! The segment also suggested that what Ayla's critics were doing was part of a bigger, genocidal plan targeting *all* white people. Ayla had laid out the steps of the purported plan in a Gab post:

1. They dehumanize you and mock your culture and faith
2. They scapegoat you and blame you for your problems
3. They play-act at killing you
4. They kill you.

THANKS TO THE reaction to the white baby challenge, Ayla became something of a martyr in the hate movement. She would eventually identify on social media as "a survivor of stalking, slander and abuse from radical journalists, media and extremist groups" who was dedicated to "paving the way for the average man and woman to reclaim the right to be normal without being terrorized." It was an attention-grabbing role that she relished, and it was in keeping with the religiosity of the personal brand she'd worked so hard to create. She even called tradlife her "ministry."

Ayla's approach to religion echoed those of contemporary Christian figures, like the Duggars of the reality show *19 Kids and Counting,* and adherents of the patriarchal Quiverfull movement, which is similar to tradlife in its encouragement of large families—a pronatalist interpretation of the prosperity gospel—and regressive gender roles.[17] Ayla's invocations of faith also sounded like those of more prominent forebears on the Christian right, from Jerry Falwell to Tony Perkins, Anita Bryant to Beverly LaHaye.[18] Where she differed from many other conservative religious figures was in her explicit discussions of whiteness.

The modern evangelical movement has racist roots. The Southern Baptist Convention was founded in the 1800s by people who defended slavery as a matter of faith. When it opened in 1971, Falwell's Liberty University, then called Lynchburg Baptist College, admitted only white students. Mormonism prevented black men from becoming priests until 1978; Brigham Young had declared that their skin color was a biblical curse. By the late twentieth century, however, Christian leaders across denominations seemed intent on dialing back their churches' racial politics. Some did this for genuinely egalitarian reasons, while others likely hoped that a more oblique approach—racism with plausible deniability,[19] as Lee Atwater once put it—would minimize claims that their faith was intolerant.

Ayla made whiteness central to her ministry. When the Mormon Church released a 2017 statement criticizing "members who promote or pursue a 'white culture' or white supremacy agenda" as being "not in harmony with the teachings of the Church," Ayla tweeted a reply: "This is a dark day. The day the LDS church turned its back on its white members. We DO have a culture to be proud of." She believed that there were good and bad types of identity politics defined by the Bible, the "ancestral book of Western people" and "a guide for building Western civilization." Good identity politics included those based on race, religion, family, and country, while bad ones included feminism, homosexuality, and communism—"all sinful things," Ayla said, "called out very plainly in the Scriptures." People shouldn't "tribe up" with one another and create their own languages, rituals, and causes just because they feel like it, and certainly not because they want to play the collective victim. "We've taken care of a lot of really egregious wrongs in our society," Ayla said in a YouTube video. "With nothing left to fight, they simply will make something up." It wasn't clear which "egregious wrongs" she was referring to.

Ayla's articulation of racial identity as a Christian value was a subdued version of more virulently racist faiths. Many members of the hate movement have coopted the rhetoric of religious salvation and applied it to whiteness. Among them are the leaders of the Christian Identity movement, a belief system that seeped into America's religious fringe after World War II. According to the creed, white people are descendants of the lost tribes of Israel, Jews are the spawn of Eve and Satan ("anti-Christs"), and Armageddon will be a clash between the rival heirs of the earth. Recognizing the potentially legitimizing power of religion, George Lincoln Rockwell anointed a Christian Identity minister in his American Nazi Party. Rockwell had been introduced to the faith by Richard Butler, a Hitler admirer who went on to found Aryan Nations in the early 1970s. At that group's notorious compound in Hayden Lake,

Idaho, Butler practiced the faith with his followers and hosted "congresses" that brought notable far-right figures together. He fostered a separatist vision of white nationalism: a movement of righteous vigilantes ready to serve the will of God by seeking to establish a white ethno-state. Thanks in no small part to Aryan Nations' prominence, Christian Identity's influence spread across the far right. Disciples included followers of the Order; Randy Weaver, the man at the heart of the 1992 Ruby Ridge standoff; and Eric Rudolph, who bombed Centennial Olympic Park at the Atlanta games in 1996.[20]

While Christian Identity is most often associated with violent men, women also shaped the faith. The LaPorte Church of Christ in LaPorte, Colorado, a frontier town settled by fur trappers between Fort Collins and the Wyoming border, offers a few notable examples. Members of the Order attended services there and went on to murder Alan Berg, a Jewish radio host in Denver, in June 1984. The church's founder, Pastor Pete Peters, had argued on-air with Berg a few months prior, an incident later presented at trial as evidence of the killers' motive. A woman named Jean Craig, a Christian Identitarian with ties to the LaPorte Church, was implicated in the crime. She had allegedly spied on Berg's home and the radio station where he worked, taking photos and jotting down information about his comings and goings. She compiled her findings in a folder and gave them to the Order, which used them to plot Berg's murder. A member of the group gunned him down in his driveway.[21]

Pete Peters, who died in 2011, viewed people who weren't white, conservative, and Christian as alien threats, a position he justified with Scripture. In a pamphlet entitled *The Bible: Handbook for Survivalists, Racists, Tax Protesters, Militants and Right-Wing Extremists,* Peters wrote, "A BIGOT AND A RACIST IS ANOTHER GREAT HERO OF THE BIBLE or at least he would be so labeled by modern standards.... There was a time in America when interracial marriage was against the law and integration was not only socially but religiously unacceptable. In those days, America had no racial problems nor a killing plague such as AIDS."[22] His wife, Cheri, spoke in less dire terms and held no official title, but her contributions to the LaPorte Church were just as important. As Leonard Zeskind writes in his book *Blood and Politics,* Christian Identitarians like the Peterses "tried to reinforce a pattern of submission and servitude for women while often relying on the same women for the most important social tasks that bound together the family, clan, or tribe. The result was a contradiction: powerful women with no independently recognized power."[23]

Cheri had a prim Midwestern accent, brown hair that she often wore teased high on her head, and a talent for recruitment and publicity. Upon her death in 1998 from cancer, her husband told his followers that much of the church's evangelical and community-building work had been Cheri's idea. She had suggested that the church disseminate a newsletter—the same one in which Pete wrote her obituary—and typed up the first edition herself. She proposed organizing summer Bible camps that became annual week-long events attracting Christian Identitarians from around the country. She also helped popularize Scriptures for America Worldwide (SFAW), the church's global outreach arm; it offered the teachings of Christian Identity to anyone with a few dollars to spare for pamphlets and other instructional materials. Cheri penned a newsletter column entitled "For Women Only," spoke at church events, and recorded mail-order SFAW audiotapes and videos.

Cheri urged women to be obedient wives and dutiful mothers, boilerplate stuff in conservative Christianity. Many of her teachings, though, were also informed by racial egotism. She told readers of "For Women Only" not to tan their skin, a lesson her grandmother had taught her. "She told me to be proud of my white skin," Cheri wrote. "In today's society, my grandmother would be what is called a 'racist.' If only we had more 'racist' grandmothers today."[24] At one Bible camp session, held in the Colorado Rockies on a sunny day in 1988, Cheri instructed women to take courage—if men of faith went to federal prison, as several Christian Identitarians recently had, their wives should stand by them no matter the consequences. Race and religion would carry them through hard times.[25] The model woman in this regard was Sheila Beam, wife of Louis Beam, a one-time Klansman who'd joined Aryan Nations; the couple was married in a Christian Identity church. When Louis was arrested in 1987 on charges of sedition—specifically, plotting to overthrow the government—Sheila presented a sympathetic face to the press and the all-white jury, which ultimately acquitted her husband.* When his trial ended, a media photographer snapped a picture of Louis holding Sheila limp in his arms outside a Texas courthouse. She was wearing a modest dress, her feet were bare, and she was hiding her face on his shoulder. Behind them stood a Confederate memorial.[26]

Cheri Peters saw race as biblically ordained; whiteness was an identity to cherish and defend from dispossession, a collection of extraordinary attributes that had a rightful place as the civilized world's racial norm. She believed that women were called by God to speak truth about their whiteness, and people who called them bigots were sinners. "I'm a racist, and I'm proud of being a racist," Cheri once declared from an outdoor lectern set against a backdrop of thick green forest. "We need to understand our genetic ability.... God is only gonna bless you when you're willing to stand for what you know to be right."[27]

Zeskind once warned that the extremism of institutions like the LaPorte Church might penetrate the religious mainstream. "They change the delivery and the packaging to make it more palatable, but the message is the same," he said in 1988. "That's the real danger."[28] Mainstream conservative Christians and the far right shared

---

* The Beams' marriage didn't last; they were divorced in 1997.

antifeminist, homophobic, and other intolerant beliefs; the ideological intersections could be gateways. Mothers, meanwhile, were a shared object of reverence. When the standoff at Ruby Ridge resulted in federal agents fatally shooting Randy Weaver's wife, Vicki,* it sparked a national conversation about violent government overreach. A Christian Identity pastor told a *Guardian* reporter, "When the Feds blew the head off Vicki Weaver I think symbolically that was their war against the American woman, the American mother, the American white wife."[29]

Ayla didn't become a Christian Identitarian. She wouldn't call herself a proud racist. "The best way to sum it up is that I'm a race realist," she told me, a term that white nationalists have used for decades to eschew the negative connotations of "racist." Still, after deciding that she was a white nationalist, much of what Ayla preached about whiteness and the connections she drew between race and faith—"we must save white Europeans and that's a Christian value"—were all but indistinguishable from the tenets of Cheri Peters's dogma.

A few examples: Cheri believed that society should "eliminate women from serving in a position God never intended for them to be in, and never allow anyone but a white Christian male to make decisions in our town."[30] Ayla shared a meme advocating the repeal of the Nineteenth Amendment in order to stop white demographic decline. The basic argument, illustrated in cartoons, was that women drag politics to the left in Western countries; if their suffrage were

---

*   The Weaver family were avowed white separatists living in northern Idaho. Randy Weaver was wanted on weapons charges for which he failed to appear in court. The Ruby Ridge standoff began when federal agents arrived to surveil the Weavers' property, leading to a shoot-out in which U.S. marshal William Degan and fourteen-year-old Samuel Weaver died. Vicki Weaver was killed the next day, hit by a government sniper while standing in the doorway of her family's cabin holding one of her surviving children. The standoff continued for another ten days. In the aftermath, both sides brought legal challenges against the other. Manslaughter charges against the sniper who killed Vicki Weaver—and who subsequently participated in the Waco siege—were eventually dropped.

gone, white people's problems, including low birth rates, would vanish. Cheri once wrote a column about Jezebel, the pagan wife of the Bible's King Ahab, under whose influence "idolatry made terrible inroads into the life and ways of Israel." Cheri wondered if Ahab had justified this evil by saying Jezebel's "culture is 'different' from ours," and she warned her readers that they "must be on guard" against the influence of other cultures. Ayla once rebuked hip-hop music and its "lack of traditional values." "Thug, ghetto, rap culture is held up as being perfectly equal with white, suburban culture. We are told there is no difference and to see a difference is racist but I'm sorry there IS a difference!" Ayla wrote. "Equality of cultures is a false God. What Beyoncé raps about is not morally equal to Amy Grant or Taylor Swift." She went on to list several more false gods, including multiculturalism, tolerance, love, and antiracism.

Lastly, Cheri once told a story about two women she knew in Bible college who became lovers. "My heart broke. To this day, I cannot understand how this could have ever happened to these two Christian girls," she said.[31] On Gab, Ayla similarly recounted an experience at an amusement park, where she and her family stood in line for a ride behind a lesbian couple. "It was heartbreaking," Ayla wrote. "Here were two beautiful daughters of God and I can't imagine how far down the path of evil they had traveled to arrive at the place they were. Wickedness is never happiness folks. It's that simple. Please pray for them."

It was an expression of pity, at least on the surface. Ayla was also issuing a reminder: Collective salvation depended on diminishing the rot afflicting her people.

6.

Ayla and I connected on Skype one afternoon in the late winter of 2017. She was in Utah; I was in New York. She wanted to record our conversation for her own purposes but gave up after a few failed attempts. It had been a bad day, technologically speaking: She'd been locked out of her Skype account and discovered that her personal information was different than what she remembered putting into the application. The outcry over her white baby challenge had just reached its zenith, and she was in the national news. "The only thing I can assume is that somebody hacked it," Ayla said.

She'd already told me in an email that she was hesitant to talk to a journalist because the media so often made errors—willful or not—in describing white nationalism. I asked her what she thought the biggest mistakes were. "Oh, wow," she said with a laugh that was deep and wide, the kind people might find infectious if it rose above the noise of a crowded room. "That's kind of a big question because it seems like almost everything."

For starters, there was the neo-Nazi issue: She wasn't sure she'd ever met someone who was a neo-Nazi or even what people like that believed. She distinguished them from people she knew who believed in national socialism, which was merely a political ideology.* She believed in differences among races—inherent strengths and weaknesses, likes and dislikes. She was white, which meant she enjoyed certain things. "Like *Lord of the Rings*," she said. "That's a great example. It's a very white European story. That's not to say that Asian people or African people can't enjoy that story, and certainly some of them do, but by and large . . . it's not their thing. They have their own things that they enjoy." She said she wasn't a white supremacist. She didn't mention the sense of fear she'd expressed on *Radio 3Fourteen*, about the world losing white people as a civilizing force.

All races deserved to be majorities in their homelands, Ayla continued, with America being a special case because it hadn't always been populated by white people. Ayla deemed it a homeland by dint of history. "America as we know it, as a country, its ideas, philosophy, laws, et cetera, they all came from European people, from European ideas," she said. "Our architecture, our language, our predominant religions, our holidays, and so forth, are white European and Christian." To the extent that this was true, America's origins of violence and prejudice didn't seem to matter to Ayla, who once said on Gab that "colonization was the best thing that ever happened to the world." Because America *felt* white to her, ipso facto, whiteness was American.

Ayla walked me through how white people might protect their American homeland. Step one: Halt immigration. Step two: "Get rid" of illegal immigrants. Step three: Allow people who aren't white to return to the countries of their ancestors if they want to. Step four: Demand assimilation. "We all need to be on the same page as much as possible, culturally, so we would really need to work on those little pockets and enclaves of people that are managing to not assimilate into our culture, make sure that they're learning English, make sure that

---

* Ayla once tweeted the hashtag #whitelivesmatter, along with a message: "My ancestors didn't die fighting Nazis so u could call me a Nazi for having the same values my ancestors had."

they're having access to jobs and employment, and that there is some self-sufficiency being taught—not simply having people be dependent upon the welfare system," she said.

Part of assimilation was discouraging interracial marriage. Ayla said she didn't want to prohibit it because you can't help whom you fall in love with. But she saw unions across races as threats to diversity, by which she meant distinct racial populations. "I don't want Africans to all start interbreeding with the Chinese, and Africans and Chinese disappear from the planet, for example," she explained. Then there were the brass tacks of marriage, a subject on which she was a self-fashioned authority. "When we marry people from similar backgrounds—and that goes for race, it also goes for culture, it goes for socioeconomic status—our marriages tend to be a little stronger," Ayla said. Then came an expected refrain: Think of the children. "What does that do to your child's sense of identity if you have different racial groups or extremely different religions, or extremely different class structures, social structures...that are competing for direction for that child, an identity for that child?" Ayla asked.

Ayla was cheerful and careful. She suggested that what she believed was what any reasonable person would believe: Nationalism was common sense—not to mention the worldview of the new U.S. president—and thus legitimate. She didn't talk about immigration in apocalyptic terms or about the forces of Satan polluting America. She didn't make "kangz" jokes. She didn't acknowledge that purifying America would be impossible to achieve without violence.

Instead, she boasted about young women reaching out to her and saying they were basing their lives on hers: "They've been raised...in this millennial generation where anything goes, and nothing is defined, and everything is kind of murky and gray, and they see definition in my life. They see that as something to aspire to." On her blog, Ayla once posted a message that she claimed came from such a person, a woman who had watched her videos. "In the space of a few days I've started questioning my SJW liberal viewpoint and I've decided that I would like to be a trad wife," the woman allegedly wrote. "I cannot thank you enough for being vocal about your beliefs because otherwise I never would have been exposed to them."

Ayla had always wanted to be a role model. White nationalism had made her one.

A FEW WEEKS after we spoke, Ayla took her ministry on the road. She went to what she described as the first-ever Mormon Right conference, attended by "about a dozen adults as well as a bushel of kids." The weekend-long conference mixed religion and politics; one session was about the alt-right and the Gospels. Ayla shared photos from the event. In most of them, only her face was visible. Other people, presumably, didn't want to be seen.

But there were white nationalists like her, people who were ready to step into the limelight. Organizers of Unite the Right were preparing for their stand in Charlottesville, scheduled for August 2017. The event's stated impetus was the proposed removal of a Robert E. Lee statue from a local park. For many attendees, however, Unite the Right was about something much bigger: demanding that America remain a majority-white nation. Its figureheads included white-nationalism poster boy Richard Spencer and Jason Kessler, a far-right internet pundit. Like Ayla, Kessler was once liberal; a graduate of the University of Virginia, he'd voted for Barack Obama and participated in the Occupy movement before getting involved in men's rights activism and the alt-right.[1]

Behind the scenes, a key organizer was Erica Alduino—the same young woman *International Business Times* had quoted a year prior about holding antifeminist views. Alduino, who would turn twenty-seven a few weeks before Unite the Right, had graduated from a Christian high school in Orlando, Florida, and become a cosmetologist. She was into cosplay—she once attended Dragon Con in Atlanta dressed up like a character from *The Legend of Zelda*—and tattoos. Inked onto her right shoulder was the word "rise," and a line of script just below her collarbone read, "I will never be silenced." By 2017, she'd joined the white-nationalist group Identity Evropa, founded by military veteran and convicted felon Nathan Damigo. Alduino participated in various activities, including the disruption of a civil rights seminar at an LGBTQ museum in southern Florida; Identity Evropa members held up a banner that said, "No regret. We apologize for nothing." Alduino also became a vetter for the application-only organization, talking to interested parties to verify their identities, confirm that they would be good additions, and introduce them to existing members.[2]

It was Alduino who created Charlottesville 2.0, the private Discord server that Unite the Right participants used to communicate, where Ayla talked about Beyoncé and "black Twitter." Alduino distributed logistical information: numbers to call to urge the city government to provide the necessary permits, links to Airbnb listings, Virginia laws on wearing masks and carrying weapons. Sometimes she issued edicts. "We should be coming with the intent to stay peaceful," she wrote.* Alduino requested photographs and relevant intel about likely counterprotesters who were coming and weighed in on the use of tiki torches at the march planned for the night before the rally. "The only reservation I have against walking around with fire on sticks this time is that we'll have potentially very violent opposition waiting for us. I really don't want our people getting burned if a brawl breaks out," she said. Alduino followed up that concern with a bit of mockery: In the style of news headlines, she wrote, "White supremacists burn down Charlottesville—destroy Lee Park" and "The Charlottesville Jewish community is terrified. Find out why at 10pm." Elsewhere on Discord, Alduino shared anti-Semitic memes and used slurs like "fag kike." In one post, she wrote, "Blacks have guns. They may shoot them sideways, but niggers are armed."[3]

---

* A male user replied, "You don't need to worry. Fighting is a man's job."

If Alduino was a quiet architect of the rally, Ayla was the closest thing it had to a female face. She was the only woman slated to speak at Unite the Right, and she planned to talk about the importance of family. She was anxious about security after the backlash to her Beyoncé-as-Kool-Aid meme and because, as the rally approached, it became clear that it was going to be a big deal. Identity Evropa, chapters of the KKK, the League of the South, a fight club called the Rise Above Movement, the neo-Nazi faction Atomwaffen Division, and the NSM—Corinna Olsen's old stomping ground—were all coming to Charlottesville, with the media in close pursuit. "A women's perspective is important," Ayla later wrote online, "but this event was quickly becoming something more, something bigger, something for the leaders of the movement, not for a mom of 6 children."

Still, Ayla traveled with her family to Charlottesville. She posted a picture on Instagram from the hotel where they were staying, taking care not to reveal where it was. At the torch vigil on Friday evening, a brawl broke out between marchers and counterprotesters; a fire didn't ensue, as Alduino had feared, but the altercation foreshadowed what might come the next day. Ayla announced late that night on the Discord server that she wouldn't be attending the rally. "My personal security detail said it's too dangerous," she explained. "But my husband and oldest son still want to go, is there a shuttle service?" (There was.)

She stayed away as thousands of people amassed in downtown Charlottesville on Saturday morning. Opposite Unite the Right supporters were concerned citizens, interfaith clergy, Black Lives Matter activists, and members of antifa, white nationalists' favorite leftist bogeymen.* What happened next is well documented but no less disturbing each

---

* Antifa is short for "antifascists" or "antifascist action." It refers to militant left-wing activists who are part of a loose and secretive nationwide network. Antifa saw a spike in support after the 2016 election, and activists have showed up to protest many far-right rallies and other events. Still, the vast majority of people who oppose white nationalism are not part of the antifa movement.

time it's recounted. The chants of "Blood and soil," a Nazi slogan. Confederate flags and swastikas. People with shields and clubs and automatic weapons. Police looking on as clashes ensued. Shots fired. Punches thrown. A declaration of emergency canceling the rally before its start time. The beating of a black man in a parking garage.

Then, a murder. James Alex Fields Jr., twenty years old, from Ohio, sat behind the wheel of a humming Dodge Challenger. It was early afternoon, sunny and hot. Fields hit the gas and plowed into a crowd of people. He shifted into reverse and sped away as fast as he'd come, his gray car shooting out of sight. Heather Heyer, thirty-two, was killed. More than two dozen people were injured. Heyer's final Facebook post went viral: "If you're not outraged, you're not paying attention." Unite the Right organizers hosted a house party that night to toast the brutal day.

White nationalists had a fast answer for everything. Ayla joined a chorus of people accusing the media of lying. They insisted that there'd been violence only because the police hadn't done their job—in fact, cops had been aggressive toward peaceful white nationalists. Alduino described helping rally-goers blinded by the harsh mist of pepper spray, using a homemade cleansing solution and rolls of gauze. On an episode of the podcast *The Daily Shoah,* Richard Spencer called Alduino a "guardian angel."[4] On her blog, Ayla pledged to learn more nursing skills so that she too could be helpful in future confrontations—a Clara Barton for white nationalists.

Unite the Right organizers and supporters had a range of excuses and explanations for Heyer's murder. They'd never met Fields, so he wasn't their problem. At the rally, he'd wielded a shield emblazoned with the emblem of the neo-Nazi group Vanguard America, but he wasn't a recorded member.[5] He'd feared for his life because he was being chased by antifa, the *real* source of terror at the event. As for Heyer, where there was minimal compassion there were also lies. "God rest her soul," Ayla tweeted. "Coroner report says she died of a heart attack, she was clearly morbidly obese, the media is spinning this hard."

This cruel lie may have originated on the far-right website Occidental Dissent. Whatever its source, the rumor spiraled across the internet. People joked on social media that Heyer had died of "landwhalitis" and "that voracious appetite." Never mind that the official cause of her death was blunt force trauma to the torso and that the manner of death was homicide.[6]

Ayla found other places to lay blame. If only men hadn't allowed Heyer to attend the event, like the ones who'd insisted it was too dangerous for Ayla to be there. "They bring their women, they put them out on the front, and now one of them is dead," Ayla said in a YouTube video. The implication was clear: The enemies of white nationalists were the enemies of womanhood. They didn't want to help other white women; they would sacrifice them in a heartbeat. Women chose that side—the wrong one, the undesirable one—at their own peril.

WHEN AYLA FINALLY delivered the remarks she'd planned for Charlottesville, she looked like she'd just arrived home from a yoga class or tossed laundry in the dryer. Her hair was in a messy bun, and she wore a gray T-shirt with a scooped neck. Her eyelashes had a thick, pristine coating of mascara. She wasn't before a crowd—she was sitting on the floor of a room in her house, leaning against a bed piled high with blankets and pillows. One of her children squalled off-screen as she began to record.

"You please tell me if this speech deserves to be shut down violently," she said, waving the creased paper on which she'd written her notes. "I'm very emotional. This is incredibly upsetting to me."

The speech wove together everything that Ayla claimed to stand for: motherhood, normalcy, tradition, faith, whiteness. Families are the building blocks of civilization, she said. It's impossible to regret having children. Guilt can only go the other way. Ayla talked about a woman she knew who had two children but wished she had a dozen. The only reason the woman didn't was because she'd been told to focus on herself and her career. She had tears in her eyes when she confided in Ayla, like a sinner confessing to a priest. Or so Ayla recalled.

Ayla said that she wanted to spread a message of redemption to all the lost souls out there, all the women who needed to find a path. "Don't let anyone convince you that you are restricted by something you used to do," she said. "Live a happy, fulfilling life full of all of those wonderful traditional values that gave so much meaning and substance to our ancestors' lives and helped create our beautiful civilization and our beautiful culture."

Ayla told her viewers that she'd planned to deliver the speech in Charlottesville with her hands raised. She said that she was going to be animated, engaging. She'd picked out a white dress to wear. If she'd been in a tent on the banks of a river, it would have been like an old-fashioned revival.

Eventually, Ayla put down her notes, going off script to talk about *us* and *them*. "We need no enemy. We want no enemy," she exclaimed. Then she talked about white people's enemies—degenerate groups with a coordinated agenda to destroy all that was good, white, and American.

Watching Ayla, it was clear that Unite the Right hadn't been discouraging. If anything, it was fuel for her commitment to racial and religious salvation. Proof that, more than ever, white women needed to be strong. A reminder that the past held the keys to the kingdom.

"My granny believed in having children. She had four," Ayla said. That's what people at Unite the Right really believed in: family and nation. The Nazi flags, the racist slurs, the violent things said on Discord—none of that mattered in comparison to white birth rates and loving your own kind. What could possibly be controversial about that? "Tell me, *please,*" Ayla demanded. "It's ridiculous."

She sighed. "Okay, that's all," Ayla said, before signing off with a smile. "Thanks for watching."

Part III

LANA

Alice laughed. "There's no use trying," she said: "one *can't* believe impossible things."

"I daresay you haven't had much practice," said the Queen. "When I was your age, I always did it for half-an-hour a day. Why, sometimes I've believed as many as six impossible things before breakfast."

—Lewis Carroll, *Through the Looking-Glass*

1.

On the evening I met Lana Lokteff, an apocalyptic thunderstorm was bearing down on Charleston, South Carolina, turning the sky the colors of a fresh bruise. It was April 2017, and Lana, who was living in the Lowcountry at the time, had suggested that we meet at the rooftop bar of a restaurant called Stars. The clouds threatened to unleash rain that would force us downstairs, into the dry safety of the main dining area. For the time being we sat on faux-wicker benches as European pop music pounded in nearby speakers and wind pummeled a white tarp suspended above our heads.[1]

Lana's husband, Henrik Palmgren, paced the roof's planked deck on a phone call. He was tall and beefy, with a thick beard. Lana had brought him unannounced. Was he supposed to be technical support? Or security? One way or the other, he was deferential to his wife and to me; he brought Lana a glass of water at one point and apologized for interrupting us.

As a journalist, it's always peculiar to encounter an online personality in real life. You can't help but evaluate what's the same and what's different in comparison to the image someone projects to the masses. In Lana's case, I'd consumed dozens of hours of video and audio segments in which she ranted about a war being waged against white people, the dangerous influence of Jews, and the scourge of rape that Muslim immigrants had unleashed in Europe. In person, she looked as I'd expected—short and trim, with long, straight blond hair and sharp green eyes. She had a piercing in her left nostril, the same place I have one. She sounded familiar too: Her tone was conversational, her enunciation precise.

What was different was the substance of what she said as we sat face-to-face. Or not different, really—it was just softened, cagier, less overtly hateful.

This was one of Lana's talents: sizing up her audience and saying what she thought they wanted to hear. She did her homework. "You're taller than I expected," she said when we first shook hands. I realized that she'd probably researched me: looked at photographs, read articles, perhaps watched the few TV spots I'd done in my career. When I spoke, she might be listening for contradictions too.

Henrik set up a recorder and tripod on a table in front of me. Lana announced that she was thinking about producing a radio segment about our conversation. I said that I'd never been recorded while conducting an interview.

"Are you nervous?" she asked with a wry smile.

Over the course of our conversation, which lasted a few hours, Lana deflected questions and tried to make her worldview sound reasonable. When I asked her if she identified as a white supremacist, she laughed. "I don't want to lord over anyone," she said, "to, like, whip black people." She flicked her wrist to illustrate what she meant. What about fascist—did she identify as that? "There's elements of fascism, from what I've studied, that I think are interesting," she replied, invoking the same aura of learnedness that I'd seen Ayla project and that Corinna once hoped to gain by reading *Mein Kampf.* "When the government rules everything, one of their big underlying principles is, is it good for the people?"

When I asked if she didn't like Jewish people, Lana said, "I think it's ridiculous to say, 'Oh, I hate this whole group of people.'" However, she did think it was fair to say that Jews tended to be hypocrites because many of them promoted mass immigration as good for the West while demanding that Israel be an ethno-state. Another generalization she found reasonable was that black Africans weren't as advanced as white Europeans and their descendants in America. "They actually did very well in the bush," Lana said. "That's how they lived probably for millions of years. It's when they get in touch with a lot of the modern world that it starts creating problems for them."

Get in touch with a lot of the modern world—a cringeworthy phrase that crammed the violence of colonialism and human bondage into the suggestion of a friendly phone call.

Honesty, in Lana's book, couldn't be bigotry. Nor could common sense. Problem being, what she considered truth was mostly opinion or outright lies. What she deemed logical were at best crude axioms. Her math didn't add up, but she made it seem like it did. "Patterns are racist conspiracy theories!"[2] she once tweeted, referring to World Bank data on countries with high rates of open defecation, all of them in Africa, Asia, and Latin America. The comment functioned on at least two levels. It mocked the correct interpretation of the statistics: Open defecation is largely a product of global inequality, which is rooted in racist history and an economic system that favors Western countries. The comment also reinforced the notion that countries that aren't predominantly white are primitive to the point of being literal shitholes, to use Trump's now-infamous terminology.

In our conversation, Lana seemed to be pushing the idea that, should people dip a toe into the far right, they would find it teeming with sensible people and ideas. That wasn't the case. Lana herself was capable of extraordinary venom, even if she kept it in relative check while speaking with me. In a 2016 appearance on David Duke's radio show, Lana agreed with the former Klan leader that Jews were "parasites" against which white people needed "to inoculate ourselves." (When I quoted her at Stars, she demurred. "Did I say that?"*) In other instances, she had fat-shamed female journalists and described immigrants of color in Europe as "repulsive...a bunch of monkeys running around."[3] On the topic of slavery, she later mocked calls for reparations and said that black people should "get over it."

Stars sat on King Street, a strip of picturesque storefronts in downtown Charleston. If you walked south on King, you would pass grand historic homes on the way to the waterfront, where the Ashley River flows into the Atlantic Ocean and Fort Sumter sits on the horizon. Walk east and north along the Battery, a seawall that was the city's defense against maritime attack during the Civil War, and you would eventually reach the site of Charleston's slave auctions; when the city outlawed the public market just over 150 years ago, an enterprising merchant opened a private one right across the street. Go a few blocks north and you'd encounter Calhoun Street, home to Emanuel African Methodist Episcopal Church, a stately white building with a needle-sharp steeple. Parishioners call the historic black church Mother Emanuel. It was here, in 2015, that Dylann Roof murdered nine people during a prayer meeting.

"Many White people feel as though they don't have a unique culture. The reason for this is that White culture is world culture," Roof wrote in his manifesto, published online before his act of terror. The document reads like a primer on white-nationalist dogma. "Europe is the homeland of White people," Roof said. "White people on average don't think about race in their daily lives. And this is our problem. We need to and have to." He described finding "pages upon pages of these brutal black on White murders" in an internet search and deciding that people of color were trying to destroy his race.[4]

Roof's ideas were remarkably similar to the maxims that, by the time he wrote them, Red Ice was broadcasting online. Roof almost

---

* In an unprompted follow-up email, she claimed that she'd been talking about *all* parasites taking advantage of America, including Israel.

certainly didn't get his ideas from the platform; he radicalized in 2012, the year Lana pinpointed in our interview as the start of her own rightward shift. Still, Lana and Roof dwelled in the same ideological corner. Roof claimed in his manifesto that when he didn't see anyone fighting to protect white people—certainly not pundits "talking on the internet"—he shouldered the job of killing racial enemies. For her part, Lana seemed content to be a digital talking head. So did Henrik. Shortly after the Mother Emanuel shooting, Red Ice broadcast an hour-and-a-half segment featuring a conspiracy theorist who claimed the massacre bore the "telltale signs of stagecraft." The guest also shared the same disinformation that had motivated Roof in the first place.

"Immediately the media says, 'Disarm white men,' as if white men are the only people who commit murders," said the guest, a right-wing blogger and shock jock named Jay Dyer. "Black-on-white murders are something like five times higher, I don't remember the exact statistic—"

"Shh, shh, you can't talk about that," Henrik, who hosted the segment, jokingly interjected.

"No, you can't," Dyer said, chuckling. "Even though it's, like, FBI statistics."

In fact, FBI data from 2015 showed that Dyer had it exactly backward: White-on-white murders happened at five times the rate black-on-white ones did. The year prior, the disparity was even wider.[5] Like so much of life in America, murder hews to racial lines. Meanwhile, the data on hate crimes show no violent campaign against white Americans. In 2017, 17 percent of reported hate crimes motivated by race, ethnicity, or ancestry were committed against white people; nearly 50 percent, by contrast, were committed against black people. Among hate crimes motivated by religious bias, nearly 60 percent were committed because of anti-Jewish beliefs, while almost 20 percent were committed because of anti-Muslim ones. A mere 2.3 percent were committed because of anti-Protestant bias.[6]

With Roof in mind, and with Mother Emanuel a half mile away from where we sat, I asked Lana about violence. Did she worry about people in her political camp committing it? "No," she said, following up the firm rejection with a comment I didn't expect: "You should never denounce an extremist on your side."

We were sitting inside Stars by then, at a high-top table near one of the restaurant's wood-paneled walls. The thunderstorm had arrived. The sounds of happy hour—glasses clinking, people murmuring, cell phones buzzing—mingled with the splatter of heavy rain on the sidewalk outside.

"When does the left do that?" Lana continued. "When do they ever denounce antifa violence or people punching people or resorting to whatever kind of violence? They never do that."

Shifting attention to antifa was a fallacious strategy the far right employed with vigor, to the point that, in 2019, Trump would suggest that the leftist cohort be labeled a terror organization. I ignored Lana's whataboutism. "So you *shouldn't* denounce people who advocate violence?" I asked.

Lana seemed to calculate a course correction, a semantic one. "Alt-right people don't. I've never heard anyone say, 'Oh yeah, let's go out and kill people,'" she replied. "People try to link people to us that aren't us." Later, in an email, Lana wrote that she wanted "to be crystal fucking clear" that she was "not implying" that Roof was on her "side." She described alleged peculiarities in the case against him, seeming to hint at a possible conspiracy against or involving him. But she also wrote, "Dylann was frustrated when he learned about the reality of interracial crime. This possibly could've been prevented by having an honest discussion about it in the media. It never happens." The bottom line, she insisted, was that "the altright has NEVER killed anyone."

Unite the Right and Heather Heyer's murder was some four months away. We were still in the first one hundred days of the Trump presidency. People who identified as alt-right, including Lana and Henrik, were riding the high of the election. Red Ice was in an ambitious phase. It had sent a correspondent—none other than men's rights blogger Matt Forney—to the Republican National Convention and partnered with Richard Spencer's National Policy Institute (NPI) to launch a media enterprise modeled on Breitbart. Lana and Henrik had been invited to speak at white-nationalist conferences. Lana described like-minded people around the country going to social gatherings, forging friendships, falling in love, solidifying their alliances. She talked about the alt-right becoming a political party.

To be one of the "us" that Lana talked about, however, meant having a certain worldview, not showing up at roll calls. This was a point of pride and a strategy. As Andrew Anglin of the Daily Stormer once put it, "The mob is the movement." When alt-right proponents wanted to suggest that they had strength in numbers, they could point to all the people agreeing with them on the internet. When they wanted to distance themselves from someone—a murderer, say—they could suggest the person wasn't *really* alt-right. They'd never met him, or chatted with him, or seen him at a conference. They washed their hands of responsibility for the online ecosystem that nurtured violence. Alt-right acolytes did this with Dylann Roof just as their ideological predecessors once had with Kevin Harpham. They would do it again with James Fields.

After Charlottesville, the alt-right label would prove useful in a new way. Amid lawsuits, digital deplatforming, and interpersonal feuds, some people tossed it aside. Their worldview didn't evaporate, and the tactics they used to promote it stayed the same: harassment, fearmongering, deceit.[7] In place of the alt-right came "something shadowier and far older," according to *Wired* reporter Emma Grey Ellis: "an underground white supremacist movement operating on society's fringes, and a culture that disavows the racists while quietly mainstreaming their ideas."[8]

Trump was a crucial part of that mainstreaming, even if, as Lana told me, he wasn't "one of our guys"—meaning, he wasn't conservative *enough* for the alt-right. His value was in his coattails, which were long and wide, and in what he was willing to say. "I think a lot of people harbor our views," Lana told me. "They just need permission to say that 'I feel them' and 'I believe them.'"

I would remember this particular comment when, in 2019, a white woman at a Trump rally in my hometown—the one where the crowd chanted "Send her back"—gave several quotes to a reporter, explaining why she supported the president. She was sixty-four, a retired nurse. "Everything he says is how I feel," the woman said. "He's speaking for me."[9]

I WANTED TO leave Stars, to observe Lana in her element, to get her to drop the party line. I offered to visit her the next day while she prepped for a radio show in her home studio or did something mundane, like grocery shopping. Lana seemed amused.

"How someone brushes their hair, and how they pick up a glass—do you write about that kind of stuff?" she asked.

Readers are more likely to see subjects as nuanced humans, I suggested, if writers show them in their real lives.

"I've never appreciated that style of writing," said Henrik, who'd finished his phone call and joined us at the table.

"Yeah, we're not novel readers," Lana agreed.

She didn't see the point in letting me talk to her outside the bar. She didn't want to risk their address being leaked. A grocery run wasn't going to happen either. "We shop at Whole Foods and Earth Fare," Lana offered.

At the time, this part of our conversation struck me as trifling. It felt loose and unproductive. Later, I realized that I was too caught up in jockeying for access to see that Lana was revealing something fundamental: She is a stage manager as much as she is a performer. She dictates what her audiences see, and she doesn't want anyone to peek behind the curtain.

An example of this careful maneuvering: Lana told me that she and Henrik had children but that they didn't talk about them in interviews. "For privacy, and there's some freaks out there," she said. In truth, they didn't have kids—not yet. A few months after our interview, Lana took a break from filming videos. She didn't attend Unite the Right, and a few weeks later, she emerged from what appeared to have been maternity leave. She joined Henrik for a segment about why their website was down; they claimed their servers had been hacked by leftist activists. Lana held a baby against her chest, wrapped in a sling. Around the same time, Lana tweeted a picture of an infant's onesie made of organic fabric and emblazoned with the 14 Words. She declared it the best baby gift ever.

Why lie about having kids? To throw me off? Perhaps. Or maybe it was because Lana sensed that she would have more capital on the far right if people either believed she was already a mother or couldn't tell for sure. A month after we met, Lana was the subject of a lengthy thread on 4chan's /pol/ forum, ground zero of racist trolling culture. The thread, in a nutshell, was a debate about Lana's white-nationalist credentials. One of the first commenters called her a "childless roastie," using the misogynistic slang term for a woman who's had so much sex with so many partners that her labia resemble roast beef. Another commenter declared, "38 years old childless woman. Some role model." But there were other users—all of them anonymous, per 4chan's policy—who pointed out that Lana's detractors didn't have proof to back up their insults. Besides, her supporters said, what *really* mattered was Lana's influence, wielded via Red Ice. "What is particularly important is that many white women go to the site," one commenter argued. "Our movement will go nowhere without some women taking part."[10]

In white nationalism, surfaces are everything: how people look, how history seems, how the future might be. The ideology is a mosaic—a mass of tiles broken so that the edges fit together or selected because, conveniently, they already do. The result is seeming coherence wrought from chaos, and people see the whole before they see the parts. Sometimes they don't care to see the parts at all.

Lana used surfaces as conduits for misinformation. She persuaded people to believe impossible things: conspiracy theories, fictions, fallacies, revisionist history. Her self-curation made her something of a cipher. It was also what made her so adept at navigating a movement rife with misogyny, conflict, and cruelty.

2.

"You're talking to an agent of Putin," Lana joked in Charleston. It was the early days of public discussion about collusion between Trump and the Kremlin and about Russian trolls spreading fake news on Facebook. Lana, though, was referring to something else: the Russian heritage on both sides of her family.

Her ancestors fled the Bolsheviks. "[She] left the house in a simple dress, with gold coins and small bits of jewelry sewn into her garments," Lana's mother, Vera, once wrote of her own mother. "She wore a very lightweight jacket, so that observers would think her simply out for a walk. This 'walk' began the very long journey"—to China and then to the Philippines, and eventually to San Francisco. Vera grew up hearing stories about the fates of people who weren't able to escape the Soviet Union, which made her staunchly oppose communism. She also heard "richly illustrated Russian fairy tales, which had come from another time—when people were not forced to leave home—for somewhere else."[1]

When Lana was born in 1979, her parents were living in Oregon and already had a son. Lana arrived on Pi Day, March 14.* She spoke Russian with her grandparents. After they died, she told me, she started to lose the language.

Her parents were libertarians and Christians. They took Lana and her brother to church and preached an exacting gospel of good behavior: no lying, no drinking, no sex before marriage. "That kind of indoctrination, looking back, is very abusive," Lana said in an interview on Renegade Broadcasting, a far-right talk radio platform. "It really keeps you in a place of fear." She said that it took her until adulthood to kick the habit of believing in Jesus Christ.[2]

When she was fourteen, her parents traded in traditional worship for metaphysical Christianity, a New Age trend that involved studying science and philosophy alongside the Bible. The Lokteffs started a home worship group called Touchstone Ministries, which her father registered as a nonprofit business. Vera later blogged about her spiritual conversion, and her testimony suggested that at least some of Lana's curiosity about obscure concepts came from her family. Vera wrote that she'd had premonitions since a young age and believed that there were multiple dimensions, which began to overlap in 1990. She talked about chemtrails and invisible technology used to control people's minds, about traveling to Pluto and seeing that time was a "soft dark black velvet" fabric that could fold into itself. Vera said that organized religion had "supernatural prohibitions" she couldn't abide, so she decided to chase the truth—"that there are many more things beyond the simple explanations of 'demons' that we living on the earth had to deal with...that Nothing was as it 'Appeared to Be.' Nothing."[3]

Grunge culture was taking the Pacific Northwest by storm by the time Lana was in high school. She later described herself as a "grunge puppy," heavily into the laissez-faire aesthetic and emo attitude that defined the generation of Kurt Cobain and Eddie Vedder. As much

---

* Her birthday was the eventual inspiration for the title of her program *Radio 3Fourteen*.

as flannel was the grunge uniform, antiestablishment views were its badges of honor. Lana started listening to *Coast to Coast AM,* the wildly popular late-night radio show hosted by disc jockey Art Bell. Broadcast from California to hundreds of stations nationwide, *Coast to Coast* featured guests who shared conspiracy theories. The show had existed for a decade by the time Lana tuned in to segments on time travel, ghosts, Bigfoot, Area 51, near-death experiences, and the Bermuda Triangle. A precursor to groundbreaking entertainment like *The X-Files* and fringe websites like Infowars, *Coast to Coast* pledged skepticism as its starting point and free speech as its raison d'être. Bell once said that he wanted to help people "get their story out, no matter how wild" and that he wouldn't counter a guest "unless someone is dangerously misinforming my audience."

But what counted as dangerous misinformation? Bell hosted numerous pseudoscientists and quasi intellectuals whose ideas were dubious at best. "Regardless of their reputation, all guests are presented as experts," Paul Arras writes of *Coast to Coast* in his book *The Lonely Nineties.* "Though he may sometimes question their theories, Bell does not question their credentials." Bell's listeners, numbering in the millions, were urged to interrogate consensus and to reconsider ideas deemed taboo or verboten. The result, Arras writes, was "weird but pleasant conversations" in "a peaceful corner of the culture wars."[4]

Peaceful, maybe, but not innocuous.

In May 1996, Bell gave airtime to William Pierce, author of *The Turner Diaries.* "It will be an interesting morning, I guarantee," Bell opened the show. "This is a very interesting man." Bell asked if Pierce thought that black, Jewish, and Hispanic people in America "must go"—a seeming euphemism for deportation, or worse—to which the National Alliance founder provided a non-answer. "Any society which is to remain healthy has to maintain a reasonable degree of homogeneity. You have to have a consensus among the people. You have to have a shared sense of history, of family," Pierce said. "We've lost that. One way or the other, we've got to get that back."

Bell, in characteristic fashion, hardly challenged his guest. "Fascinating," he said after a programming break, as a way of diving back into their conversation. Toward the end of the show, Pierce praised Hitler for restoring Germany to "moral and spiritual health," and Bell followed up by asking what his guest thought about "the final solution." Pierce said that the Nazis wanted "to free German society from the very disproportionately strong Jewish influence that had built up during the period of the Weimar Republic." And he sympathized with that: "The Jews have by working together, having a strong sense of racial solidarity, by cooperating with each other, had a great advantage toward doing that sort of thing in every country that they have moved into."

"The very thing you admire!" Bell interjected. "Natural selection!"

"Right," Pierce said with a laugh. "When it is something that is done by my people to strengthen their own position, but not when it's done by somebody else so that it weakens my people and affects my people. Now, if a group of people in their own part of the world do this, I don't worry about it, I don't resent it." Pierce then suggested that the Holocaust was only "partially true."[5]

The episode was an early example of how, via alternative media, the hate movement's ideas could creep into mainstream conversation. Two decades later, Lana would mimic the format of *Coast to Coast* on Red Ice, broadcasting lengthy shows featuring a mix of commentary, conversation, and listener questions. Meanwhile, as an interview subject, Lana sounded a lot like William Pierce. "Jews as a class, I mean, they have ultimate privilege," she told me. "They're dominating in all kinds of fields." In her conversation with Renegade Broadcasting, she suggested that Jews had it out for white people, to the point that they dictated foreign policy in favor of war. "They want to make the goy look bad and take down Western civilization because they're bitter for things that happened in the past, because they were kicked out of so many places in Europe and for good reason," Lana said, scorn filling her voice. "They want us to fight the war from the Arabs and then hopefully maybe that would kill, you know, several million more goy."

She punctuated her comments with a laugh.

THE ROAD FROM grunge-loving teenager to anti-Semitic pundit was a meandering one. When she graduated high school in the late 1990s, Lana went to Portland State University. She planned to study physics and philosophy, but that didn't last long. She dropped out because, as she later claimed, she found the curriculum too narrow. Lana didn't want to be taught groupthink—she wanted to expand her horizons. A few years later, on a personal website written in the third person, she described leaving "the 'indoctrination institution' to pursue her own research. A veil lifted from her eyes when she discovered a world of suppressed alternative theories not only in relation to physics but to the universe and humanity's existence at large."[6]

Lana moved to Los Angeles to try a career in entertainment. She first worked as a model but didn't like the fashion world. "Everyone does cocaine, and there's all these slimy men," she once said. She transitioned into the film and music industries, where she saw entertainment projects rejected by executives because the ideas behind them were "too deep" or threatened to "wake people up" from the trance of modern life. Lana was, in her own words, "too creative" for that. So she left.

Lana went back to Bend, Oregon, where her parents and brother were. The city was growing fast—between 1990 and 2010, its population more than tripled. Bend was known for its proximity to parks, campgrounds, and ski resorts. Lana immersed herself in a different scene. Local music was a small but vibrant world, dominated by bands performing at bars, breweries, and hole-in-the-wall clubs. Groups rarely strayed—or made it—outside the city, which was isolated by all the nature that tourists loved. "You've gotta travel a long ways from Bend to do a gig that isn't a Bend gig," an artist once told a local newspaper.[7]

The Lokteff family saw an opportunity. Lana had dabbled in the music business and liked to sing; her brother was trained as a sound mixer. In the early aughts, the family established Piggyback Records, a label and recording studio located in the Lokteffs' home. They planned to expand eventually, into a dedicated complex on several acres.

Lana was the "schmooze queen" of the operation, and Piggyback signed a handful of local bands. The label's website described rockers tromping in and out of the Lokteffs' house, which was "surrounded by sage, coyotes, and an awesome view of the Cascades." Rehearsals took place in the living and dining rooms. Heavy shoes and equipment wore down the carpets; amps blocked the route to the house's stairs. When the musicians took breaks, they emptied the pantry of snacks and crowded onto the couch to watch *South Park*. "Basically, our parents have adopted a lot of new children," the Lokteff siblings wrote online.[8] "They seemed to have their shit together, but they were trying very hard to impress," a musician who knew the Lokteffs back then told me. "They were always name-dropping and trying hard to convince you they had something you needed."[9]

Sometimes the siblings rehearsed their own music in an abandoned movie theater, located in an old shopping center called Mountain View Mall. The brother-sister duo called themselves Thirty Day Notice and described their sound as "somewhere between pleasantly hypnotic & slightly disturbing." On their website, they listed as inspiration for their lyrics "ancient civilizations, secret societies, the soul, fringe science, aliens, mythology, symbolism, parallel universes, sacred geometry, dystopian societies, government black ops, cataclysms, out of body experiences, consciousness and more." Lana did all the singing, and her voice oscillated between a coo and whisper. As one reviewer put it, "Lana's airy vocals lull you into a reverie with auditory brain massage." *Eugene Weekly* compared her to Shirley Manson of the band Garbage.

Lana collaborated on a record with Keith Hillebrandt, a sound designer who had worked with Nine Inch Nails. *Eugene Weekly* described the music of Magdalene's Dream, the duo's name, as a "pulsating, throbbing mix of shadowy electronica . . . that's as smooth as waves gently rocking a boat, as deep as the ocean and as sexy as 4-inch stilettos." In the record's artwork, Lana posed in a slinky Goth getup. Her hair was dyed black with a streak of pink at the front. Also black were the large bird's wings—meant to look like a raven's, perhaps— attached to her ensemble.

Lana considered herself something of a feminist back then. *I'm going to take care of myself, no guy is going to take care of me, I'm not going to have kids, I'm going to travel the world,* she recalled thinking. Piggyback's business faltered within a few years, and Lana went to Fiji with her brother, where they recorded music in a solar-powered studio.

During her time overseas, in the mid-aughts, Lana discovered Red Ice. Founded in 2003 by Henrik in his native Sweden, the website had been rudimentary at first, more like a personal, angst-filled blog. It included poetry describing a "new world order" and humans "living in a prisoned freedom." The verses pleaded for people to wake up to reality—a vast, undefined concept:

Venice is Sinking
the snow falls as rain
Atlantis is Rising
please open up the eye

Henrik turned his site into an aggregator of fringe news and gave it the tagline "Resist the Flood of Ignorance." He posted articles by thinkers with varied political leanings, links to sites like Infowars, and material presented at Conspiracy Con, held annually for several years starting in 2001. Red Ice covered everything from September 11 to UFO landings, vaccine safety to the Illuminati, the Rothschilds to mind control. A sidebar on the site's main page included a ticker calculating the rising cost of the Iraq War. "The purpose of Red Ice," Henrik wrote, "is to follow, track and comment on information, news and other world changing events from present day to the year 2013 and perhaps beyond"—a reference, seemingly, either to the myth that the ancient Mayans prophesied the world's end in December 2012 or to Grigori Rasputin's claim that its demise would come in August 2013. Henrik added audio to Red Ice's repertoire a few years before the maybe-apocalypse. In his online radio show, he hosted guests with possible insight into the alarming juncture where he believed humanity found itself: "Speeding towards some kind of convergence, we are also approaching a crossroads where a 'second renaissance' or a technotronic dark age seems to be the available options."

Lana was enthralled by the man she heard on the radio. *I want a guy like that,* she thought. She contacted him and asked if he wanted to collaborate on a project; Henrik made music and videos under the name Leeq.[10] That initial communication spawned emails, long Skype sessions, and a budding romance. Henrik invited Lana to Sweden. She arrived in 2009. Before long, they were dating, and she was working at Red Ice.

At first, Lana took a back seat to Henrik. When they covered protests at the United Nations' climate conference in Copenhagen, Lana was behind the camera as Henrik wandered through crowds with a microphone.[11] He asked people if they'd heard about "climategate," referring to a trove of hacked emails from a research unit at the University of East Anglia that climate-change skeptics claimed supported their arguments.* Henrik had targeted environmental policy-making before, suggesting that it was part of a bigger conspiracy: He once wrote in a Web journal that carbon taxes were stepping-stones toward taxing people's breathing. "This is the way the control grid will be implement[ed],"[12] he said.

Lana would later praise Henrik for expanding her worldview. "He

---

* "A fair reading of the emails reveals nothing to support the denialists' conspiracy theories," the journal *Nature* stated in an editorial.

really opened me up to a plethora of incredible researchers,"[13] she said. What united those thinkers was an oppositional stance vis-à-vis elites and institutions, no matter the intellectual pitfalls required. In their view, some truth was always being suppressed. Falsehoods were thought crimes—taboo, alluring—and refusing to acknowledge reality was a virtue. Like *Coast to Coast,* where Art Bell believed in the principle "Let the audience decide," Red Ice treated expertise as a matter of perception and confidence. It was in the eye of the beholder, and in the mind's eye.

"The tiniest bit of knowledge can make us feel like an expert," authors Steven Sloman and Philip Fernbach write in their book, *The Knowledge Illusion.* "Once we feel like an expert, we start talking like an expert. And it turns out that the people we talk to don't know much either. So relative to them, we are experts."[14] On and on the cycle goes, reinforcing knowledge that isn't. "This," Sloman and Fernbach note, "is how a community of knowledge can become dangerous."

WHY DO PEOPLE believe what isn't true? Philosopher Baruch Spinoza believed that humans aren't skeptical by nature—they're instinctively credulous. More than three centuries after Spinoza published his ideas, a growing body of behavioral science literature reveals how right he may have been. Everyone has "the potential for resisting false ideas," a trio of researchers note in a paper about Spinoza's theory, "but this potential can only be realized when the person has (a) logical ability, (b) correct information, and (c) motivation and cognitive resources."[15]

No one, it seems, is immune from the psychic glitch of sometimes believing that what's wrong is right. Among the chinks in our intellectual armor is a susceptibility to repetition. Research shows that people become more credulous of an idea the more times they encounter it. In what's known as the illusory truth effect, people are more likely to perceive statements that they've encountered on multiple occasions as true *even if* they already know the statements are false. "Reading a statement like 'A sari is the name of the short pleated skirt worn by Scots' increased participants' later belief that it was true," a 2015 study notes, "even if they could correctly answer the question 'What is the name of the short pleated skirt worn by Scots?'"[16]

Kilts aside, this is the essence of propaganda: Repeat, repeat, repeat, and make people believe. In the context of white nationalism, the work of the United Daughters of the Confederacy (UDC) shows how repetition can displace truth. At the turn of the twentieth century, the UDC presented a false version of the causes and consequences of the Civil War as often as it could, to any audience available. Cofounder Caroline Meriwether Goodlett once wrote in a letter, "It is my earnest prayer that it may continue to be the crowning glory of Southern womanhood to revere the memory of those heroes in gray and to honor that unswerving devotion to principle which has made the Confederate Soldier the most majestic figure in the pages of history." Those pages bore the UDC's influence: The organization lobbied for the creation of state commissions to determine which textbooks schools could distribute, then ensured that the selections were "fair and impartial" to the Confederacy. The UDC's historian general warned against any volume that "calls a Confederate soldier a traitor, a rebel and the war a rebellion; that says the South fought to hold her slaves; that speaks of the slaveholder as cruel or unjust to his slaves; that glorifies Lincoln and vilifies Jefferson Davis."[17] Meanwhile, the UDC's youth arm held ritualized chapter meetings. Members saluted the Confederate flag and recited catechisms, each one like a hammer on the nail of false historical memory—for instance, "Q: How were the slaves treated? A: With great kindness and care in nearly all cases."[18]

The UDC capitalized on wishful thinking, another cognitive proclivity that works against truth. Research shows that people often interpret information as supporting a choice they want to make or the way they wish to see things.[19] After the Civil War, there were white people in the South who craved a narrative of redemption and counterparts in the North who sought one of reconciliation.[20] The UDC's tale of honor and amity provided both.

UDC-approved textbooks were used widely until the 1970s, and not only in the South. Generations of Americans were denied an accurate education about the Civil War. The UDC is still active today, and it has expressed sadness "that some people find anything connected with the Confederacy to be offensive." The organization's headquarters are in Richmond, Virginia, in a regal rectangular building that looks like a tomb. The fruits of the UDC's work, however, seem to be very much alive. A 2011 poll found that 48 percent of white Americans still believe that the main cause of the Civil War was states' rights, not slavery. In 2018, an SPLC study found that "only 8 percent of high school seniors surveyed could identify slavery as the central cause of the Civil War. Most didn't know an amendment to the U.S. Constitution formally ended slavery. Fewer than half (44 percent) correctly answered that slavery was legal in all colonies during the American Revolution."[21]

A particularly obstinate psychological combination is an inaccurate belief held with high confidence, or the "I know I'm right" syndrome. The further from reality someone's belief is, the less likely they are to course correct. In fact, trying to get them to do so can backfire spectacularly: Research shows that people sometimes double down on their misperceptions when presented with the truth.[22] "I know that what is contained herein will be bitterly denied," former Union soldier James McElroy wrote in his 1879 account of life in a brutal Confederate prison, an early challenge to the narrative of the Lost Cause. "I know that hell hath no fury like the vindictiveness of those who are hurt by the truth being told to them."[23]

Loyalty, too, can overpower logic and knowledge. People filter information through preexisting convictions, feelings, and affiliations. Psychologists call this motivated reasoning. The classic example is a sports fan who blames the other team for instigating rough play, no matter what actually happened on the field. A more extreme example is a conspiracy theory. We tend to associate conspiracy theories with cranks in tinfoil hats, perhaps because we don't want to admit that we'd ever be prone to that kind of thinking. In fact, as Richard Hofstadter wrote in a seminal *Harper's Magazine* essay in 1964,[24] "the paranoid style of American politics" is significant precisely because it is expressed "by more or less normal people." A recent case in point is a 2012 poll that indicated 85 percent of Republicans believed government unemployment statistics were being manipulated in favor of the Obama administration. The stronger their political knowledge—the better educated they were—the *more* likely people were to believe in the conspiracy theory.[25]

People embrace conspiracism for the same reasons they find God or start reading the future in the stars: They've experienced anxiety, ostracism, or a sense of losing control. They are seeking stories to explain what's happening. Narratives become sources of power, validation, even superiority. Socialization has primed them for this moment; skepticism of authority is already ingrained in their existence.[26] Perhaps they grew up in an environment that championed antiestablishment ideas. Maybe they had a series of bad encounters with powerful entities. Or perhaps they were conditioned by global unrest, social instability, financial insecurity, political polarization, and declining trust in institutions. Life in contemporary America may be enough to incline a person toward conspiracism.

That includes the theories and lies of the hate movement. Fear of a "white genocide" isn't that many mental steps away from wondering why there are a growing number of Spanish-language TV channels, why public schools let Muslim students wear hijabs, or why women are having fewer children. What if something bigger were going on, something nefarious, something that people in positions of power didn't want everyone else to see? What if white Americans could point to it and say, *It must be stopped*? Never mind that the theory is old and worn, that the Klan warned of racial "replacement" a century ago[27] and David Lane wrote a treatise on the subject in the 1990s. What matters is the sense it seems to make, and the power and purpose it imparts to believers.

If anxiety is conspiracy theories' fuel, technology is their propulsion. The internet offers an open, easy-to-use market in which to shill unfounded ideas, some that are spanking new and some, like white genocide, that are older than the Web itself. In the 2014 book *American Conspiracy Theories,* researchers describe studies showing that a third of Americans believed Obama wasn't born in the United States and that roughly the same number believed the September 11 attacks were an inside job.[28] Assuming that the respondent groups didn't overlap precisely, that meant an alarming number of Americans believed in at least one conspiracy theory. Today, unfounded theories saturate the internet, each more far-fetched than the next: Pizzagate, QAnon, Ruth Bader Ginsburg dying and liberals putting her body double on the Supreme Court. So huge is the burst of conspiracism that in June 2019, the FBI released a bulletin calling it a security risk. "Based on the increased volume and reach of conspiratorial content due to modern communication methods, it is logical to assume that more extremist-minded individuals will be exposed to potentially harmful conspiracy theories, accept ones that are favorable to their views, and possibly carry out criminal or violent actions as a result," the bulletin stated. "The Internet has also enabled a 'crowd-sourcing' effect wherein conspiracy theory followers themselves shape a given theory by presenting information that supplements, expands, or localizes its narrative."[29]

Making money and gaining attention are additional incentives for people to get involved with what might be called the conspiracy economy. Influencers "write blogs, teach seminars, promise quick-fix financial and legal packets, and sell nutritional supplements and other magical products meant to counteract the malicious effects of whatever 'they' are doing to us," journalist Anna Merlan writes in her book *Republic of Lies.* Conspiracists are like snake oil salesmen of the digital age, and they often imbibe what they're selling.

Sometimes these hucksters get an endorsement from the most powerful person in America. Trump has floated numerous right-wing conspiracy theories online and in public appearances. "A lot of people are saying" is a typical lead-in to whatever unfounded notion the president is promoting. Among these conspiracy theories is what Trump has described as "land and farm seizures and expropriations and the large scale killing of farmers" in South Africa—*white* farmers, that is. The theory reverberated through the media after Trump tweeted about it in August 2018. Not everyone who reported on the president's claim clarified that it was false: Farm murders, a postapartheid trend affecting mostly Afrikaner landowners and their families, were at a two-decade low. It wasn't always clear whether killings that did occur were racially motivated. And while land reform was a hot political issue, the South African government wasn't seizing white people's property.

The idea that the opposite was true originated on the far right. Since the end of apartheid, white nationalists had held up South Africa as evidence that, when white people lose power in places where they've long held it, annihilation is nigh. Anders Breivik, the perpetrator of the July 2011 massacre at a Norwegian summer camp, cited the "genocide" of Afrikaners in his manifesto. Other white nationalists shared stories and images—most of them fake, exaggerated, or misattributed—of brutalized women and children on South African farms. The intended effect was emotional. Depictions of victimhood grab people's hearts, not their minds.

How farm murders in South Africa wound up on the U.S. president's Twitter feed was something of a game of telephone. Trump tweeted about the conspiracy theory seemingly after hearing about it from Tucker Carlson, who promoted it on his popular Fox News show. Before Carlson talked about it, Ann Coulter did. Before Coulter mentioned it, chauvinistic blogger Mike Cernovich did. And before he talked about it, outfits like Stormfront and Red Ice did.

Lana was talking about farm murders as early as 2014. By then, she was making a name for herself as an alt-news pundit. Not just any fringe notion would do, however—Lana was focused on cornering the conspiracy economy's most racist sector.

3.

The first episode of Lana's solo Red Ice show, *Radio 3Fourteen,* aired in May 2012. By way of introduction, Lana thanked Henrik for championing her; the couple had gotten married the year prior. The show's early guest list read like a roster of alt-news favorites: astrologists, herbalists, esoteric artists, sacred archaeologists, fantasy writers, and town criers warning about everything from hormones in the water to secret messages in the media. Lana identified herself as an anarchist, with no love for mainstream liberals or conservatives. Her guests' politics tended toward the far left or libertarianism.

Then, a few months into the program, Lana began lumping feminism in with the conspiracy theories that *Radio 3Fourteen* featured. It's certainly possible that she had a personal axe to grind with the cause of women's empowerment. She agreed with the opinions of her guests, who embraced Red Ice's fuck-the-man ethos but believed the enemy overlord was actually a woman. Unlike Ayla, however, Lana didn't share her life story in detail or describe an emotional transformation.

Then again, why would she? Lana wasn't in the business of filming testimonials in her kitchen. Red Ice had been in the alt-news game for almost a decade; it had slick website graphics, good sound equipment, and other trappings of a real media operation. The hosts' partisan agnosticism suggested a conspiracist mentality open to theories across the ideological spectrum—or, more accurately, around it. As stories of radicalization show, there isn't much space between the far left and far right when it comes to notions of wild plots and agendas. People on each side might oppose one another, until they straddle the divide between them and find it surprisingly narrow.

To some extent, in targeting feminism, Lana was capitalizing on a digital trend. As she was shaping *Radio 3Fourteen*'s identity, the digital manosphere was expanding—in size, in notoriety, and in its range of voices. Leading the way were websites like Return of Kings and forums like r/TheRedPill. Misogynistic trolls flexed their muscles by insulting women on social media, behavior that would explode with Gamergate, a coordinated campaign of cyber harassment targeting female video-game developers and journalists. Some women gladly jumped into the fray. Janet Bloomfield launched *Judgy Bitch,* staking out territory in the online grass roots of antifeminism. Other female denizens were Phyllis Schlafly's niece Suzanne Venker, creator of the now-defunct blog *Women for Men,* and YouTuber Karen Straughan, who went on to host the antifeminist podcast *Honey Badger Radio.*[*]

Antifeminism was a hot topic on the fringe internet that *Radio 3Fourteen* could tackle. Lana interviewed Paul Elam of A Voice for Men, a men's rights website, and affirmed his complaints about feminists demonizing men and wanting "everything, with a capital E." Another guest, a woman with ties to Infowars, called feminism a form of "psychological warfare" deployed by the ruling class to divide and conquer the masses. A third guest said that Western societies were

---

[*] Female supporters of the men's rights movement sometimes call themselves honey badgers, a reference to a viral 2011 YouTube video about the tenacious mammals that fight snakes and destroy beehives. A voice-over declares, "Honey badger don't care. Honey badger don't give a shit."

doomed to fail if they kept blurring the lines between gender roles, and he decried feminism as a Marxist movement.

Lana, too, saw the specter of communism. She talked about how communists had killed her family in Russia, and she suggested that social equality was a dangerous concept because it was a fantasy. Some people were better than others at certain things, depending on their talents, abilities, and identities. Preaching and enforcing equality, Lana asserted, risked making everyone and everything in a society mediocre. In one of her earliest conversations about the dangers of feminism, Lana scoffed to her guest that Betty Friedan and Gloria Steinem were communists and Jews. The signifiers hung in the air as implicitly loathsome, no explanation required.

With antifeminism, red-baiting, and anti-Semitism, the telltale signs of Lana's foray into white nationalism were accumulating. Still, whiteness wasn't yet one of *Radio 3Fourteen*'s top-line concerns. On his own Red Ice podcast, Henrik had done a series of interviews in 2011 with guests who warned that multiculturalism was destructive. If you force races and cultures to mix, they claimed, nothing good comes of it. Unless, that is, you benefit from racial conflict or the specter of it because it makes you look like a victim. "Is anti-Semitism and racism hyped up and invented?" one Red Ice guest pondered, according to promotional text for his interview.

Behind the scenes, Red Ice's rightward shift was accelerating. Lana told me that 2012 was an important year "for some reason." Perhaps that reason was the same event that Dylann Roof described in his manifesto as "what truly awakened" his racism. "I kept hearing and seeing his name, and eventually I decided to look him up," Roof wrote. "I read the Wikipedia article and right away I was unable to understand what the big deal was." The "him" in question was Trayvon Martin. "How could the news be blowing up the Trayvon Martin case," Roof asked, "while hundreds of these black on White murders got ignored?"

Martin was seventeen when George Zimmerman shot and killed

him in February 2012. The death of a black teenager and the authorities' initial decision not to charge Zimmerman with a crime spurred protests and petitions. Zimmerman was ultimately tried and acquitted, after which President Obama said, "If I had a son, he would look like Trayvon." Three activists on Twitter created the hashtag #BlackLivesMatter. A movement was born. Backlash followed in the form of #WhiteLivesMatter and #AllLivesMatter, and in accusations that BLM was a radical, violent organization.

There is a world in which Lana might have sided with people angry about Martin's killing, the ones arguing that if American justice was rigged against anyone to the point of conspiracy, it was a young black man. Instead, Lana saw virtue on the other side of the matter—or perhaps what she saw was potential. "When you're truth seeking, you go wherever you feel you need to go to, where the truth is pointing to," Lana told me. "It was pointing towards there being an attack on white people."

A WAVE OF hyperdemocratic social media was sweeping the internet the year that Martin was killed. Twitter had 140 million users who generated more than one billion tweets every three days.[1] Reddit had some thirty-seven billion page views and four hundred million unique visitors. 4chan's /pol/ celebrated its first birthday. YouTube reached four billion daily views and reported that sixty hours of video were being uploaded to the site every minute.[2] As journalist Andrew Marantz explains, these platforms became "the most powerful information-spreading instruments in world history," run by people who "refused to acknowledge that expanding scope of their influence and responsibility. They left the gates unguarded, for the most part, trusting passersby not to mess with the padlocks."[3] Instead, people smashed the padlocks. Some laughed hysterically as they did. Others plotted mayhem and violence.

The same tools that helped popularize BLM empowered the racist opposition. White Lives Matter was a reactionary hashtag *and* the name of an organization run by a Tennessee woman with ties to the NSM. Far-right thinkers and provocateurs used digital channels to promote their ideas as antidotes for the discomfort and fear some white Americans felt when they saw black protesters demanding humane treatment from law enforcement. They aggregated their bigotry in pseudointellectual Webzines like Richard Spencer's *Radix,* shared it on largely unregulated message boards, and compressed it into viral memes. Early in his presidential campaign, Trump began pulling this material into the spotlight. He retweeted the account @WhiteGenocideTM and shared an infographic with fake statistics about black criminality; researchers traced it back to a now-defunct Twitter account with the bio "We should have listened to that Austrian chap with the little mustache."

Red Ice had common ground with the new keyboard warriors in that its proprietors were clamoring for attention and keen to share provocative opinions about race. In the middle of 2014, as BLM seized headlines with the deaths of Michael Brown and Eric Garner, Red Ice dove headfirst into pro-white advocacy. The site's shifting gears caught the attention of other people in the alt-media space. Jason Colavito, an author and blogger, wrote a post entitled "Red Ice Radio's summer of anti-Semitic white pride." He detailed several segments that had featured bigoted guests "under the banner of 'alternative history' and 'forbidden truth.'" Among them were John Lash, a "self-educated freelance scholar" who claimed that ancient mythology foretold white genocide; Kyle Hunt, a former Google employee who organized antidiversity protests under the banner of the White Man March; and Jeanice Barcelo, a "birth activist" who suggested that Jews were breeding white people out of existence while simultaneously stealing Nordic sperm for their own use. "It will be interesting to see which figures from the higher echelons of fringe history return to Red Ice Radio now that it's clear that the program is a platform for racist and anti-Semitic views," Colavito wrote.[4]

In fact, it didn't matter. Red Ice had found a new niche, one that would bring it more notice than ever before. The company had no plans to turn back. Lana made this clear in a game-changing segment on *Radio 3Fourteen* that aired in May 2014, with the title "The War on Whites." Lana interviewed Tim Murdock, a Michigan-based podcaster and meme creator best known on the fringe internet for promoting the phrase "Diversity is a code word for white genocide." Their conversation, however, was less important than Lana's opening monologue. The mere fact of it was unusual: Lana typically introduced her guest and jumped right into the interview. This time, she spoke for five minutes.

"It's quite common for a white person in these insane politically correct censored times to be labeled a racist if you do not approve of mass third-world immigration into your country, or if you dare to hold on to your European heritage culture and tradition and express concern to preserve it," Lana said. She surveyed the greatest hits of racist fearmongering, focusing on the victimization of white women—Muslim men raping them in Europe, black men raping them in South Africa. And she talked about America: "We're supposed to sit back and be thrilled and say, 'Come on in,' while us whites have to deal with being called a racist because we disapprove of those who are actively destroying what our ancestors have worked so hard to create," Lana said, "that which now foreigners want to profit on while telling us to get out of the way, whitey, because you stole everything so it's time for you to take it up the ass."

Her tone grew more indignant the longer she spoke. Lana said that white people needed to "clean out Zionist rats from our governments who seek to destroy us"; that Obama was "intentionally trying to work up the hatred against us"; and that white children were being taught in schools and by pop culture that their skin color was "a cancer." She reserved special disdain for "white race traitors who suffer from a pathological mental disease"—that is, the conviction that white supremacy is a serious problem.

"To my fellow whites," Lana concluded, "get keen to this agenda or we just may lose what we've built up over thousands of years. It's happening now before your eyes. So if you're offended by this program, I don't care. That time is over."

The segment was akin to a campaign kickoff. Lana seemed to have found her cause and her voice. She later joked about some longtime Red Ice listeners accusing her of ruining the platform—of being a CIA agent or honeypot who wrecked the whole enterprise by marrying Henrik and pushing him to the right. Henrik waved the idea off. In its quest to "break away from the mainstream as much as possible," he said, Red Ice and *both* of its hosts had decided that race was a pressing issue. The most pressing one, in fact.

Radio 3Fourteen began to feel less like an homage to *Coast to Coast* and more like a survey of the various entry points into white nationalism. Antifeminism was one that Lana returned to numerous times. But what if a viewer was more concerned about, say, the vilification of Southern heritage? Lana resurrected the UDC's agenda and declared that slavery was not all bad—slaves were allowed to marry and have children, after all. "I wish the South would secede again," Lana said. "That would be great. But now the feds are such gangsters, they're never going to let that happen." The sentiment seemed likely to appeal to another right-wing crowd: the separatist and survivalist set.

What if a listener was pondering why Jewish people talked so much about anti-Semitism? Lana called the Holocaust a "religion" that no one was allowed to doubt, and she criticized the "massive brainwashing operation" that insisted Nazis only did terrible things. "I used to be there, too," Lana said in a monologue. "This is where most truthers, anarchists, left and right, CNN and Fox, Christian and atheists, join as one: on the Nazi issue. It is politically correct to demonize Hitler."

Sick of government telling you what to do? Here, Lana employed a combination of fawning and scolding. "I have to congratulate yet another guest of mine who's managed to make it on the Southern Poverty Law Center's website," she said to Craig Fitzgerald, the founder of a racist anarchist group in New York. "When I need to find interesting guests, I should just go to the SPLC website and check their intelligence reports for dangerous people because I like all the people they warn us about." Fitzgerald was chuffed. Lana asked him what came to mind when he thought of Europe. "I think of my ancestral homeland that I'm yearning to go back to, but I don't know when I'll have enough revenue, money, to do so," Fitzgerald replied. Lana, though, was looking for a different answer. "Many who are ready to defend multiculturalism have never been to Europe," she said. "These people flop their big fat mouths at me without understanding that Europeans are literally well on their way to becoming a minority in their homelands. . . . And who is allowing mass immigration? Government—so government is the problem here. Yet anarchists don't want to touch the subject of race differences." Translation: Fitzgerald was smarter than other people in his anarchist cohort, who leaned too far left. They needed to get enlightened about the evils of diversity; otherwise, they were idiots, and not the useful kind. Lana similarly criticized "naïve" conspiracy theorists and "airhead New Age-y people." If they were shrewd, they'd see that the far right, not left, served their interests. And who didn't want to be shrewd?

Lana interviewed early adopters of the alt-right label. She agreed with Richard Spencer when he told her that SJWs—or "granola communists"—did white nationalists a favor by being "a bunch of people who no one would conceivably want to sleep with." Andrew Anglin told her that the label neo-Nazi "sounds kind of gay, like white supremacist." Lamenting "apology culture," Anglin said that white people needed to stop "running away from accusations of racism or anti-Semitism" because it made them look like "the loser." Lana agreed. "There's no respect when someone's backing down," she said, then raised her voice to a squeak in an impersonation of a liberal. "*I'm sorry, but I like all races!*'—you know, just looks laughable."

Lana's interview questions were self-satisfied, leading, and mostly void of genuine curiosity, suggesting no room—or need—for disagreement. She interspersed them with orations that urged listeners to be bold and liberated. She positioned white nationalism as a coveted code or empowering prize. The people who understood, who really *got* it, should blog, make YouTube videos, and get the word out. They should mock their critics and test the limits of discourse. The white race depended on them provoking liberals and shaping the future. "When people accuse you of being something like a Nazi, just run with it and use it against them, pump it up, and even have fun with it," Lana said. "People censor themselves instead of just cutting loose and saying all those words we've basically been told, 'They're naughty' and 'You can't say that.' But if we don't use those words, then that Overton window, it's hardly going to be open."

Lana was a DIY propagandist suggesting that other people follow her lead, promising that they'd be better and stronger for it. "We're not limiting ourselves to talking about what's safe," Lana once said of Red Ice. The implication was clear: *Neither should you.*

LANA struck me as the strategic descendant of another opportunist, a woman named Elizabeth Tyler. Born in 1881 in rural Georgia, Tyler had no formal education, was married several times starting at age fourteen, ran "sporting houses" (brothels) in Atlanta, and worked in tenements promoting eugenic science under the veil of "hygiene." After meeting an itinerant huckster named Edward Young Clarke at a carnival, she joined him in a new PR venture called the Southern Publicity Association. In 1920, the KKK hired the Southern Publicity

Association to create a Propagation Department, which recruited and charged Klan members a ten-dollar initiation fee. Membership and income skyrocketed; eighty-five thousand people joined the Klan in the first six months of Tyler and Clarke's involvement. Within a few years, the Klan was a multimillion-dollar business.[5]

Tyler's chief skills were in marketing and conscription. She owned a Klan newspaper called *Searchlight* and sent weekly missives to "kleagles," recruiters around the country tasked with expanding the KKK's reach. Tyler encouraged them "to study their territories, identify sources of concern among native-born Protestant whites, and offer the Klan as a solution," writes Kathleen Blee. The "sources of concern" could be anyone: "Mormons in Utah, union radicals in the Northwest, and Asian Americans on the Pacific Coast." Tyler told kleagles to recruit "their friends, and their friends' friends," to find allies in local ministers, and to use churches as staging grounds. In 1921, a congressional report said of Tyler, "In this woman beats the real heart of the Ku Klux Klan today.... She has a positive genius for executive direction."[6]

The same year, during a visit to the Empire State, Tyler bragged to a reporter about New Yorkers "flocking" to the KKK. "Counting letters and callers, I have had at least 700 inquiries in two days," Tyler told the *New York Times*. "And 95 per cent of the persons who sought to line up with the Ku Klux Klan were women. Why not?... The Klan stands for the things women hold most dear."

Tyler may have been exaggerating about her correspondence, though it's impossible to say to what extent. What mattered was that she was projecting strength and esprit de corps. She wanted women reading the article to believe that the Klan was respectable, powerful, even progressive. Tyler noted that a women's KKK would soon exist. Its members would have "equal rights" and "the same ritual and costumes" as the traditional fraternal order. Tyler told the *Times* reporter that she regretted not bringing her silk Klan attire with her to New York, where that very evening she was going to the movies. "It isn't half as dreadful as it has been pictured," she said of the robe.[7]

The article about Tyler ran next to an item about an incident in the small town of Greenwood, South Carolina. A white mob there had dragged two black women—"negresses," the paper called them—out of a local jail and whipped them.[8] Flogging was one of the Klan's favorite tactics of terror in the South. If the reporter interviewing Tyler had asked about extrajudicial whippings, what would the "first lady" of the KKK have said? Perhaps she would have sounded like Lana nearly a century later, speaking to me in Charleston: *You should never denounce an extremist on your side.*

4.

Zeynep Tufekci was on YouTube one day in 2016, watching videos of Trump rallies, when something strange happened: The platform began recommending or auto-playing videos promoting white supremacy and Holocaust denial. It was material that Tufekci, a sociologist at the University of North Carolina, never would have sought out. She ran a handful of experiments. She would create a new YouTube account, watch videos from mainstream sources, and see where the platform suggested that she go next. It pointed her toward what she described as "hard core" videos that endorsed conspiracy theories and fake news—the disinformation that, come November, would wreak havoc on American politics. In a 2018 *New York Times* op-ed about her experience, Tufekci wrote that YouTube "promotes, recommends, and disseminates videos in a manner that appears to constantly up the stakes." The platform, she concluded, could be "one of the most powerful radicalizing instruments of the 21st century."[1]

Tufekci's anecdotal findings were similar to the results of a *Wall Street Journal* investigation that found, for example, that watching a CNN clip about September 11 led to recommendations for videos with titles like "Footage Shows Military Plane Hitting WTC Tower on 9/11—

13 Witnesses React" (5.3 million views).[2] Was YouTube's algorithm to blame? Or was something more basic going on? A 2019 political science paper urged researchers to consider the dynamics of supply and demand. "YouTube has affordances that make content creation easy for fringe political actors who tap into an existing base of disaffected individuals alienated from the mainstream," the paper states. What's more, "alternative voices on YouTube discuss topics mainstream media fails to touch, which may help them feature more prominently in search results and recommendations."[3]

I've been down the rabbit hole that Tufekci and others have identified more times than I can count, clicking on video after video. At a certain point, there's a plateau—or maybe it's a nadir. Racist pundits repeat the same tropes, cite the same falsehoods, make the same generalizations. The queue of disinformation can feel endless, which seems to be the point. If a person likes what they hear, there's plenty more where it came from.

This is what Tim Murdock described in his 2014 interview with Lana as "consistent messages"—a flood of digital material that hits the same points. Repeat, repeat, repeat, and make people believe. And who delivers the messages matters. "Women are just as effective, if not more," Murdock told Lana. "You can get away with saying a lot more than I can get away with."

Red Ice began posting its audio content on YouTube as early as 2009, and it added live video streams a few years later, after the platform's pivot to the far right. Viewers could now see Lana and Henrik at work in their studio, where heavy curtains blocked the windows during taping. There were plush chairs for the hosts, computers where they could chat with viewers, and lighting that turned the space an electric blue. The couple's dynamic was easygoing, sometimes flirty. It might have been relatable were it not for the noxious things they said. Alongside the denial of white privilege, the claims of white genocide, and the appeals to white identity, there were other consistent messages: Muslims are dangerous, Jews are manipulative, communists are conniving, feminists are ugly, black people are violent, the LGBTQ community is degenerate, liberals are snowflakes. To name a few.

In 2016, on *Red Ice Radio*'s tenth birthday, Lana and Henrik held a live fundraiser; their platform is supported by donations and monthly subscriptions, each of which Lana described to me as the equivalent of "the cost of a hipster coffee." The hosts decided to celebrate the occasion with a cake. The confection had a backstory: Lana recounted a recent incident in which a gay Texas pastor had accused a Whole Foods bakery of writing "fag" in frosting on a cake that he ordered. It turned out to be a hoax, and Lana was inspired.[4] She said that she asked an employee at her local Whole Foods if he would put the word "faggots" on Red Ice's birthday cake. "You should have seen this guy, who was a leftie," Lana told Henrik with a laugh. "The plugs in the ears, the clothes, you know, the hipster kind of guy. He couldn't even help me anymore. He was so paralyzed because I thought that saying 'fag' was funny."

According to Lana, Whole Foods wouldn't do what she asked, so a friend of hers put the word onto the cake before the livestream. Viewers could see the result for themselves. The cake sat on Henrik's desk; it was round with white frosting, piped edges, and lettering that said, "Red Ice Radio 10 Years Faggots." The slur was written in a soft pink hue.

The homey scene, an inside joke, PC culture run amok in a grocery store near you—it all suggested a sense of community. "I ask girls all the time, 'How did you find us?'" Lana told me, referring to the women she knows on the far right. "They search around online. They'll find some of the bait and some of the memes out there, and kind of go down this little rabbit hole, and they find us. And then they realize, 'Oh my God. There's all these people that thought like I do. Now I can be vocal.'"

LANA EXPANDED HER reach by collaborating with other racist pundits. She and Henrik attended the annual NPI conference, hosted by Richard Spencer and held in Washington, D.C. When Trump won the Republican nomination, Red Ice celebrated, and on election night, Lana and Henrik broadcast a livestream for more than seven hours. The coverage included appearances by friends and some of the biggest names in the hate movement. There were relative newcomers and members of the old guard, including Jared Taylor, active on the scene since the early 1990s, when he launched the racist journal *American Renaissance*. Soon after Trump's win, Red Ice was in the room where Spencer elicited a Nazi salute.

Lana was especially in demand; she received more attention as a white nationalist than she'd ever gotten as a musician or conspiracy generalist. She appeared on popular alt-right programming, including the podcast *Fash the Nation*. David Duke introduced her on his radio hour as a "harder-hitting" Ann Coulter, with a "movie-star quality." White nationalists who admired her said that Lana ticked off all the right boxes. "Young, attractive, intelligent un-brainwashed women in our camp," a Stormfront user wrote, "is what the enemy fears like the bubonic plague."

One of Lana's hallmarks was talking about sex, both explicitly and not. During a live podcast at one NPI conference, Lana mocked a protester she'd seen outside the event. "He was yelling, 'Fascist scum!' and he looked like a total homeless scumbag talking to guys who are looking pretty slick and pretty hot in their suits," Lana said. Later, she described conference attendees as "funny, edgy, well-dressed, and actually pretty handsome." It was impossible not to read the contrast as intentional. Men had outnumbered women at the NPI event, but Lana said that was to be expected. "Generally, society builders have been men—guys that sit and think of the intellectual framework, the infrastructure," Lana explained on a Red Ice program. "Once you build it, then the ladies come, that's just always how it works." To women, she extended an invitation: "I encourage a lot of you young girls to get there next year and to get matched up with some of these young guys." ("It's important," Henrik added. "We need the babies, folks!")

Lana was presenting herself as the ultimate guys' girl of the far right. She could hang with the boys but not overstep, wield influence without sacrificing femininity, and play matchmaker in a movement obsessed with reproduction. When I met her in Charleston, Lana explained her persona by comparing herself to me. "You and I are different kind of women, in that we're more political. We ask questions," she said. "That's not the norm for most women. They really do want to be beautiful, attract a guy, be taken care of, have their home, have their children." It's not that most women don't care about the wider world, Lana added, "they just don't want it to affect them." White nationalism, in Lana's view, augured a future when life would be easier for white women, free of bewildering distractions and distasteful complexity.

Lana made a concerted effort to find female guests. YouTube's algorithm, perhaps, did some of the work for her; listeners also made recommendations. She found women who agreed with her and ones who were close enough ideologically—or vulnerable enough personally—that a nudge might bring them over to her side. Some women already had strong online followings; others gained them in the months following their Red Ice appearances.

Ayla was an early find, first appearing on *Radio 3Fourteen* in the fall of 2015. From there, Lana amassed a constellation of white-nationalist women. The particulars of their stories varied, but the broad strokes were consistent: They had all felt lost, besieged, empty, probing, insecure, frustrated, or unmoored. White nationalism had transmuted their grievances or anger into a lofty purpose. When she invited them on *Radio 3Fourteen,* Lana gave the women a stage and validation. The effect, it seemed, was intoxicating and emboldening.

Lana's methods reminded me of a statement that Gertrud Scholtz-Klink, the head of the Nazi women's league, once made about appealing to women. "Take it from me," the former Third Reich official said in an unapologetic 1981 interview, "you have to reach them where their lives are—endorse their decisions, praise their accomplishments."[5]

PRETTY WHITE GIRLS get a bad rap—that was the consensus of a klatch of women Lana assembled for an April 2017 Google Hangout that she streamed for Red Ice viewers. The rap was particularly bad in pop culture. Take Regina George, the villain of the iconic comedy film *Mean Girls,* played to vicious perfection by actress Rachel McAdams. She manipulates her friends and cheats on her boyfriend. She creates an insult-filled "burn book" that almost tears her high school apart. But it didn't have to be that way. Regina George didn't have to be mean, beautiful, and white. Hollywood *made* her that way, Lana insisted. "The evil girl in school is always the pretty blond girl. She's the bad one, she's the bitchy one," Lana said. "It's the mixed-race or the multicultural or the leftie ugly girl with her little cat glasses and purple hair that are the good ones."

The "war on beauty," as Lana described it, was a leftist conspiracy targeting women like the guests who'd joined her that day. Each of their faces filled an on-screen box in the Google Hangout. One was Brittany Nelson (a.k.a. Bre Faucheux), a far-right vlogger and fantasy fiction writer. Nelson agreed that *Mean Girls* had an agenda. "The girls who got along and hailed themselves as being good people, they were outcasts," she said. Like the one with "raccoon eyeliner"— Nelson dragged two fingers around the edges of each of her eyes to demonstrate the repugnant thickness—and "goth hair." (Fans of the movie will remember this as actress Lizzy Caplan's character, Janis.)

Lana had plucked Nelson out of relative internet obscurity. A Louisiana native, Nelson once dabbled in beauty blogging, reviewing lipsticks and nail polishes on her website Tribal Faerie, while working toward a master's degree in the United Kingdom. She was a petite brunette who sometimes went red, with a husky voice and a fondness for pearls. "Women who like to look nice (like myself) should not be berated for it," she wrote in a 2013 blog post.[6] "Just because I take time to get ready in the morning doesn't make me dumb, or unintelligent, or into myself. It means I like things that are shiny and sparkly!!" The Twitter feed she kept back then was a stream of random thoughts on school, dating, hitting daily word counts, and smoothie ingredients.[7] There were also photos of her dogs and personal responses to tweets posted by celebrities, including comedian Kathy Griffin and figure skater Johnny Weir. Nelson expressed support for LGBTQ rights and cheered *The View*'s Joy Behar for challenging conservative Christian pundit Pat Robertson on social media.

When she came back to the United States after graduate school, Nelson lived at home and looked for work. Complaining about being in close quarters with her mom, Nelson tweeted, "I need a job! Get me outta here!!" But she couldn't find a gig. In a blog post, she recounted telling a friend, *I can't support myself without help from my parents. . . . I had fifteen job interviews and they all said I don't have enough f*cking "experience."* Her friend replied, *That's our whole generation. No one is doing good on any of those things right now.* In another post, Nelson said that she'd been "lied to" about what success would require. "When I first got out of school, everyone told me that if you go to college, you will get a job. And if you get a Masters (which I did), you are guaranteed an even better job or a promotion down the road. Well, that's just not true anymore," she wrote. "Now, with the influx of degrees, a piece of paper saying you studied at Uni doesn't mean shit because tons of other people have the same thing."

In her free time, Nelson worked on her fiction as much as she could and sent out query letter after query letter. Nothing stuck. "Got my first representation rejection in less than 24 hours!" she tweeted in 2013. A few weeks later: "I am beginning to think that all these 'How to Write a Great Query Letter' sites overall encompass that agents don't know what they want!!" She decided to self-publish her first novel, *The Elder Origins,* described on Amazon as "a historical fantasy with sinister blends of medieval warfare, young love, Native American legend, and vampire lore that will excite anyone with a taste for the macabre and alternate versions of history."[8] Nelson later wrote that she loved being able to set her own deadlines and expectations for her work but resented the "stigma" that self-publishing carried. Why did people feel like they had license to criticize her grammar, even though they knew she didn't have an editor?

Nelson built a profile on BookTube, a YouTube subculture in which users videotape themselves reviewing books. Her taste ran the gamut, from *The Hunger Games* to the Pulitzer Prize–winning *All the Light We Cannot See,* though she knocked the latter for having young "protagonists who don't protag." Nelson soon found that the digital book community could be off-putting. "People are selfish when story lines don't go their way," she once said of online reviewers. "Whatever happened to going along the ride that the author takes you on?? Rather than getting angry about what YOU want to happen." She resented readers telling her how to write. "[I] might never be a best selling author. I might not be a New York Times Best Selling author. [I] might never reach the income I want to from my writing. And I certainly won't be everyone's flavor when it comes to my stories," she wrote in November 2015. "But saying that there is a 'proper' or 'correct' way to write puts a really nasty taste in my mouth."

By the following summer, her tone had grown markedly more bitter, and her politics seemed to be sliding to the right. She posted "Unpopular Opinions," a video in which she described giving up on feminism because it had been "hijacked by a bunch of freaking nut bags." Several weeks later, she wrote about what she saw as publishing's fixation on diversity—white writers were called racist if they didn't have diverse characters and were accused of cultural appropriation if they did. It was a Catch-22, and to what end? "Every single culture in existence has resisted diversity by means of killing each other, segregating against one another, and saying it was even immoral to even be around one another," Nelson said in defense of books with only white characters. "Taking comfort in one's own ethnic group or race is not racist."[9]

The video got thousands of views within a week. Many other BookTubers were furious; some recorded video responses saying as much. But when Lana saw the video, it piqued her interest. She invited Nelson on *Radio 3Fourteen,* where Nelson said "pure anger" had inspired her antidiversity tirade. She claimed that, in college, when she'd suggested that the curriculum judged "white civilization" more harshly than others, she was accused of being ethnocentric. Lana chuckled knowingly. "It's only wrong when whites do it, right?" she asked.

"How *dare* you?" Nelson shot back in mock horror. "Check your white privilege."

After her appearance on *Radio 3Fourteen,* Nelson made a personal video expressing her devotion to the far right. For several months, she'd been reading blogs and watching videos that excoriated feminism, liberalism, and diversity. Recognizing the purported evils wrought by the left—"the collapse in national identity, the destruction of the nuclear family...and the very real threat of white genocide"—had left her despondent. "I couldn't even go to the mall to buy myself a pair of jeans," she said, "without noticing the trends that I had been reading about taking place all around me." Nelson had felt alone in her despair until she went on *Radio 3Fourteen.* Talking with Lana had been like "taking in an entire glass of water after months and months of chronic thirst," Nelson said. She'd lost friends as a result of her political coming-out, but no matter: "My days of engaging in white guilt are over."

By the time Nelson appeared in the Google Hangout with Lana a few months later, she had set book reviewing aside. Her YouTube bio read, "Conservative. Traditionalist. #AltRight Enthusiast. American Nationalist. Pro Gun. Anti-Left. Right Wing Blogger. Author. YouTuber. Completely Deplorable." Nelson was aspiring to be what

Lana described in the Hangout as "the ideal alt-right woman"—she "has a good relationship, she keeps a little fashy household, but she's also fighting back." Sure, it could be hard work for a smart white woman to record a video or bang out a few tweets each day, especially if there were kids and a husband to take care of (as there should be). Yet a woman with the skill to juggle obligations and the toughness to withstand naysayers "needs to take time to do battle," Lana said, "against anti-white politics." Racist women could have it all.

Within a few months, Nelson would launch a YouTube channel that she called 27Crows Radio and become the cohost of the podcast *This Week on the Alt-Right*. She started a romantic relationship: Lana set her up with an alt-right believer who lived in the same city that Nelson did. They exchanged messages on Twitter and agreed to meet. After he watched her on Red Ice, the prospective beau told Nelson that he wanted to buy her dinner. On their first Valentine's Day together, he gave her the biggest bunch of roses she'd ever seen.

Another guest in the Google Hangout was Rebecca Hargraves (a.k.a. Blonde in the Belly of the Beast), a vlogger[10] in the "liberal, fascist hellscape" of Seattle who sometimes recorded videos with a photographed backdrop of vibrant pink and white flowers. She'd first appeared on *Radio 3Fourteen* in early 2016, soon after she started a YouTube channel with a video titled "Living in Libtard USA." She followed that up with "Feminism Is for Idiots and Uglies." She presented herself as the antithesis of what she abhorred: Hargraves wore carefully applied makeup, with tasteful black lines drawn around her eyes, mascara applied to her lashes, and pink gloss smoothed on her lips.

Hargraves had grown up in a largely white and Asian suburb of St. Louis, Missouri, where black students were bused into her district for middle school. "They were often from broken homes, they were interested in crime, disinterested in academics, they were highly sexualized from an extremely young age," she once said in a video. "My friend was successful because her black family moved her out of a black neighborhood and taught her to adopt the values of the white community." After graduating from the University of Missouri, Hargraves worked in finance in New York City, but by age twenty-three, she saw the endgame of the corporate life that she believed feminism had pushed on her: She'd be a slave to her job and either not have kids or be an absent mother.

Hargraves decided to move to the West Coast to reevaluate her life; she ate healthily, stopped drinking alcohol, and decided that she'd been too dominant in her romantic relationships. She also had encounters she didn't like with people of color—for instance, an Uber driver in a niqab who wouldn't let her get in the car with the pet Chihuahua that she carried around in a bag. A man she went out with briefly broke up with her in a text that said, *I cannot date you anymore because I do not believe that you will teach our children that all cultures are equal and to love everyone equally.* "He was right," Hargraves told her YouTube viewers. "I'm absolutely not going to teach my children that—that's garbage."*

She became an online pundit because she felt like she couldn't speak her mind among friends and acquaintances. "I feel like I need to discuss these things or I'll lose my mind," she told Lana in their first conversation. Lana sympathized: "It's amazing how much hate you can come up against with these liberals." Hargraves agreed. "It's a huge double standard," she said.

---

* In early 2020, a pregnant Hargraves launched a YouTube show called *Motherland,* cohosted with Robyn Riley, a vlogger with tens of thousands of followers on her own channel, which she billed as a "creative experiment in free speech." In the first episode of *Motherland,* Hargraves said she was inspired to create the show after watching other motherhood videos that were too apolitical for her taste. "Nobody's talking about cultural issues," she said. Riley chimed in to say that mommy vloggers who were political tended to be "radical feminist[s]." A commenter on the video, identifying as a woman named Stephanie, wrote, "I feel like I've been waiting for this channel my whole life. The perfect marriage of motherhood and red pill."

The exchange fit neatly into a rubric that Lana described to me. When selling white nationalism to other women, she explained, it was important to focus on "the really simple double standards." Simple, I suppose, in the sense that they were tapered to the point of falsehood, or premised on inaccurate statistics, or derived from personal anecdotes instead of rigorous study. "Girlfriends don't go out and have drinks and talk politics like this," Lana said, again referring to the conversation she and I were having. "But I notice when I'm in a group of normie* girls, if you will, and I just start asking questions, present some of the alt-right topics, a lot of them respond."

The subtext seemed to be that women were dumb and malleable. Lana would never have said that outright. When it came to recruitment, she preferred serving up compliments to shaming. She told women that their blond hair and blue eyes—or, if they didn't have those traits, their white skin—were rare and enviable. "A lot of these white girls are tired of being told that white is boring, white is common, white is not diverse," she told me. If flattery didn't work, Lana tried other techniques. She asked women: Wasn't it terrible that the mainstream media attacked "average housewives" like Ayla? Weren't they worried about the dearth of alpha men in liberal circles? Surely they yearned for racial sisterhood, like what black and Jewish women had. All of those suggestions, Lana claimed, might push white women her way.

Another option for recruitment was outright fearmongering. "There's a joke in the alt-right: *How do you red-pill someone? Have them live in a diverse neighborhood for a while*," Lana told me. If women did that, they'd understand. "Women are scared of rape," Lana continued. "They're scared of crime."

She made a similar point in conversation with Hargraves, asserting that America's more diverse areas supported Trump while heavily

---

* "Normie" is a far-right term for someone who hasn't been red-pilled and isn't in the hate movement.

white ones tended to support "communist" or "cuckservative"[*] candidates. Hargraves attributed this supposed trend to "the luxury of being in the elite. There's not a lot of intermingling with low socio-economic backgrounds. They don't really see a lot of the problems that diversity does cause." Neither woman cited statistics. But figures were available, and they proved the assertions wrong. During the 2016 primary season, a *New York Times* analysis of U.S. counties found that "one of the strongest predictors of Trump support is the proportion of the population that is native-born. Relatively few people in the places where Trump is strong are immigrants."[11] The findings held fast through the election: Cities with larger shares of white voters went for Trump. Generally, the less white a county's population, the more heavily it opposed him.[12]

The far right has always appealed to feeling, not fact. It conflates personal experience with hard evidence, and it inflates acolytes' sense of self. "A lot of these liberal women, they're not risk-takers, even though they have piercings or blue hair," Lana once said. "What we do, the things we talk about, I don't think it can get any more high-risk." Her statement underscored white nationalists' quest to be seen as rebels for a righteous cause. Lana presented the mission to reverse decades of progressive change as simultaneously common sense and insightful, rational and radical.

The subtler effect of her orchestration—particularly bringing far-right women together in conversation—was to assure female viewers that ideas wider society might deem offensive feel normal if you're in the right crowd. "It's okay to think like us," Lana said. "If you do, there's a whole tribe here that you can join of girls that actually have your back."

---

[*]   "Cuckservative" is slang for a Republican who isn't sufficiently right-wing.

In *Under the Banner of Heaven,* Jon Krakauer writes of the individual who becomes a fanatic, "A delicious rage quickens his pulse, fueled by the sins and shortcomings of lesser mortals, who are soiling the world wherever he looks." Replace "him/he" with "her/she" and the quote applies to much of *Radio 3Fourteen*'s programming. Lana and her female guests made it their business to remind viewers that they were better than anyone who opposed their movement—intellectually, spiritually, and genetically. And should an adversary come after one of their own, they would degrade them mercilessly.

When Unite the Right organizer Erica Alduino joined Lana for an episode, they both criticized a black female protester at a speech Richard Spencer had recently delivered. The woman wouldn't give up the microphone until Spencer answered her question, which was "Do you think that you are better than I am?" Lana said the protester reminded her of "gangsters...in the ghetto" who "size each other up." Alduino lamented, "That's part of their culture, though."

When Florida schoolteacher Dayanna Volitich (a.k.a. Tiana Dali-chov) was exposed as a far-right podcaster and lost her job—not long after Lana was a guest on Volitich's program, *Unapologetic*—Lana declared it an abomination. "Two girls...do a simple podcast, just talking about leftism and how we need to take the schools back, [and it's] national news!" she said in a Red Ice video. Ayla got involved too, videotaping herself calling the school that had fired Volitich and leaving a message for the administration condemning its decision.

When tradwife Sarah Dye (a.k.a. Volkmom) was identified as part of Identity Evropa, with ties to a member who had painted swastikas on an Indiana synagogue, protesters appeared at a stand she and her husband operated at a local farmer's market. Lana invited Dye on *Radio 3Fourteen,* where she praised her guest for being "brave" and described white nationalists as "gracious" and "well-rounded." Lana also showed clips of "trashy" protesters and laughed at them. "We're dealing with sick people," she said, "and we need to treat them that way."

Insults weren't always prompted by any particular offense—

sometimes they were about policing beauty. Hargraves once tweeted a picture of plus-size model Ashley Graham in a bathing suit. "A particularly tragic case," Hargraves said, "bc she has a pretty face and would be a real fox if she lost 50 pounds. A little fat-shaming would go a long way here."

In a Twitter message, I asked Lana why she and other far-right women attack physical appearance. Lana had recently compared Christine Blasey Ford, during her congressional testimony about alleged sexual misconduct by Supreme Court nominee Brett Kavanaugh, to Dana Carvey in *Wayne's World*. "Lighten up," Lana told me, adding that "trauma" wasn't a guy "rubbing up against her or whatever decades ago." When I asked her the same question after she publicly called a female journalist fat, Lana replied that the target of her cruelty was "clearly unhealthy. What would her fellow comrades say about having to pick up the medical bills for her unhealthy lifestyle habits in their socialized medical system? I sure don't want to pay for it."

On its face, the comment was about leftism. Deeper down, it seemed to be about Darwinism and eugenics. Lest there be any doubt about Lana's views, she once dedicated an entire Red Ice video to criticizing interracial relationships. She described race mixing as part of a plot to erase whiteness from the earth. "That, folks, constitutes as genocide. It's more devious than blatant in-your-face mass murdering, but give it time," Lana warned.[13]

Men like Josef Mengele and Madison Grant were the best-known purveyors of racist science and policy at the height of the eugenics movement's popularity. Women, though, were on the real front lines, incorporating eugenics into the fabric of everyday life. The U.S. Eugenics Record Office trained more than 250 field-workers in the 1920s to go door-to-door in minority communities conducting interviews, taking photographs, observing physical appearances, and compiling family histories. Eighty-five percent of those workers were women. In fact, as historian Elizabeth Gillespie McRae writes, some scientists at the ERO believed that "women's power of intuition and emotional sensitivity made them more adept at judging and assessing the feebleminded and detecting bad 'germplasm,' a supposed biological product of interracial mixing."

Seven female field researchers worked on a 1926 study called "Mongrel Virginians," which McRae describes as concluding that interracial relationships "had rendered a portion of the population less intelligent, less restrained, less industrious, and less moral than their 'purer' white or black neighbors." The findings were used to justify segregation and violence under the auspices of Virginia's Racial Integrity Act (RIA), which prohibited race mixing and classified only people with no trace of non-European blood as white. Women helped enforce the RIA over the next forty years. Their work as midwives, nurses, public registrars, and schoolteachers often put them in close contact with suspected miscegenators and their offspring. White women kept an eye out for ambiguous skin tones so that they could report people they believed had broken the law. "Individual vigilance," McRae notes, was crucial "in determining and upholding racial identity."[14]

When Lana posted the video about interracial relationships, she was either living in Virginia or in the process of moving there. Two hours south of her new home was Sweet Briar College, the all-women's school where the researchers on the "mongrel" study had been based. About the same distance west was Caroline County, where Mildred and Richard Loving, an interracial couple, famously challenged the RIA. The Supreme Court ruled in their favor in 1967, effectively nullifying miscegenation laws nationwide.

Did Lana know this history? Perhaps not. More troubling was the possibility that she did and just didn't care.

5.

A Stormfront user once said of Lana, "She reminds me of the 14 words." The user punctuated the comment with a smiley face.[1] Lana reminded me of something—of someone—else. In Margaret Atwood's *The Handmaid's Tale*, a woman named Serena Joy is married to the man who keeps the novel's protagonist as a sex slave. Before America became a dystopian theocracy called Gilead, Serena Joy was a musician who sang hymns on the radio. Then she turned political, urging people to have faith in the old ways, in the Gospels, in God. "Her speeches were about the sanctity of the home, about how women should stay home. Serena Joy didn't do this herself," Atwood's narrator says, "but she presented this failure of hers as a sacrifice she was making for the good of all."[2]

Lana would surely reject my comparing her to Serena Joy. When the TV adaptation of *The Handmaid's Tale* premiered, around the time of my trip to Charleston, Red Ice produced a short video declaring it "anti–white male agitprop." Lana laughed off Atwood's public comments about the show's relevance in the Trump era. "Are you seriously going to tell me women are still oppressed while you can sit here talking about how oppressed women are?" Lana said. "This could easily be a show about Islam."

Unlike Serena Joy, Lana has never been a Bible-thumper. In fact, she described herself to me as having "a problem with a lot of Abrahamic religions in general" and being "more of a pagan." Which isn't to say that she had a problem with individual Christians—she extolled white nationalism as "incredibly diverse, just not racially," with "pagans, Christians, atheists, agnostics and even a few Satanists." She spoke of ideological diversity: free-market capitalists and national socialists working together.

When Lana talked about faith, she invoked the natural world—all that was pure, primal, and sensuous. "Why the fear in discussing what nature made?" Lana asked in an early *Radio 3Fourteen* episode. "To me race is metaphysical, the formation of different biological expressions is miraculous. Racial differences are the manifestations of the spiritual expressed in physical form. Racial awareness is spiritual to me—it's mysticism when you combine the knowledge of one's family lineage as well as a spiritual effort to delve into your people's primordial and mythical times."

The quote owed a debt to the Nazi concept of *Rassenseele* ("racial soul"), wherein the Nordic master race was spiritually distinct from inferior beings like Jews and black people. Alfred Rosenberg, the Third Reich's most prominent racial ideologue, believed that "religion of the blood" was the truest possible faith. Genetics, not a shared belief in a particular god or pantheon, were the ideal preconditions for a spiritual community.[3] Rosenberg was hanged after the Nuremberg trials, but his ideas lived on, including in Savitri Devi's writings and advocacy. Devi traveled the world and kept company with other wealthy Nazi apologists, including Françoise Dior, niece of fashion designer Christian Dior.

Another female contemporary of Devi's seized on the idea of racial souls, but rather than mingling with the racist upper crust, she exerted influence through the grass roots. Else Christensen was born in Denmark in 1913. She became a professional handweaver and amateur philosopher, and she supported the Third Reich. After World War II, Christensen and her husband, who had spent time in a detention camp for his Nazi sympathies, moved to Canada. She was a health-care worker and studied right-wing political ideas in her free time. Christensen established contacts with activists in North America and Europe, including neo-Nazi Willis Carto and members of George Lincoln Rockwell's ANP. She read tracts about Norse mythology and was drawn to the god Odin, ruler of Valhalla. She also embraced Carl Jung's idea of a "collective Aryan subconsciousness."[4]

Christensen fashioned a new theology urging Aryan people to save themselves from the ravages of modernity—capitalism, pollution, multiculturalism, Judeo-Christian beliefs—by reverting to a tribal state and honoring the gods of their ancestors. She believed that the ideal social order was commune-style living in which group welfare was paramount; protecting borders of all kinds was vital to racial and spiritual survival. Historian Mattias Gardell writes that, to Christensen, "a pure individual nurtures a pure mind in a pure body and lives a wholesome life in purity with an equally pure partner in a pure—that is, heterosexual and monoracial—relationship. This pure family provides a wholesome environment for bringing up pure and healthy children and is the primary building block of a pure racial organism living in harmony with a pure unpolluted ecological system."[5]

This all might have amounted to little more than offensive personal musings, but in her retirement, Christensen decided to start a movement. In 1969, she founded the Odinist Fellowship, which she considered a religious organization. When her husband died two years later, she relocated from Canada to a mobile home in Crystal River, Florida. She began delivering lectures and self-publishing a newsletter called *The Odinist*. The first issue was printed in August 1971 and cost thirty cents, or one dollar for four copies. An essay on the front page declared, "The Man of the West has forgotten how to think for himself, how to take [an] honest stand, and how to have the courage of his convictions."[6]

Christensen encouraged the people her teachings reached to start their own Odinist chapters. By the early 1980s, she'd devised another evangelical strategy. Now in her seventies with thinning white hair, sporting reading glasses on a lanyard around her neck, Christensen visited prisons to recruit Odinists. She staged religious services and informational seminars for audiences that were literally captive. As a result of the converts she gained, Odinism became recognized as a religion under Florida law.

Christensen insisted that she wasn't a white supremacist. Like Lana, she claimed to honor "the diversity of Nature, including the natural variations of human beings." When people criticized her support for the Third Reich, Christensen lamented that she was enduring "the cheapest of all shots that can be aimed against anyone who finds something positive to say...or who merely desires some degree of objectivity in dealing with this grossly maligned movement."

Problematic on its face, Christensen's faith took a dark turn when several members of the Order swore allegiance to it. One of them was David Lane. Behind bars, Lane devised his own variation of the religion, which he called *Wotansvolk* ("Odin's Folk"). He incorporated violence into the creed, describing it as a means of separating the white race from its enemies. He advocated leaderless paramilitary resistance and denounced Christianity as kumbaya nonsense. "God is not love," he said. "Compassion between species is not the law of nature. Life is struggle and the absence of struggle is death."[7]

The success of Lane's sect was due in no small part to his wife, Katja, who once described *Wotansvolk* as a "vehicle to unite our race, give us a singular sense of identity as well as destiny."[8] A one-time Vietnam War protester with undergraduate degrees in Spanish and Portuguese literature and a master's in economics, Katja had met her husband through prison correspondence. She published Lane's religious writings under the auspices of what the couple called 14

Words Press. She also delivered speeches on his behalf and organized a prison outreach program to spread Lane's ideas. She corresponded with prison chaplains nationwide, provided *Wotansvolk* reading materials to inmates, and offered legal advice when penal authorities challenged a prisoner's right to practice the religion.[9] By the early aughts, whole gangs of white inmates had converted to the faith. "[Katja] spent much of her day by the computer, updating the *Wotansvolk* Web page, communicating electronically with fellow Odinists and sympathizers in the United States and abroad," Gardell writes.

Initially a complement of sorts to Christian Identity, by the turn of the millennium, Odinism had become the more influential racist faith.[*] It was a belief system for skinheads uninterested in anything that looked like their parents' religion; a pathway to radicalization for the environmentally conscious and incarcerated; an affirmation that whiteness wasn't America's original sin but something ancient and vital; and a tradition rich in symbols and rituals that weren't white hoods and cross burnings. "The most cursory glimpse at White-racist publications, Web pages, and White-power lyrics reveals muscular heathens, pagan gods and goddesses, runes and symbols, magic, and esoteric themes in abundance," Gardell noted in 2003. Paganism rooted in bigotry was "on its way to reducing earlier racist creeds . . . to the status of an old man's religion."[10] That was ironic considering who had accelerated its spread in the first place. Else Christensen died in 2005. She was buried under a gravestone bearing the moniker her followers had given her: "folk mother."

Today, there's a *Wotansvolk* settlement in rural Tennessee, a

---

[*] Creativity, a third racist religion that became prominent at this time, was neither Christian nor rooted in pagan mythology. It held that the laws of nature designate a racial hierarchy—"that race, not religion, is the embodiment of absolute truth and that the white race is the highest expression of culture and civilization," according to the SPLC. Some Creators advocated racial holy war (RAHOWA). The religion lost considerable strength in 2005, when its leader, Matthew Hale, was sentenced to forty years in prison for encouraging an FBI informant to kill a federal judge.

self-proclaimed "Odinic wolf cult" near Lynchburg, Virginia, and nodes of pagan alliances all over the country.[11] A researcher who went undercover in the far right for the organization Hope Not Hate described attending events where people prayed to Odin and drank mead from a Viking horn.[12] Some hard-core racists mimic the masculine ideal of a Norse warrior by committing violence. Anders Breivik, the perpetrator of the 2011 terrorist attacks in Norway, identified as an Odinist; a member of the "wolf cult" once set a black church on fire. Yet Odinism has never become a unifying theology, certainly not among white nationalists concerned with keeping a foot in the social mainstream. Its primary significance seems to be its impact on the grab-bag imagery and language of the far right.

Pagan symbols and mythological figures show up on posters, websites, flags, and lapel pins; an attendee at the 2015 NPI conference showed off a pendant shaped like Thor's hammer that he wore on a necklace.[13] When black actor Idris Elba was cast as a Norse god in the movie *Thor,* the Council of Conservative Citizens (CCC), a racist organization, urged a boycott to protest cultural appropriation. "Marvel has now inserted social engineering into European mythology,"[14] the CCC declared. More recently, on social media, the same alt-right followers using #DeusVult, a Crusades-era Christian battle cry, romanticized the figure of the pagan fighter. The term *volk*/folk was invoked in memes and online chatter as referring to white people descended from ancient European civilizations, downplaying the term's connection to Nazism. A *volkisch* emphasis on honoring nature and one's ancestors implied that acolytes merely wanted to live in harmony with the earth, one another, and their history. Pagan emblems and ideas also served as reminders that white nationalism wasn't strictly an American project. They summoned alliances among white people everywhere, suggesting that individuals of common stock should have common cause. That cause was restoration, a vague notion that could mean everything from adopting old traditions—languages, recipes, holidays, rites—to ridding white society of contaminating influences.

Thanks to Henrik's Swedish heritage, Red Ice had Norse mythology in its DNA. The company's name came from a legend about the creation of the world occurring in the space between fire and ice. After its rightward shift, Red Ice regularly featured guests who supported racist paganism. Among them was Carolyn Emerick (a.k.a. Völkisch Folklorist), a writer who insisted that the Holocaust was a hoax; that she would "not abide" her "exceptionally pure bloodline... being flushed down the shitter after 400 years of racial purity in the New World"; and that population control in Africa could start with Prince William neutering his brother, who by the time Emerick made the comment was in a relationship with Meghan Markle.[15] Red Ice itself became rich in the iconography and language of white restoration. The tagline of Christensen's *The Odinist* was "New Values from the Past," and one of Red Ice's slogans was "The Future Is the Past." Lana and Henrik appeared in a promotional photo for their company as a Viking couple. Wearing chain mail and leather, he carried a spear; she had a sword and shield. Henrik was in the foreground, facing the viewer directly. Lana was behind him and turned to the side—a helpmeet or sidekick, but no less powerful.

The image captured another way that paganism has influenced white nationalism: by prescribing distinct roles for men and women in the movement. According to various far-right figures, ancient Northern European populations knew that, by design, the sexes weren't equal, physically or otherwise. Freyja, the Norse goddess associated with love, fertility, and war, was the female archetype—fierce, fruitful, and complementary to her male counterparts. Today, this view manifests in the hate movement as a celebration of misogyny, which supporters describe as natural and necessary. Men are strong and rational, women yielding and emotional; men are good at navigating politics, women at nurturing family units; men make decisions, women provide counsel. Social harmony depends on the sexes embracing their roles: When everything is in its right place, the world comes into balance. Believers argue that this is no less true in the twenty-first century than it was in the time of the Vikings.

The same goes for the *act* of sex. In the far-right imagination, intercourse is required for there to be white babies, certainly, but it's also necessary for prosperity and security. Lana articulated this idea at a 2017 conference in Stockholm, Sweden, not long before we met in Charleston.[16] "What really drives men is women, and, let's be honest, sex with women," Lana explained to a room of white nationalists. Sex, in short, is what motivates men to fight for racial survival.

Lana asked the audience to imagine the vesica piscis, the shape created when two circles intersect, as in a Venn diagram. Lana explained that it adorned the doorways and windows of many old European churches. "It lured people in, making them feel warm," she said. "To get graphic, the vesica is reminiscent of the vagina." Lest anyone doubt the revolutionary power of female bodies, Lana invoked centuries' worth of wars waged, freedoms protected, and civilizations supposedly built on behalf of white women. "It's the ultimate romantic gesture," she said.

David Lane once wrote, "Nothing makes a woman happier than to be desired by a great warrior." Consciously or not, Lana was echoing that opinion and presenting herself as a desirable white woman. At the Stockholm conference, she wore her hair down, hanging over her cheek on one side and tucked behind her ear on the other. She was clad in a demure white blouse and crocheted black shawl. She toggled between being forceful—minorities can "get the fuck out" of Europe, she said at one point—and playful, like when she talked about the vesica piscis. As ever, she flattered the men in the room, assuring them that women wanted to sleep with them. "Like in school, when the pretty girl dated the guy no one noticed before, all of a sudden, everyone noticed that guy. Well, nationalism has become that guy," she said. "We have winning arguments, and remember, women choose winners."

To women, Lana offered insight and a warning. Deep down, she said, they wanted only three things: beauty, family, and home. "Exactly what nationalism gives to women. We value the beauty of Western civilization and the refined human form," Lana said. "A nation is your extended family, your tribe, your support system. The comfort of your home and way of life remains uncertain without your people as your neighbors. The Left provides us with nothing but ugliness, conflict, violence, and anti-nature false constructs."

While women "are too emotional for leading roles in politics," Lana argued, they have always had political power, should they choose to tap into it. To that end, she had instructions: Be like Freyja or a Viking wife. "Be loud," she said. "When women get involved, a movement becomes a serious threat."

LANA's STOCKHOLM SPEECH garnered some ninety-five thousand views and more than one thousand comments on Red Ice's YouTube channel before the platform took it down. Sites like the Daily Stormer shared it too. Some viewers described Lana as an "Aryan goddess" and compared her to Joan of Arc. Several encouraged her to go into politics. One even joked, "I'm with her."

There were also sexist replies. Some were objectification masked with adulation: Men said they wanted to sleep with Lana or touch her flowing blond hair. Other comments were cruelly blunt. "If women are busy giving speeches and making YouTube broadcasts," one read, "they are not going to have time to give birth." On the Daily Stormer, a commenter who took it upon himself to rate Lana as "maybe a 7" said he didn't have any interest in "spending 15 minutes listening to a female who isn't singing and/or playing a musical instrument."

It wasn't the first time that Lana had been subjected to the far right's misogyny. In December 2015, Colin Robertson, a young Scottish alt-right blogger who called himself Millennial Woes, invited Lana and Ayla onto a livestream. The conversation's topics ranged from

Robertson's gallstones to American suffragettes, whom Lana criticized as "spinsters, women who couldn't get married, gay females who were teaming up with Marxists." Forty minutes in, the comments from viewers turned ugly. "These women are the same old tainted, fucked-up strong womyn," one Chad Thundercock wrote. A viewer with the handle Don Trump commented, "This Lana cunt needs to wash her mouth before speaking badly about MGTOW." That's the acronym for "men going their own way," a virulent subculture of the manosphere in which men swear off women entirely. Lana had on more than one occasion pointed out that not having sex wasn't conducive to propagating the white race. MGTOW acolytes—or miggies—weren't pleased with her take.

Henrik, who was also on the livestream, noticed the comments targeting his wife and went on the offensive. "These guys are, like, fucking losers," he said. "Get a fucking life, you idiots." Lana jumped in, her tone shifting from chatty to scathing. "You cowards are hiding behind your avatar trying to talk trash about us," she said. "You're a disgrace, and you will be wiped out of this society once men finally step up and get their act together."

When I asked Lana about the incident, she told me that she had a female stalker who was responsible for the mean replies; she declined to elaborate further. Generally speaking, Lana dismissed on-line commenters as mere "agitators"—an ironic stance for someone in a movement built in no small part on the backs of internet trolls. She mused about infiltration, suggesting that commenters might be part of the Jewish Internet Defense Force or even FBI agents.

Her answer sidetracked the real matter at hand: the divisive potential of far-right women. Lana seemed to agree heartily with her movement's gender politics. She disavowed feminism—white women didn't need it, she told me, because "our men have already propelled us like crazy." When I asked about sexist comments made by high-profile men in the alt-right, Lana countered by paraphrasing David Lane: Men in the movement "love women," she said, "and they want a future for women and children." How could love be sexist? Lana rolled her eyes when she talked about Trump's "grab 'em by the pussy" comment. "Feminists are always bragging about their vaginas, and showing their vaginas, and walking around topless," she said. "All of a sudden, they become Puritans when the guy says the word 'pussy.'"

Countering Lana's replies might fill a book of its own. There would be a chapter on how misogyny and love can be intertwined. Another on why a woman embracing her body isn't an invitation for a man to touch it. How a woman might have a rape fantasy and simultaneously fear being violated. Who gets to use the word "pussy" and how. Suffice it to say, there was an unbridgeable gap in our conversation. I got the sense that when Lana talked to other women, ones who had already found antifeminism, tradlife, or other inklings of white nationalism, the span was often more manageable.

But what about the kind of misogyny that, in the long run, would likely minimize someone like Lana in the very movement to which she'd dedicated herself? One of the talking heads at the Stockholm conference was Paul Ramsey (a.k.a. RamZPaul), a middle-aged man with black thick-rimmed glasses and some sixty thousand Twitter followers. Ramsey once said that he didn't believe women should be allowed to vote or participate in politics—period. That stance was shared by Greg Johnson of the racist publishing company Counter-Currents, who was once caught on tape complaining about women having too few children and too late in life. As a remedy, he suggested what can only be called a school-for-birth program. "Women are postponing childbearing because of education and their careers," Johnson said. "Say you give a woman a free year of education for every child she bears and takes care of in the home up to the age of six. Okay, so maybe by the time she's thirty she's ready to go off to college or something."[17]

Lana, I realized, faced competing audiences: racist men who were skeptical or disdainful of female strength, and racist women wary of a cause that might sideline them. She used public appearances to reassure both groups, which required twisting logic and concocting rationaliza-tions as needed. Lana didn't apologize for being voluble but confessed to having overactive "guy brain," the assertive and argumentative part of herself. She boosted women like Ayla, Rebecca Hargraves, and Brittany Nelson, who claimed to feel empowered in traditional gender roles. She said that many of the highest-rated *Radio 3Fourteen* episodes had female guests, which in her mind was a sure sign that male viewers liked them. She didn't argue that women should lose the right to vote; in our interview, she pushed the matter into the future, saying that in an ethno-state white households would vote as units. As for rejecting groups like MGTOW, Lana's effort felt feeble at best.

I wondered if she would at least condemn domestic abusers. Over the course of my research, I heard her rail against what she called the Hollywood stereotype of white nationalists as wife beaters who live in trailer parks. What about Richard Spencer? In divorce proceedings, Nina Kouprianova, Spencer's wife of eight years and a nationalist pundit in her own right, accused him of physical and emotional abuse. She had recorded him threatening to break her nose and suggesting that she kill herself. "You have nothing to offer the world," Spencer told her. "You are profoundly disgusting." In an interview with journalist Lyz Lenz, Spencer didn't deny saying awful things, but he insisted that there was important context. For instance, his wife "wouldn't listen," and he didn't *actually* break her nose. "It's tough talk, words said in anger," Spencer told Lenz. "There is a red line between actually doing something."[18]

In a Twitter message, I asked Lana about the abuse accusations. She brushed them off. "Who knows what's true in that marriage," she told me.

MY INTERVIEW WITH Lana in Charleston became part of a *Harper's Magazine* article I wrote about the women of the alt-right. The article focused heavily on the contradictions that women in the movement navigate, and it pointed to historical precedents where they didn't succeed. Misogyny forced Elizabeth Tyler out of the Klan that she'd built. Tyler and Edward Young Clarke, her business partner, were both married to other people but were having an affair. Clarke's former secretary—a man—suggested that this gave Tyler undue power. "Her experience in catering to [men's] appetites and vices had given her insight into their frailties," the secretary wrote.[19] Klan leaders didn't like a woman wielding so much influence anyway, and they forced Tyler's resignation over charges of embezzling funds. She died in 1924. Later, when Gertrud Scholtz-Klink proposed titles that women could hold in the Nazi Party, male superiors objected because the honorifics were too similar to men's. "They perceived any autonomy on the part of the women as a threat," historian Geraldine Horan writes.[20]

After my article was published in August 2017, Red Ice addressed it in its programming at least twice. Lana waved off my comparisons to white-nationalist women of the past, because they lived long ago and she had nothing to do with them. She and Henrik also made several false claims seemingly intended to make me look like a rube or a liar. They said that I was shocked when Lana was friendly to a black bartender at Stars and that I'd gone undercover in my reporting, neither of which was true. What I found most interesting in their reactions, though, were the illogical leaps made in service of an agenda. "They're talking about how basically nationalism holds women back," Lana said of the article. "So you're saying communism was liberating for women? Stalin, Mao, Castro, that was all about female empowerment?" There are plenty of political ideologies and structures outside white nationalism and communism—liberal democracy, for one. But reinforcing the purported existence of a battle between far-right good and leftist evil, and lumping my article in with the latter, worked to Lana's advantage. There was no need, and no room, for other possibilities. "Ambiguity vanishes from the fanatic's worldview," Jon Krakauer writes. "A narcissistic sense of self-assurance displaces all doubt."[21]

To prove that white nationalism wasn't hostile to women's interests, Lana convened a Google Hangout that she broadcast online. Ayla was there; Nelson was too. Two other women joined, and Lana made a point of saying that she'd invited several others who couldn't make it. Their mere existence, it seemed, was supposed to help prove my research wrong—even as real-world events suggested that it was right.

Around the same time Lana recorded the Hangout, far-right vlogger Tara McCarthy publicly decried male trolls who were harassing vocal women in the movement. "Men in the alt-right are going to have to decide whether they will continue to passively/actively endorse this behavior, or speak out against it," McCarthy said on Twitter. "If you want more women speaking publicly about ethnonationalism, I suggest you choose the latter." Vlogger Lauren Southern faced so much backlash for promoting traditionalism while not being married at the age of twenty-two that she felt compelled to make a video entitled "Why I'm Not Married." Then, in early 2018, Nelson vanished from the internet under murky circumstances, shortly after she recorded podcast episodes criticizing chauvinistic movements like MGTOW. I asked Lana what had happened, and she told me that Nelson was "fine. Planning a wedding. Lots of weddings and babies lately." When Nelson reappeared several months later, she was indeed married. In a Red Ice segment, she said family stuff had kept her from far-right advocacy. Lana made a point of mentioning past "attacks on some single women in our circle."

In the Google Hangout about my article, Lana walked an ideological tightrope. "I would love to be able to just do things around the house and feed my other creative interests and spend time with children," she remarked. "But that's not the times that we live in, because now we're all called to say something against . . . this anti-white system that wants to come after our children, that wants to destroy their future."

It was hard to imagine Lana, who'd sought a spotlight for so much of her life, gladly disappearing into her home should a white ethnostate ever exist. I wondered if the pursuit of white nationalism—the struggle, as believers would call it—was the endgame for people like Lana. Did she crave the energy and tenacity of a movement more than its stated goals? Perhaps so, which posed considerable risks should the world ever go—*really* go—the far right's way.

There was another reason Lana reminded me of Serena Joy in *The Handmaid's Tale.* In Gilead, Serena Joy's life is different than it was before, because the new order followed through on its pledge to install a brutal patriarchy. Women aren't allowed to read, much less be involved in public life. "She doesn't make speeches anymore. She has become speechless," the narrator says of Serena Joy. "She stays in her home, but it doesn't seem to agree with her."

"How furious she must be," the narrator continues, "now that she's been taken at her word."

6.

In the nightmare, it's a dazzling day—sunny, cloudless, probably in the summer, though I don't feel any heat. I'm preparing to host a dinner party. In some versions of the dream, it's an outdoor barbecue. I learn that I have new neighbors, and I decide to introduce myself and invite them to the meal. No sooner do they open the door of their home than I realize that they're white nationalists. I panic as I introduce myself, my mouth saying, *Hi, how are you,* while my mind becomes a combat zone. One side says, *Invite them over; you don't want to be rude. Isn't that how you change hearts and minds?* Except *fuck that,* the other side jumps in—*that's just "white niceness,"* as an acquaintance of color once aptly described it.

Every time I've had the dream, I've woken up before I had to make a decision. Except once. In that case, I decided not to invite the couple, but they hosted their own barbecue at the same time as mine and invited their white-nationalist friends. We all found ourselves sharing the evening in side-by-side yards—two groups of people with antipodal worldviews, unsure of how to communicate.

The nightmare came to life when, in the summer of 2018, I received an email out of the blue from a woman I'd never met. I've agreed not to reveal her name out of concern for her safety; I will call her Kay. She had stumbled across a small item in her local newspaper, a property-transfer notice. The names of the people who'd purchased a home not far from Kay's were familiar. She looked them up on-line. That's how she remembered who they were, and how she found me. I had written about the couple in my *Harper's Magazine* article. The wife was the better-known figure of the pair. A congressman had even retweeted a comment she made about Swedish children being "adorable & everyone knows it."[1]

The couple were Lana and Henrik. They'd moved to Harrisonburg, Virginia, with their baby boy. (In 2020, Lana gave birth to a second son.) "So far I would guess fewer than 100 folks realize who Henrik and Lana are, although word is spreading quietly," Kay wrote. "Of course they are free to live wherever they want. . . . We are not looking to borrow trouble, but we want to be aware."

Aware, that is, of Lana's worldview and possible motives for moving to a small city that's home to three colleges. After Unite the Right the previous year, white nationalists had continued making headlines by posting recruitment flyers on college campuses, urging white students to organize. One of the ringleaders of that effort, a man named Patrick Casey, frequently appeared on Red Ice; information gathered by leftist activists indicated that he lived in Harrisonburg. Kay wondered if Henrik and Lana's arrival presaged a Unite the Right–style event in their city. She and other concerned neighbors wanted to be prepared.

After receiving the email, I messaged Lana on Twitter and asked how she liked her new home. "We do not live in H'burg but have a property there," she claimed. "[It] is actually a massive refugee relocation center and had a major crime increase. It used to have potential. . . . The only good thing about Shenandoah Valley is the beautiful nature." The last point was a matter of opinion, but the rest of what Lana said ranged from flat-out lies to skewed facts. Church World Service had been resettling refugees in Harrisonburg and the surrounding area for thirty years, which was a problem only for someone who didn't like refugee resettlement as a general practice. A 2018 *USA Today* article listed Harrisonburg as a place where violent crime was "soaring"—up 37 percent between 2011 and 2016—but it also noted that "violent and property crime rates in Harrisonburg remain far lower than the national rates . . . and among the lowest in the country."

And Lana *did* live there, at least some of the time. The property-transfer notice wasn't the only proof. Neighbors had seen her around town, spoken to her, and even invited her and Henrik over to their homes. I know because I went to visit.

THE LAST TIME I'd been in Virginia was on the heels of Trump's election, when I saw a white woman use a racial slur at a gas station. Now, as I drove south toward Harrisonburg, the midterm elections were approaching. On a highway overpass, people waved Trump banners to the traffic below. Trump had supporters running for office, including Corey Stewart, cochair of the president's Virginia campaign in 2016. Stewart hoped to defeat Democrat Tim Kaine in Virginia's Senate race—or "kick [his] teeth in," as he once put it. Stewart's agenda was anti-immigration and pro–Confederate history. He had supported the preservation of the Robert E. Lee statue in Charlottesville, rubbing shoulders with the organizers of Unite the Right. Stewart later voiced the same opinion that Trump did about the event ("fine people on both sides"). I spotted several Stewart for Senate yard signs and bumper stickers as I entered Harrisonburg.[*]

Kay had invited a small group of people for breakfast at a cavernous hotel and convention center on the campus of James Madison

---

[*] Corey Stewart narrowly lost the Republican nomination to Ed Gillespie. As of this writing, he is the director of the pro-Trump PAC Keeping America Great. He told the *Washington Post* that he left electoral politics because it "sucks," and that he wasn't interested in becoming a bureaucrat in the Trump administration because "the problem with these jobs is that they don't pay very much."

University. Student servers ferried coffee and water to the table; the food was on a buffet, piled on steaming metal platters. The group Kay had convened was mostly middle-aged and white; a few people were Jewish, and several worked in education. No one wanted to graffiti Lana and Henrik's house, stage a protest, or yell angry things at them. They came with pen and paper, ready to take notes. I came with a recorder, hoping to gain insight into what it meant to face down white nationalism in your own backyard. Mostly, it seemed to involve confusion. The breakfast was a long, winding conversation about a single question: What did people who cozied up to neo-Nazis want in Harrisonburg?

I can imagine Lana reading this, perhaps live on Red Ice, and laughing at the concerned citizens' expense. How silly, she might say, that a bunch of sensitive liberals were anxious about her living among them. They should blame the media for turning her into a villain. In reality, she's just a wife and mother who records videos; she's never hurt anyone.

"The negative outcome of a public act or utterance that spreads prejudiced or hateful ideas is the same, no matter the motivation or intent," researcher Chip Berlet writes in the book *Home-Grown Hate*.[2] This truth was made plain in a story that I heard in Harrisonburg. When Lana and Henrik first moved into their new home, a black couple lived next door. They'd come from out of town too, likely drawn by the same factors that attract many new arrivals: Harrisonburg is quiet but not sleepy. Property values are good. The Shenandoah is storied and bucolic. The road where the couple chose to live is particularly picturesque. It snakes up a ridge with panoramic views to the east and west. From a front window or a back porch, sunrises and sunsets must be stunning. But when they discovered who their new neighbors were, the black couple put their house on the market and relocated.[*]

---

[*] I made several efforts to speak with the couple, and a contact in Harrisonburg communicated with them on my behalf. Ultimately, the couple could not be reached for an interview.

Lana didn't wear a Klan robe or keep a Nazi flag flapping in the breeze outside her home. Her belief system, however, was all but indistinguishable from women who did. She inflicted injury by unilaterally limiting the definition of *harm* and then doing what fell just outside it. If a person was hurt by what she said or did, it wasn't her problem.

Except, of course, it was. Lana provoked fear and antipathy as a matter of business. Bigotry had become her livelihood.

HARRISONBURG HAS A large Mennonite population. Two of the city's colleges are Mennonite institutions. This affected how some residents reacted when they found out that white nationalists—prominent ones—had moved to town. Mennonites are committed to pacifism and loving thy neighbor. A church in Harrisonburg was the origin of a protest sign staked in the lawns or placed in the windows of many Trump opponents nationwide. It declares in three languages, "No matter where you are from, we're glad you are our neighbor."[3]

After finishing the breakfast meeting, I visited a few people around town. One Mennonite grandmother, who served me freshly baked cookies in her wood-paneled kitchen, hugged her arms to her body and shook her head when she told me that deciding how to engage with overt racists was a test of her faith. Neighbors confirmed that Lana and Henrik were honest about their beliefs—not proselytizing, per se, but finding opportunities to discuss their views on white identity, immigration, and other relevant topics. Maybe, some residents suggested, the city could respond by incorporating lessons about tolerance and antiracism into public schools. That way, kids would know what to do with hateful ideas if they encountered them.

After I left town, I stayed in touch with several of the people I'd met. Over the next year, whenever I contacted them, I got a version of the same response: Things are quiet up on the ridge. People seemed surprised, relieved, or both. They still cared, very much so. But in the absence of something tangible to oppose—a rally, racist flyers, Lana or Henrik running for local office—it was hard to know where and how to direct their concern.

From their home, Lana and Henrik kept running Red Ice. Many of their most popular videos featured only Lana, the clear star of the operation. Some of the YouTube videos garnered views numbering in the hundreds of thousands, and a few were creeping toward one million views when YouTube banned them for offensive content. In a signal of the conservative media establishment's ever-tightening relationship with the far right, Lana hosted former Fox News contributor and bestselling author Michelle Malkin on *Radio 3Fourteen*.

Lana's rhetoric didn't soften as her profile rose—quite the opposite. She spoke at a conference sponsored by *American Renaissance* in rural Tennessee, where she mocked transgender people and said that "sickly" progressives feared the far right because "we represent their deepest fear: putting them back into the shadows where they belong." Around the same time, a sociologist ran an analysis comparing the manifesto of a terrorist who murdered fifty people at a mosque in New Zealand with the language of online bigotry. The results showed that Lana was "one of the influencers with the most similar rhetoric"—far more, even, than her husband's.[4]

People in Harrisonburg were still wondering why the couple had chosen their city. Was it the colleges, with all those young, impressionable minds? The proximity to other white nationalists based in Virginia, or maybe to bodies of power in Washington, D.C.? Or was it because of the Mennonites, whose most orthodox adherents live a modest, communal existence much like the one many white nationalists aspire to have?

There was a more mundane guess. It seemed just as plausible, maybe more so. Like many American communities, Harrisonburg is nice—a nice place to live, a nice place to raise a family, a nice place to build a community. It's nice right up until, as Lana and Henrik's neighbors learned, it isn't.

CONCLUSION

The Way Through

No thanks, god bless.

That's how Ayla rejected one of my requests for a follow-up interview. She wasn't always so friendly in our exchanges. "Have you no shame???" she asked in one email, lambasting my reporting about tradlife. Around the same time, in late 2018, she recorded a YouTube video in which she told viewers that I was lying about her. She encouraged people to "politely contact" me and provided my email address should they want to do so. It was mildly surreal to sit at my desk, a battered thrift-store purchase piled high with books and articles about white supremacy, watching on my laptop screen as Ayla called me dishonest. I started my journalism career as a fact-checker; I don't take the accusation lightly. But there was no proof of error—there was only invective. Ayla's video was titled "Never EVER EVER Trust the Media, a Personal Note."

A barrage of emails from Ayla's defenders never came, but I did get a private message on Instagram from a stranger. It arrived in early 2019. "So anyway, you're kind of a cunt," it began.

According to this person, a woman, I was guilty of "slandering" Ayla and "putting her family in danger" because I didn't like "her more traditional conservative politics." The sender let me know that she wasn't religious. "Sometimes I wish there was a God, so I knew you'd get your punishment in the afterlife," she said, "but I'd rather not believe in a creator who'd made a devious sociopath like you."

I looked her up. She was a college student in Colorado. I mentally added her name to the list of adversaries I'd managed to make while writing this book. I had been accused by other people I didn't know of applying "strands of Jewish left wing intellectualism to white Nationalism."[1] A male blogger called me a "snowflake" for whom "facts are so inconvenient."[2] On /pol/, users dubbed me "blue-pilled" and a "commie." Another commenter did some Googling to determine if I was Jewish—I'm not—while another described where I live as "(((Brooklyn NYC)))," deploying the echo marks that white nationalists use to designate Jewish people online.[3]

Some of the women I approached for interviews, including Brittany Nelson and Rebecca Hargraves, declined my request or never spoke to me at length. "If I had a dollar for every seemingly kind journalist that approached me that I declined, only to be flooded with relief when I read the subsequent story," Hargraves wrote in an email. Several months after speaking with me in Charleston, Lana told her followers not to do media interviews, unless they planned to record what a reporter said and "do something fun with it." In a subsequent Twitter message to me, sidestepping a request for a follow-up conversation, Lana wrote, "None of this benefits me in the end. It only benefits you. Let's not pretend." I pointed out that journalism wouldn't exist if reporters interviewed subjects only for mutual benefit—it would be indistinguishable from public relations. Lana didn't reply.

My last correspondence with Ayla, who since we first spoke had relocated from Utah to the East Coast, was a series of emails about fact-checking the book. On March 16, 2020, I wrote the following:

As I've mentioned a few times in the past, I am writing a book about women and white nationalism in which you are featured.

Ultimately, I have organized the book around the stories of three women, yourself included. The book details how and why each of the women came to support nationalism and what their activism has involved. Many other women are featured, though less prominently. The book draws from a range of sources, including interviews, correspondence, blogs, videos, social media, books, and articles. There is a wealth of material in the text beyond the three main stories, pertaining to history, sociology, psychology, and other relevant topics. The book has been fact-checked and copyedited.

Last we left it, you indicated that you didn't want to speak to me further—which I acknowledge in the book—and that is your choice, of course. Still, in addition to telling you about the book's substance, I want to offer you the opportunity to respond to some queries from the fact-checker. Please let me know if you would be willing to do so.

A few hours after I sent the email, Ayla replied, "I am willing to respond to an independent fact-checker." Ten minutes later, she sent another message: "Correction. I will not be speaking with anyone." I followed up to clarify. Three days later, she responded:

To whom it may concern,

I do not authorize Ms. Darby's project, a book which features myself, because of Ms. Darby's egregious, damaging carelessness and inaccuracy in her past coverage of me. Furthermore, I do not give her permission to profit from misrepresenting myself or my family.

There are dead ends in every reporting project, but ones like this I found uniquely telling. Indeed, they were part of the story. Lana, Ayla, and other white-nationalist women I encountered subscribed to the "fake news" narrative that Trump has amplified as president, the notion that most journalism is deliberately distorted to undermine right-wing voices and ideas. Trump has gone so far as to call the media "the real enemy of the people"—the *volk,* that is—and his verbal attacks have fomented aggression among his supporters. The *Columbia Journalism Review* has described a "climate of hate toward the press at Trump rallies."[4] The women who declined interview requests likely did so because they saw me as part of the "lamestream media."

I suspect, however, that there was another reason they dismissed my work. White nationalists have always wanted to tell their stories on their own terms—unscrutinized, mythologized. Now more than ever they have a stage with an open mic. While writing the book, I thought often of a comment I read on YouTube, left beneath a far-right video by a supportive viewer: *No need to talk to any media ever. We are our own media now.*

According to Lana and Henrik, Red Ice had more than three hundred thirty thousand YouTube subscribers and one million monthly views before the platform removed the company's channel in October 2019. Facebook banned Red Ice a month later. As of this writing, the company and both of its proprietors are still on Twitter. Red Ice's video and audio content is available elsewhere, including on the company's main website and BitChute, a platform established to accommodate content creators who dislike YouTube's speech policies. Plus, there are followers and fans who use their own accounts to promote Red Ice on platforms that have kicked it off.

In 2017 and 2018, Ayla had accounts terminated by Facebook and Twitter, where she once had more than thirty thousand followers. She remained active on other platforms and used prohibitions of her content to promote her brand as the "most censored Christian mom in America." In July 2019, she decided to take a break from "public life." A few months later, she scrubbed numerous videos from her YouTube account. She took to describing herself as "politically retired." But Ayla made the political a domestic concern; there was little distinction between the two realms. White pride could be ministered at dinner tables, during playdates, through electronic mailing lists, and on private texts. Stepping out of the public eye wasn't a retreat—it was a shift in focus. When some of her social media followers begged her not to go, Ayla said that she didn't know what the future held; she might be back soon enough. In the meantime, she offered to send a newsletter about tradlife to anyone who provided their address.

LANA'S AND AYLA'S online moves are pertinent to a question that lingers here, at the end of the book: What can America *do* about the hate movement? Tech companies can identify and ban hate speech, but this process inevitably becomes a game of Whac-a-Mole. It's not enough, and it never will be. Similarly, bringing the law to bear on hate speech and crimes is necessary but remedial—levying penalties for specific wrongdoing won't vaccinate America against far-right extremism.

It's possible to imagine the hate movement fracturing along its own fault lines, especially internecine conflicts and power struggles. Red Ice and Richard Spencer's Breitbart-style project seemed to fizzle around the time Spencer began clashing publicly with some other alt-right figures and then faced charges of domestic violence. Could personal rifts, so common on the far right, be harbingers of something more definitive?

"An emphasis on the disorganized aspects of Aryanism obscures its strategic and structured dimensions," argue the authors of the book *American Swastika*.[5] Today, that emphasis downplays the endurance and adaptability of the hate movement over time. It ignores the internet's unparalleled propaganda power and the implications of hate as a social bond. It overlooks that white Americans' group consciousness is ascendant and that the mere existence of the Trump administration is evidence of the political salience of explicit appeals to white interests. The idea that white nationalism is going anywhere, much less anytime soon, is wishful thinking.

I will confess to being a pessimist by nature, and while reporting on the far right, I found it difficult not to feel despondent. Magnifying my gloom were encounters with white people who identified as moderate or liberal who made statements that I recognized as precisely the kind of bait white nationalists use to make their case to the mainstream. At a dinner party, a friend of a friend I'd never met before, a little younger than I, went into full All-Lives-Matter mode. She made false equivalences—for instance, that "ban white men" was just as dangerous as saying that America should ban Muslims or black people. Attempts to bring power disparities and other context into the conversation were met with retorts about people just needing to be nicer to one another. In another instance, standing in a breakfast buffet line, a middle-aged writer told me that I needed to be very careful with my book lest it hurt women (white ones, presumably). Of *course,* she said, what white-nationalist women supported was wrong, but everyone was complicit in something, right? Lowering her voice, she added that America never would have had slavery if Africans hadn't sold their own people to European traders. I could imagine some of the women featured in my book saying those words, verbatim.

The least Americans can ask of one another is to have frank conversations about whiteness, no matter how difficult or uncomfortable. People concerned about the rising tide of hate can also get involved in antiracist initiatives that seek to empower populations of color, tackle inequality, facilitate dialogue about prejudice, and root discriminatory ideas out of American life.* They can demand better media coverage of race and vote bigots and xenophobes out of office. They can support the work of groups like Life After Hate, which helps people leave far-right groups. But first and foremost, combating hate requires understanding it—not what it seems to be or what we hope it amounts

---

*   White nationalists despise—and perhaps fear—this kind of action so much that one of their rallying cries is "antiracist is a code word for antiwhite."

to, but what it actually *is*. That includes who supports it, why they do, and how their experiences reflect a reality we all share.

Women are the hate movement's dulcet voices and its standard bearers. As purveyors and keepers and caretakers, they arguably tap into a wider spectrum of power than men do. They would be hate's secret weapons, except there's a difference between hiding and not being seen. Outsiders discount or overlook the women of white nationalism at America's peril. The same goes for minimizing or ignoring the factors that push some women toward a politics of exclusion and hate.

In our pluralist, capitalist, ever-shifting society, identity is a crucible in which people forge the future. For women, as ever, the stakes are particularly high. As the century barrels on, could white women prove increasingly vulnerable to hate's allure? What might the consequences be? Lana put her vision of the threat succinctly in her 2017 Stockholm speech. "It was women that got Trump elected," she said triumphantly. "And I guess to be really edgy, it was women that got Hitler elected."*

So MUCH OF history is made up of small moves. Hope, too, dwells in increments. There is hope if white Americans can confront the true face of hate and their own complicity in bigotry, however oblique. There is hope if they can see white nationalism as a crisis of individual and collective responsibility. If that sounds kumbaya, so be it. Once upon a time, the word didn't conjure cynicism. It summoned strength and resistance.

---

* Adolf Hitler lost a presidential race, but the Nazis earned enough votes in a parliamentary election in 1932 to become the dominant party in the Reichstag. Hitler was appointed chancellor the following year. Research indicates that the party's ascent to power was due in no small part to its success in garnering support from women, particularly those of the Protestant middle class. Between 1928 and 1932, the Nazis won an increasing number of votes from women, who reported casting ballots out of self-interest and concern for the future of German society.

There is a strain of kumbaya in the stories of people who've exited the hate movement. In my interviews, women who used to be white nationalists described a hand they didn't expect, thrust through the surface of hate's murky pool, offering them its grip. Maybe it was a love interest or a childhood friend who showed up to remind them of how life might have been different. Maybe it was someone who gave them an opportunity—a job, a platform—that made them realize they didn't need hate. Or maybe it was family.

Rae, who radicalized as a teenager and found community in the racist music scene, met with me on a hot July day in 2018. We sat on a bench outside a new public library, all glass and wood surfaces, in the West Coast town where Rae lived with her husband and kids. She had long dark hair that hung to her waist and tattoos on her arms, but none that were racist. "I was proud of that, at least," she quipped.

Rae said that when she had her first baby, a girl, she began to see the world differently. "I realized how vulnerable she was and how shitty the world was, and I had to do something to make it better," Rae explained. For so long, she'd thought that supporting hate was that "something," because it meant speaking truth about how minorities were standing in white people's way, making life hard in America. But now, at home caring for her daughter, worrying about money and the future, Rae began to wonder: Did her community of hate misidentify what was problematic in her life? Maybe it wasn't people with black or brown skin or Jews with their purported monopoly on successful careers. Maybe the problem was being working class in an economic system that cared about what it got from someone like Rae, not what it could provide her.

Rae had exited hate several years before we met. In the intervening time, she'd become an advocate for economic policies that support families. She'd built a career working and volunteering for progressive initiatives. She'd voted for Obama. She wanted to help other people leave the hate movement.

After they found that first grip, Rae and other women with whom

I spoke found another, then another. There were setbacks—a grasp lost or a hand that wouldn't let go when it was time to move on. Still, the women kept finding a way forward.

———

IT WAS LIKE that for Corinna.

The mosque she attended when I met her was a world away from everything that made her life challenging. No one asked about her past. She didn't have to think up topics of conversation, which always made her uncomfortable, because no one got tired of talking about what they believed, the dogma that gave their lives meaning. The kinship that the women at the mosque offered was genuine, and they didn't want anything in return from Corinna. They just seemed glad she was there, practicing Islam alongside them.

The day after I first went to prayers with Corinna, we returned to the mosque for an exercise class. It was held in a small, drab gym. The floor was painted, peeling, and dotted with equipment that sagged from disuse: a badminton net, a basketball hoop, a cornhole deck. Corinna had volunteered to lead a calisthenics session when she heard several women at the mosque talking about how they wanted to be healthier but didn't know where to start. Exercise was something she knew, something she was good at.

Wearing a hijab, workout gear that covered her arms and legs, and a pair of Nikes, Corinna led a half-dozen women in simple exercises. There were jumping jacks, modified push-ups, and a round of lunges. She had the women grab bottles of water to use in bicep curls. Corinna was a good teacher—clear, firm, encouraging. "Challenge yourself a little bit each time," she said as the women did reps. With every exercise, she showed the proper body positioning to avoid an aching back and pulled muscles: arms straight, abdominals engaged, head up.

I settled onto the sidelines with my notebook. At one point, the women asked who I was, scribbling while they tried to work up a sweat. Without hesitating, Corinna said that I was a journalist writing about women who had transformed their lives. The group nodded knowingly. I assumed they thought that Corinna was talking about her religious conversion. She and I hadn't agreed on the description of my project, but it was right.

When a call to prayer emanated from the gym's loudspeaker, the women rushed to the middle of the floor. They left their shoes in a pile and stood in a line on a blue tarp. One used her cell phone to find the direction of Mecca. "A little to the left!" she instructed, and the group edged that way. Then they fell silent. I could hear the crinkling of plastic, gentle whispers, and the whir of traffic outside.

The prayer began. The women stood hip to hip, all except Corinna. She was at one end of the line, where she'd left a gap between her body and the rest of the group. The woman closest to her glanced over. She was tall and willowy, a black woman from Niger. She extended a hand, sending a ripple through her abaya. She grasped Corinna's arm and tugged her close.

ACKNOWLEDGMENTS

Sisters in Hate was born during an inauspicious coffee date. Katia Bachko, recently installed as an editor at *Harper's Magazine,* invited me to pitch feature ideas. It was January 2017. I was between jobs and eager for a meaty freelance assignment. I told Katia about some women I'd started following online; they were supporters of the alt-right, which didn't immediately square with the media's depiction of the movement as a bastion of toxic masculinity. A few weeks later, I was interviewing Lana Lokteff, Ayla Stewart, and other white nationalists. That September, my story appeared on the cover of *Harper's.* By then I had a new job, which I also owed to Katia: At the same coffee confab, she'd told me that her old employer, the *Atavist Magazine,* was looking for an editor. So I must extend my first, hearty thanks to Katia. She brought her keen editorial eye to my nugget of an idea and single-handedly proved that there are times when networking actually *works.*

I wouldn't have written a book—ever—if my friend and agent Adam Eaglin hadn't convinced me that I could. It took a few months, but he won, and I'm glad that he did. He had a vision for *Sisters in Hate* that was as exciting as it was daunting. I owe him a lifetime of wine dates and dog videos for encouraging me. Thanks to the rest of the team at the Cheney Agency for their enthusiastic support of the project.

Vanessa Mobley of Little, Brown was the first editor I met with, and I was thrilled when the book landed in her hands. She understood immediately that I wanted to write a text that was urgent but empathic, angry but grounded. She was a brilliant sounding board, reviewer, and confidante. I appreciated the guidance, notes, and encouragement from others at Little, Brown, especially Sabrina Callahan, Reagan Arthur, Elizabeth Gassman, Shannon Hennessey, Jessica Chun, and Karen Landry.

Fact-checkers are the real heroes of nonfiction reporting. Rachel Poser checked the *Harper's* story with patience and fortitude. Kate Wheeling stepped up to the plate to check the book. She handled even the most taxing material with grace, clarity, and compassion. I am forever in her debt. The same goes for my copyeditor, Susan Buckheit, who, among making other vital contributions to the book, pointed out that there are, in fact, gay characters in the Sweet Valley High series.

My eternal gratitude goes out to the colleagues who supported me through reporting and writing, including with drinks when I very much needed them: Evan Ratliff, Jefferson Rabb, Jonah Ogles, Sean Cooper, Ben Huberman, Michelle Weber, Mike Dang, Mark Armstrong, Cheri Lucas-Rowlands, Krista Stevens, and Carolyn Wells, as well as the staff at *Longreads,* the *Atavist's* wonderful sister publication. I am also grateful to the Virginia Center for the Creative Arts (VCCA), which allowed me the time, space, and tranquility to work on the book and nothing else for a few weeks. I was lucky enough to share a portion of the manuscript for the first time with other VCCA residents, and their feedback was the push I needed to meet my manuscript deadline with confidence. Special thanks to Finola Merivale for Barry's Tea and *No Such Thing as a Fish,* both of which proved crucial to my mental health.

To the many friends and loved ones who tolerated my talking about this book and its themes ad nauseam, I promise to be a more elevating conversationalist in the future: Kyle Knight, Jake

Scobey-Thal, Katie Flahive, Megan Greenwell, Meredith Shiner, Saidi Chen, Peter Finnerty, Sarah Mehta, Lauren Goodwin, Ryan Brier, Jamal Berkenkotter, Merritt Wever, Rachel and Alexia Korberg, John Kilbane, Katie Engelhart, Ari Urus, Sam Dolbee, Brian McGinn, Jess Rather, Glenna Gordon, Lauren Markham, Carly Knight, Emily Eckert, Kevin Cornish, Michael Leviton, and my in-laws Scott and Cindi Sobel, Killian Sobel, and Kylie and Marc Kline. A special thanks to Michelle Legro, who read an early manuscript and provided feedback that made the final version infinitely better. You will not find a better friend than a magazine editor willing to read your book in their "free time."

I would be utterly lost without the many experts who generously provided the insight and context necessary to navigate topics ranging from hate to conspiracy theories: Wendy Lower, Kathleen Belew, Kathleen Blee, George Hawley, Keegan Hankes, George Michael, and Brendan Nyhan, among others. There are many scholars and journalists whose research I read eagerly and to whom this text owes a great debt; their names and the titles of their indispensable works can be found in the book's endnotes.

I couldn't have written *Sisters in Hate* without the participation of Corinna Olsen, Lana Lokteff, and Ayla Stewart. I am appreciative that they gave me their time and shared their stories, to the extent that they were willing. I am also grateful to the other women I interviewed, some of whom are former white nationalists who wished not to be named. Rae, especially, was generous with her time. Thanks to the family members, friends, teachers, and other sources who talked to me about the book's subjects, and to the residents of Harrisonburg who welcomed me in their city.

My parents, Leonard and Catherine Darby, raised me to be curious and open-minded—not to tolerate difference but to celebrate it. They taught me to work hard, and they have never stopped telling me they are proud of me. They have been supporters of this project even when, as parents, it scared them. They also named me

"Seyward"—pronounced "say-word"—which probably meant that I was destined for a life immersed in language. I owe them everything.

Last but never least is my husband, Corey Sobel. I've always considered him the real writer in our relationship. He writes novels by hand, while mine cramps at the mere thought. Words are his oxygen. He gets up every day eager to create and consume language in equal measure. I have spent more than eleven years in awe of what he is capable of. All the while, he has treated me like the writer I so often doubt that I am. He is my biggest fan, my most perceptive critic, and the adult in the house who remembers to walk the dog, feed the cat, and do the laundry when I'm chasing an elusive fact or source. He is my person.

NOTES

Author's Note: *Sisters in Hate* was reported over the course of three years. In addition to conducting extensive interviews and reading dozens of books and articles, I reviewed a wealth of far-right websites, personal blogs, and posts on social media and messaging platforms, including Twitter, Instagram, YouTube, Facebook, Reddit, 4chan, Gab, Stormfront, Discord, Telegram, and BitChute. With very few exceptions, when I quoted online posts, I left errors of grammar, spelling, and syntax untouched. Some of the digital material was available only via the Wayback Machine or another online archive. I downloaded or took screenshots of many items, anticipating that their creators might delete them at some point, and I took extensive notes to which I could later refer. In the endnotes that follow, I have tried to state which content, as of this writing, is no longer readily available.

INTRODUCTION

1   See, for instance, Jack H. Lepa, *The Shenandoah Valley Campaign of 1864* (Jefferson, NC: McFarland & Company, 2003).
2   This is from the poem "Lynchburg": Mary Mackey, *Breaking the Fever: Poems* (East Rockaway, NY: Marsh Hawk Press, 2006).
3   "Presidential Election Results: Donald J. Trump Wins," *New York Times,* last updated August 9, 2017, https://www.nytimes.com/elections/2016/results/president.

4 Lawrence Hammack, "Confederate Battle Flag Polarizes Rockbridge County and Lexington," *Roanoke (VA) Times,* July 23, 2015, https://www.roanoke .com/news/virginia/confederate-battle-flag-polarizes-rockbridge-county-and -lexington/article_98929a38-595f-5b6f-815d-cac293dcd000.html.

5 Caitlin Dickerson, "A New Martin Luther King Jr. Parade Divides Virginia Town," *New York Times,* January 16, 2017, https://www.nytimes.com/2017 /01/16/us/parades-lexington-virginia-martin-luther-king-jr-robert-e-lee .html.

6 Dara Lind, "Nazi Slogans and Violence at a Right-Wing March in Charlottesville on Friday Night," Vox, August 12, 2017, https://www.vox.com/ 2017/8/12/16138132/charlottesville-rally-brawl-nazi; the video referenced in this article, posted by Twitter user @_Dr._Bill_, is no longer available.

7 Barbara Perry, "'Button-Down Terror': The Metamorphosis of the Hate Movement," *Sociological Focus* 33, no. 2 (May 2000): 113–31.

8 George Hawley, "The Demography of the Alt-Right," Institute for Family Studies, August 9, 2018, https://ifstudies.org/blog/the-demography-of-the -alt-right.

9 J. M. Berger, "The Alt-Right Twitter Census: Defining and Describing the Audience for Alt-Right Content of Twitter," VOX-Pol Network of Excellence, 2018, https://www.voxpol.eu/download/vox-pol_publication/Alt RightTwitterCensus.pdf.

10 "Rae" (pseudonymous source), interview with author, July 10, 2018.

11 Mariel Padilla, "Student Wins $725,000 in Lawsuit over 'Troll Storm' Led by the Daily Stormer," *New York Times,* August 10, 2019, https://www.nytimes .com/2019/08/10/us/taylor-dumpson.html.

12 "Extremist Files: Andrew Anglin," Southern Poverty Law Center, https://www.splcenter.org/fighting-hate/extremist-files/individual/andrew -anglin.

13 Seyward Darby, "The Rise of the Valkyries," *Harper's Magazine,* September 2017, https://harpers.org/archive/2017/09/the-rise-of-the-valkyries/.

14 Monica Hesse, "Wolfie James and the Insidious Role of Female White Nationalists," *Washington Post,* August 14, 2019, https://www.washingtonpost.com /lifestyle/style/wolfie-james-and-the-horrifying-softer-side-of-white-supremacy /2019/08/14/19c86a68-babe-11e9-b3b4-2bb69e8c4e39_story.html.

15 Nell Irvin Painter, *The History of White People* (New York: W.W. Norton & Company, 2010), ix, 383.

16 Frances Lee Ansley, "Stirring the Ashes: Race, Class, and the Future of Civil Rights Scholarship," *Cornell Law Review* 74, no. 6 (September 1989): 993–1077.

17 F. Scott Fitzgerald, *The Great Gatsby* (New York: Scribner, 1925), 13.

18 Kathleen Belew, *Bring the War Home: The White Power Movement and Para-military America* (Cambridge, MA: Harvard University Press, 2018), 60–61.

19 Ashley Jardina, *White Identity Politics* (Cambridge: Cambridge University Press, 2019), 8, 16, 116, 261.

20 "QuickFacts," United States Census Bureau, last updated July 1, 2018, https://www.census.gov/quickfacts/fact/table/US/PST045218.

21 Jardina, *White Identity Politics,* 96, 262.

22 Leonard Zeskind, *Blood and Politics: The History of the White Nationalist Movement from the Margins to the Mainstream* (New York: Farrar, Straus and Giroux, 2009), xviii.

23 "The Year in Hate and Extremism," Southern Poverty Law Center, March 18, 2020, https://www.splcenter.org/news/2020/03/18/year-hate-and-extremism-2019.

24 "Hate Groups Reach Record High," Southern Poverty Law Center, February 19, 2019, https://www.splcenter.org/news/2019/02/19/hate-groups-reach-record-high.

25 Jana Winter and Hunter Walker, "Here's the Data on White Supremacist Terrorism the Trump Administration Has Been 'Unable or Unwilling' to Give to Congress," Yahoo! News, August 8, 2019, https://news.yahoo.com/heres-the-data-the-trump-administration-wouldnt-give-congress-on-white-supremacist-terrorism-235254627.html?soc_src=hl-viewer&soc_trk=tw.

26 Zolan Kanno-Youngs, "Homeland Security Dept. Affirms Threat of White Supremacy After Year of Prodding," *New York Times,* October 1, 2019, https://www.nytimes.com/2019/10/01/us/politics/white-supremacy-homeland-security.html?smid=nytcore-ios-share.

CORINNA

1.

1 This section draws extensively on interviews and correspondence between Corinna and the author that took place between 2018 and 2020.

2 "Stormfront: A History," Southern Poverty Law Center, March 26, 2015, https://www.splcenter.org/hatewatch/2015/03/25/stormfront-history.

3 Benj Edwards, "The Lost Civilization of Dial-Up Bulletin Board Systems," *The Atlantic,* November 4, 2016, https://www.theatlantic.com/technology/archive/2016/11/the-lost-civilization-of-dial-up-bulletin-board-systems/506465/.

4 Patricia Anne Simpson and Helga Druxes, *Digital Media Strategies of the Far Right in Europe and the United States* (Lanham, MD: Lexington Books, 2015), 27.

5   "Stormfront: A History."

6   Phyllis B. Gerstenfeld, Diana R. Grant, and Chau-Pu Chiang, "Hate Online: A Content Analysis of Extremist Internet Sites," *Analyses of Social Issues and Public Policy* 3, no. 1 (December 2003): 29–44.

7   See Jessie Daniels, *Cyber Racism: White Supremacy Online and the New Attack on Civil Rights* (Lanham, MD: Rowman & Littlefield Publishers, 2009); see also Jessie Daniels, "The Algorithmic Rise of the 'Alt-Right,'" *Contexts* 17, no. 1 (February 1, 2018): 60–65.

8   Corinna Olsen (@NorwayLuray), "Q's about WN vs. Supremacy," Open Forums: General Questions and Comments, Stormfront, March 21, 2008, https://www.stormfront.org/forum/t471121/.

2.

1   Thomas Burt, interview with author, November 23, 2019.

2   Corinna Olsen, "Harley," Facebook photo album, https://www.facebook.com/eatliftgrow/media_set?set=a.149456088446122&type=3.

3   Burt, interview.

4   Gavin Evans, "The Unwelcome Revival of 'Race Science,'" *Guardian* (U.S. edition), March 2, 2018.

5   Angela Saini, *Superior: The Return of Race Science* (Boston: Beacon Press, 2019), 202.

6   Kathleen Blee, "Positioning Hate" (paper presentation, Conference to Establish the Field of Hate Studies, Spokane, WA, March 20, 2004).

7   Linda Gordon, *The Second Coming of the KKK: The Ku Klux Klan of the 1920s and the American Political Tradition* (New York: Liveright Publishing Corporation, 2017), 8.

8   Arie Kruglanski, Katarzyna Jasko, David Webber, Marina Chernikova, and Erica Molinario, "The Making of Violent Extremists," *Review of General Psychology* 21, no. 1 (March 2018): 107–12.

9   Dinitia Smith, "The Women Behind the Masks of Hate," *New York Times,* January 27, 2002, https://www.nytimes.com/2002/01/26/books/the-women-behind-the-masks-of-hate.html.

10 Joseph A. Schafer, Christopher W. Mullins, and Stephanie Box, "Awakenings: The Emergence of White Supremacist Ideologies," *Deviant Behavior* 35, no. 3 (March 2014): 177.

11 "Rae" (pseudonymous source), interviews with author, July 10–11, 2018.

12 Corinna Olsen (@NorwayLuray), "Are There Any Affordable White Neighborhoods Anymore?" General: Lounge, Stormfront, April 13, 2008, https://www.stormfront.org/forum/t481275/.

13 Alan Taylor, "American Nazis in the 1930s—The German American Bund," *The Atlantic,* June 5, 2017, https://www.theatlantic.com/photo/2017/06/american-nazis-in-the-1930sthe-german-american-bund/529185/.

14 Frederick J. Simonelli, *American Fuehrer: George Lincoln Rockwell and the American Nazi Party* (Urbana: University of Illinois Press, 1999), 11–12, 17.

15 Donna Alvah, *Unofficial Ambassadors: American Military Families Overseas and the Cold War, 1946–1965* (New York: New York University Press, 2007), 95–96.

16 The Injustice System, "Stokely Carmichael Black Power Speech & Debate W George Lincoln Rockwell" (audio recording), ca. 1966, Internet Archive, https://archive.org/details/StokelyCarmichaelBlackPowerSpeechDebateWGeorge LincolnRockwell.

17 Simonelli, *American Fuehrer,* 3.

18 Savitri Devi, *The Lightning and the Sun* (Calcutta, India: Temple Press, 1958), 419.

19 Kathleen Belew, *Bring the War Home: The White Power Movement and Paramilitary America* (Cambridge, MA: Harvard University Press, 2018), 6–7.

20 "FAQ," New Order (website), https://neworderorg.wordpress.com/faq/; this website is no longer available.

21 "National Socialist Movement 'Gathering' in Portland," Rose City Antifa, February 25, 2014, https://rosecityantifa.org/articles/national-socialist-movement-gathering-in-portland/.

22 Anna Diamond, "The Original Meanings of the 'American Dream' and 'America First' Were Starkly Different from How We Use Them Today," *Smithsonian Magazine,* October 2018, https://www.smithsonianmag.com/history/behold-america-american-dream-slogan-book-sarah-churchwell-180970311/.

23 natsocmov, "NSM to Rally in Arizona: Nov. 13th—V.2," AltCensored (website), October 1, 2010, https://altcensored.com/watch?v=npcMKCctUWo; another video of the event, once available on YouTube, has been removed: https://www.youtube.com/watch?v=f9TdkiDffqM&bpctr=1550856959.

24 Burt, interview.

25 Carol Tavris and Elliot Aronson, *Mistakes Were Made (but Not by Me): Why We Justify Foolish Beliefs, Bad Decisions, and Hurtful Acts* (Boston: Houghton Mifflin Harcourt, 2007), 5, 71.

26 Joseph Bernstein, "The Baraboo Nazi Prom Photo Shocked The World. The City's Response Shocked Its Residents," BuzzFeed News, April 2, 2019, https://www.buzzfeednews.com/article/josephbernstein/baraboo-nazi-prom-photo.

3.

1   Maxine Bernstein, "Anti-Racist Group Argues Shooting of Portland Man Was a Neo-Nazi Attack," *Oregonian* (Portland, OR), April 2, 2010, https://www.oregonlive.com/portland/2010/04/anti-racist_group_argues_shoot.html.

2   Elinor Langer, *A Hundred Little Hitlers: The Death of a Black Man, the Trial of a White Racist, and the Rise of the Neo-Nazi Movement in America* (New York: Metropolitan Books, 2003), 34–35, 228, 234.

3   Alice H. Eagly and Antonio Mladinic, "Are People Prejudiced Against Women? Some Answers from Research on Attitudes, Gender Stereotypes, and Judgments of Competence," *European Review of Social Psychology* 5, no. 1 (January 1994): 1–35.

4   David Sadker and Karen R. Zittleman, *Still Failing at Fairness: How Gender Bias Cheats Girls and Boys in School and What We Can Do About It* (New York: Simon & Schuster, 2009), 21.

5   Otto H. Olsen, "The Ku Klux Klan: A Study in Reconstruction Politics and Propaganda," *North Carolina Historical Review* 39, no. 3 (July 1962): 340.

6   Timothy Tyson, *The Blood of Emmett Till* (New York: Simon & Schuster, 2017), 1–7.

7   William Bradford Huie, "The Shocking Story of Approved Murder in Mississippi," *Look,* June 1956, https://web.archive.org/web/20170208225152/ and http://www.pbs.org/wgbh/amex/till/sfeature/sf_look_confession.html.

8   Wendy Lower, *Hitler's Furies: German Women in the Nazi Killing Fields* (New York: Houghton Mifflin Harcourt, 2013), 196.

9   Stephanie E. Jones-Rogers, *They Were Her Property: White Women as Slave Owners in the American South* (New Haven, CT: Yale University Press, 2019), xvi.

10   "Women Extremist Organizations Stake Their Claim on the Web," *Intelligence Report,* Southern Poverty Law Center, September 15, 1999, https://www.splcenter.org/fighting-hate/intelligence-report/1999/women-extremist-organizations-stake-their-claim-web.

11   General: The Women's Forum, Stormfront, https://www.stormfront.org/forum/f167-62/.

12   Evelyn Schlatter, "Better Homes and Aryans: April Gaede Wants to Be a Publisher," *Hatewatch* (blog), Southern Poverty Law Center, November 16, 2010, https://www.splcenter.org/hatewatch/2010/11/16/better-homes-and-aryans-april-gaede-wants-be-publisher.

13   Kathleen Blee, *Inside Organized Racism: Women in the Hate Movement* (New York: New York University Press, 1998), 133.

14 Red Ice TV, "Lana Lokteff—How the Left Is Betraying Women—Identitarian Ideas IX," Internet Archive, February 27, 2017, https://archive.org/details/youtube-BjnH99slHmE.

15 Mark Potok, "The Year in Hate & Extremism, 2010," *Intelligence Report,* Southern Poverty Law Center, February 23, 2011, https://www.splcenter.org/fighting-hate/intelligence-report/2011/year-hate-extremism-2010.

16 Elizabeth Wheaton, *Codename Greenkil: The 1979 Greensboro Killings* (Athens: University of Georgia Press, 1987), 46.

17 Ferrel Guillory, "Nazi's Showing in N.C. Race Embarrasses GOP," *Washington Post,* May 14, 1980, https://www.washingtonpost.com/archive/politics/1980/05/14/nazis-showing-in-nc-race-embarrasses-gop/84295cd5-37c3-449c-b8b6-cea599978b14/.

18 Harold Covington, "A Special Message from HAC," *Homeland Blog,* Northwest Front, November 8, 2010, http://northwestfront.org/2010/11/a-special-message-from-hac/.

19 "Extremist Files: April Gaede," Southern Poverty Law Center, https://www.splcenter.org/fighting-hate/extremist-files/individual/april-gaede.

20 April Gaede (@AprilGaede), "Book Suggestions for Children and Young Adults," General: Education and Homeschooling, Stormfront, January 6, 2012, https://www.stormfront.org/forum/t857678/; and April Gaede (@AprilGaede), "Non PC Homeschooling Books," General: Classified Ads, Stormfront, January 2, 2012, https://www.stormfront.org/forum/t856843/#post9867371.

21 Jesse Pearson, "Hello, White People!" Vice, November 30, 2004, https://www.vice.com/en_us/article/yvba8m/hello-v11n10.

22 Nancy S. Love, *Trendy Fascism: White Power Music and the Future of Democracy* (Albany: State University of New York Press, 2016), 68–69.

23 Patricia Anne Simpson and Helga Druxes, *Digital Media Strategies of the Far Right in Europe and the United States* (Lanham, MD: Lexington Books, 2015), 231, 237.

24 Aaron Gell, "Minor Threat," *GQ,* February 14, 2006, https://www.gq.com/story/prussia-blue-hitler.

25 "Young Sisters Spread Racist Hate," ABC News, November 1, 2005, https://abcnews.go.com/Primetime/story?id=1231684&page=1.

26 "Extremist Files: April Gaede."

27 Mark Potok, "Closed Circuit," *Intelligence Report,* Southern Poverty Law Center, November 20, 2013, https://www.splcenter.org/fighting-hate/intelligence-report/2013/closed-circuit.

28 David Holthouse, "High-Country Extremism: Homeland on the Range,"

Media Matters for America, November 15, 2011, https://www.mediamatters
.org/diversity-discrimination/high-country-extremism-homeland-range.

29   "'Not White Enough': White Nationalist Family Arrives in Kalispell from Ca-
lif.," Associated Press, September 6, 2006, https://helenair.com/news/state
-and-regional/not-white-enough-white-nationalist-family-arrives-in-kalispell
-from/article_05b0d0a4-9500-57fa-9d9b-f30995af5f2b.html.

30   Holthouse, "High-Country Extremism."

31   Michael Jamison, "Protesters Rally as White Separatists Watch Nazi Film in Kalispell Library," *Missoulian* (Missoula, MT), April 30, 2010, https://missoulian
.com/news/local/protesters-rally-as-white-separatists-watch-nazi-film-in-
kalispell/article_1de7f0ac-540a-11df-bc72-001cc4c03286.html.

32   *Nazi Pop Twins* (documentary), channel 4, July 2007, https://www
.dailymotion.com/video/x27dfok.

33   David Holthouse, "Tales from the Creeps: A White Nationalist Horror Story,"
Hatewatch (blog), Southern Poverty Law Center, October 31, 2008,
https://www.splcenter.org/hatewatch/2008/10/31/tales-creeps-white-nationa
list-horror-story.

34   "Oregon Neo-Nazi Leader Hides Identity as Pornographic Model and Actor," Portland Independent Media Center, July 30, 2010, http://portland
.indymedia.org/en/2010/07/401293.shtml.

35   "NSM Member, Bodybuilding Porn Star Turned NS," News & Discussion:
This Just In, Vanguard News Network Forum, August 5, 2010, https://www
.vnnforum.com/showthread.php?t=114631.

4.

1   Harold Covington and Corinna Olsen, "Radio Free Northwest—April 28th
2011," *Homeland Blog,* Northwest Front, April 28, 2011, http://northwest
front.org/2011/04/radio-free-northwest-april-28th-2011/.

2   Richard Lucas, *Axis Sally: The American Voice of Nazi Germany* (Philadelphia:
Casemate Publishers, 2010), 50, 73, 77–78.

3   Susan Heller Anderson, "Mildred Gillars, 87, of Nazi Radio, Axis Sally to Allied
Audience," *New York Times,* July 2, 1988, https://www.nytimes.com/1988/07/
02/obituaries/midred-gillars-87-of-nazi-radio-axis-sally-to-an-allied-audience
.html.

4   Harold Covington, "Radio Free Northwest—May 5th 2011," *Homeland Blog,*
Northwest Front, May 5, 2011, http://northwestfront.org/2011/05/radio-free-
northwest-may-5th-2011/; and Harold Covington, "Radio Free Northwest—
May 26th, 2011," *Homeland Blog,* Northwest Front, May 26, 2011, http://north
westfront.org/2011/05/radio-free-northwest-may-26th-2011/.

5   Harold Covington, "Radio Free Northwest—July 28th 2011," *Homeland Blog,* Northwest Front, July 28, 2011, http://northwestfront.org/2011/07/radio-free-northwest-july-28th-2011/; and "Ga. Police Shut Down Girls' Lemonade Stand," Associated Press, July 15, 2011, https://www.cbsnews.com/news/ga-police-shut-down-girls-lemonade-stand/.

6   See, for instance, Jessica Robinson, "Man Admits He Attempted to Bomb MLK Parade Because of Race," Oregon Public Broadcasting, September 7, 2011, https://www.opb.org/news/article/man_admits_he_attempted_to_bomb_mlk_parade_because_of_race/.

7   "Rightwing Extremism: Current Economic and Political Climate Fueling Resurgence in Radicalization and Recruitment," Office of Intelligence and Analysis Assessment, U.S. Department of Homeland Security, April 7, 2009, https://fas.org/irp/eprint/rightwing.pdf.

8   Keegan Hankes and Sam Zhang, "Waning Storm: Small Population of Active Users Post Count High as Registrations Decline," *Hatewatch* (blog), Southern Poverty Law Center, March 8, 2017, https://www.splcenter.org/hatewatch/2017/03/08/waning-storm-small-population-active-users-post-count-high-registrations-decline.

9   Spencer Ackerman, "DHS Crushed This Analyst for Warning About Far-Right Terror," *Wired,* August 7, 2012, https://www.wired.com/2012/08/dhs/; and Janet Reitman, "U.S. Law Enforcement Failed to See the Threat of White Nationalism. Now They Don't Know How to Stop It," *New York Times Magazine,* November 3, 2018, https://www.nytimes.com/2018/11/03/magazine/FBI-charlottesville-white-nationalism-far-right.html.

10   Brian Montopoli, "Peter King: I Won't 'Surrender to Political Correctness,'" CBS News, March 10, 2011, https://www.cbsnews.com/news/peter-king-i-wont-surrender-to-political-correctness/.

11   Eric Lach, "Did MLK Day Bomb Suspect Leave Online Trail of Hate?" Talking Points Memo, March 10, 2011, https://talkingpointsmemo.com/muckraker/did-mlk-day-bomb-suspect-leave-online-trail-of-hate.

12   Hadding Scott, "April Gaede on Covington and His Followers," *Setting the Record Straight* (blog), http://noncounterproductive.blogspot.com/p/april-gaede-on-covington-and-his.html.

13   Harold Covington, "Radio Free Northwest—November 11th 2010," *Homeland Blog,* Northwest Front, November 11, 2010, http://northwestfront.org/2010/11/radio-free-northwest-november-11th-2010/.

14   Corinna Olsen, *Axis Sally Raw* (blog), http://axissallyraw.com; the blog has been taken down, but pieces of it have been posted on the Web forum white nationalist.org.

15   Pete Simi, Kathleen Blee, Matthew DeMichele, and Steven Windisch, "Ad-

dicted to Hate: Identity Residual Among Former White Supremacists," *American Sociological Review* 82, no. 6 (August 29, 2017): 1167–187.

16   Noelle Crombie and Shane Dixon Kanavaugh, "Emboldened White Nationalists? Look No Further Than This Liberal Oregon College Town," *Oregonian* (Portland, OR), December 29, 2017, https://www.oregonlive.com/pacific -northwest-news/2017/12/post_292.html.

17   Hunter Wallace, "Harold's Bad Karma," Occidental Dissent, June 18, 2013, http://www.occidentaldissent.com/2013/06/18/the-northwest-front-and- the-bowel-movement/.

5.

1   Mark Potok and Laurie Wood, "Leaving White Nationalism," *Intelligence Report,* Southern Poverty Law Center, August 21, 2013, https://www.splcenter.org/ fighting-hate/intelligence-report/2013/leaving-white-nationalism.

2   Corinna Olsen, "The Worst Thing I Have Ever Seen," *The Last Person You Want to Meet* (blog), January 18, 2015, https://iamcori.com/the-worst-thing -i-have-ever-seen/.

3   Corinna Olsen, "You're Normal," *The Last Person You Want to Meet* (blog), March 3, 2015, https://iamcori.com/youre-normal/.

4   Corinna Olsen, "You'll Find Something Else," *The Last Person You Want to Meet* (blog), October 20, 2018, https://iamcori.com/youll-find-something -else/.

5   Corinna's social media quotes are from her Twitter account (@6PointMePlease) and her Facebook account (Corinna Luray Olsen, https://www.facebook.com /eatliftgrow).

AYLA

1.

1   Beyoncé (@beyonce), "Sir Carter and Rumi 1 month today," Instagram photo, July 13, 2017, https://www.instagram.com/p/BWg8ZWyghFy/?utm_source =ig_embed.

2   Kate Storey, "The Secret Meaning Behind Beyoncé's Pregnancy Photo Shoot," *Harper's Bazaar,* February 2, 2017, https://www.harpersbazaar.com/ culture/news/a20368/beyonce-pregnancy-photo-symbolism-decoded/.

3   This section draws extensively from a Skype interview and correspondence between Ayla and the author that took place between 2017 and 2020. It also

includes references to posts made by Ayla on YouTube (https://www.youtube.com/user/adorableayla), Twitter (@apurposefulwife; defunct), Instagram (@wifewithapurpose), and Gab (@wifewithapurpose), and on the blogs *Mother, Lover, Goddess* (defunct), *A Wise and Glorious Purpose* (defunct), and *Wife with a Purpose* (wifewithapurpose.com).

4   Spell Buckaroo (@JuhLeeSeeUh), Twitter, July 14, 2017, https://twitter.com/JuhLeeSeeUh/status/886004244909879297.

5   "Saltine Fury: Mediocre Mayo Packets Are Big Mad at Queen Bey's Glorious Twin Reveal," Bossip, July 14, 2017, https://bossip.com/1571868/saltine-fury-mediocre-mayo-packets-are-big-mad-at-queen-beys-glorious-twin-reveal/.

6   "Charlottesville 2.0," Discord Leaks, Unicorn Riot, https://discordleaks.unicornriot.ninja/discord/server/4.

7   Kevin Roose, "This Was the Alt-Right's Favorite Chat App. Then Came Charlottesville," *New York Times,* August 15, 2017, https://www.nytimes.com/2017/08/15/technology/discord-chat-app-alt-right.html.

8   "Charlottesville 2.0," Discord Leaks.

9   Adam Serwer, "What Americans Do Now Will Define Us Forever," *The Atlantic,* July 18, 2019, https://www.theatlantic.com/ideas/archive/2019/07/send-her-back-battle-will-define-us-forever/594307/.

10 This video, originally accessed on Ayla's blog *Wife with a Purpose,* is no longer available (https://wifewithapurpose.com/2017/06/26/new-video-why-leftists-are-losers-who-dont-try/).

11 Elizabeth Gillespie McRae, *Mothers of Massive Resistance: White Women and the Politics of White Supremacy* (Oxford: Oxford University Press, 2018), 14.

2.

1   Lee Benson, "About Utah: Beaver's Water Is Worth a Stop," *Deseret News* (Salt Lake City, UT), November 18, 2009, https://www.deseretnews.com/article/705345308/Beavers-water-is-worth-a-stop.html.

2   Childhood friend of Ayla's (anonymous source), email message to author, June 26, 2019.

3   Ibid.

4   Professor of Ayla's (anonymous source), interview with author, March 7, 2018.

5   Daniel W. Drezner and Henry Farrell, "Introduction: Blogs, Politics and Power: A Special Issue of Public Choice," *Public Choice* 134, no. 1/2 (February 2008): 2.

6   Katy Vine, "The Raid on YFZ Ranch, Ten Years Later," *Texas Monthly,* April 6, 2018, https://www.texasmonthly.com/the-culture/raid-yfz-ranch-ten-years-later/.

7 "California and Same Sex Marriage," Church of Jesus Christ of Latter-Day Saints, June 30, 2008, https://www.mormonnewsroom.org/article/california-and-same-sex-marriage.

3.

1 Toni Bentley, "'Vindication': Mary Wollstonecraft's Sense and Sensibility," *New York Times,* May 29, 2005, https://www.nytimes.com/2005/05/29/books/review/vindication-mary-wollstonecrafts-sense-and-sensibility.html.

2 "A Word for Men's Rights," *Putnam's Monthly Magazine* 7, no. 38 (February 1856): 208–13.

3 "Low Cut Gowns and High Morals; Suffrage and Sex," *Courier* (Harrisburg, PA), May 11, 1913, https://www.newspapers.com/clip/4445584/josephine_jewell_dodge_on_immorality/.

4 See, for instance, Janet Saltzman Chafetz and Anthony Gary Dworkin, "In the Face of Threat: Organized Antifeminism in Comparative Perspective," *Gender and Society* 1, no. 1 (March 1987): 33–60.

5 Andrea Dworkin, *Right-Wing Women* (New York: Perigree Books, 1983), 34–35, 203–09, 236.

6 Adrienne Rich, *Of Woman Born: Motherhood as Experience and Institution* (New York, Bantam, 1977), 290.

7 Louise Michelle Newman, *White Women's Rights: The Racial Origins of Feminism in the United States* (Oxford: Oxford University Press, 1999), 65.

8 Linton Weeks, "American Women Who Were Anti-Suffragettes," NPR, October 22, 2015, https://www.npr.org/sections/npr-history-dept/2015/10/22/450221328/american-women-who-were-anti-suffragettes; and Chafetz and Dworkin, "In the Face of Threat," 54–55.

9 Kathleen Blee, *Women of the Klan: Racism and Gender in the 1920s* (Berkeley: University of California Press, 1991), 52.

10 Robbie Gill Comer, *The Equality of Woman* (Little Rock, AR: Women of the Ku Klux Klan, Inc., Imperial Headquarters, 1923/24), http://images.library.wisc.edu/WI/EFacs/WiscKKK/RiverFalls/KlanEphem/reference/wi.klanephem.i0009.pdf.

11 Blee, *Women of the Klan,* 145–46.

12 Rachel Gillett, "A Hidden Chapter: Women of the Klan," *History Today* 69, no. 7 (July 2019), https://www.historytoday.com/archive/feature/hidden-chapter-women-klan.

13 See, for instance, David W. Southern, *The Progressive Era and Race: Reaction and Reform, 1900–1917* (Hoboken, NJ: Wiley-Blackwell, 2005).

14 Linda Gordon, *The Second Coming of the KKK: The Ku Klux Klan of the 1920s*

and the American Political Tradition (New York: Liveright Publishing Corporation, 2017), 6; and Thomas R. Pegram, *One Hundred Percent American: The
Rebirth and Decline of the Ku Klux Klan in the 1920s* (Chicago: Ivan R. Dee,
2011), 10–11.

15 Sharon Otterman, "A Booming Church and Its Complicated, Ugly Past,"
New York Times, September 15, 2017, https://www.nytimes.com/2017/09/
15/nyregion/zarephath-christian-church-new-jersey-pillar-of-fire.html.

16 Kristin E. Kandt, "In the Name of God; An American Story of Feminism, Racism, and Religious Intolerance: The Story of Alma Bridwell White," *American
University Journal of Gender, Social Policy & the Law* 8, no. 3 (2000): 753–94.

17 Jerome L. Himmelstein, "The Social Basis of Antifeminism: Religious Networks and Culture," *Journal for the Scientific Study of Religion* 25, no. 1 (March
1986): 1–15.

18 Marjorie J. Spruill, *Divided We Stand: The Battle Over Women's Rights and
Family Values That Polarized American Politics* (New York: Bloomsbury, 2017),
84–85, 186.

19 Dworkin, *Right-Wing Women,* 216.

20 Jane Junn, "Hiding in Plain Sight: White Women Vote Republican," *Politics
of Color* (blog), *Journal of Race, Ethnicity, and Politics,* November 13, 2016,
http://politicsofcolor.com/white-women-vote-republican/.

21 Victoria M. Massie, "White Women Benefit Most from Affirmative
Action—and Are Among Its Fiercest Opponents," Vox, June 23, 2016,
https://www.vox.com/2016/5/25/11682950/fisher-supreme-court-white
-women-affirmative-action; and Jessie Daniels, "White Women and Affirmative Action: Prime Beneficiaries and Opponents," RacismReview,
March 11, 2014, http://www.racismreview.com/blog/2014/03/11/white
-women-affirmative-action/.

22 Janell Ross, "It's Not Just Men: White Conservative Women Have Played
Key Role in Abortion Policy Changes This Year," NBC News, August 13,
2019, https://www.nbcnews.com/news/nbcblk/it-s-not-just-men-white
-conservative-women-have-played-n1038746.

23 Summer Meza, "Who Voted for Doug Jones? White Women Backed Roy
Moore," *Newsweek,* December 13, 2017, https://www.newsweek.com/
doug-jones-roy-moore-alabama-senate-race-special-election-results-demo
graphics-746366.

24 Alexis Grenell, "White Women, Come Get Your People," *New York Times,*
October 6, 2018, https://www.nytimes.com/2018/10/06/opinion/lisa
-murkowski-susan-collins-kavanaugh.html.

25 Helen Andelin, *Fascinating Womanhood: How the Ideal Woman Awakens a Man's
Deepest Love and Tenderness* (Santa Barbara, CA: Pacific Press, 1963), 7.

26 Jennie Chancey and Stacy McDonald, "Passionate Housewives: Desperate for God," *Passionate Housewives Desperate for God* (blog), 2007, http://passionate housewives.blogspot.com/2007/09/passionate-housewives-desperate-for-god .html.

27 Angie Maxwell and Todd Shields, *The Long Southern Strategy: How Chasing White Voters in the South Changed American Politics* (Oxford: Oxford University Press, 2019), 148.

28 Phyllis Schlafly, "What's Wrong with Equal Rights for Women?" *Phyllis Schlafly Report* 5, no. 7 (February 1972), https://eagleforum.org/wp-content /uploads/2017/03/PSR-Feb1972.pdf/.

29 Janet Saltzman Chafetz and Anthony Gary Dworkin, *Female Revolt: Women's Movements in World and Historical Perspective* (Totowa, NJ: Rowman & Allan-held, 1986), 65.

30 Ann Coulter, *How to Talk to a Liberal (If You Must)* (New York: Crown Forum, 2004), 392.

31 Christina Hoff Sommers, "What's Wrong and What's Right with Contemporary Feminism" (lecture, American Enterprise Institute, November 19, 2008, https://web.archive.org/web/20090117085529/http://aei.org/docLib /20090108_ContemporaryFeminism.pdf).

32 Janet Bloomfield, "Women don't build, invent, or produce anything of real economic, social or political value BUT WE SHOVE HUMANS OUT OUR VAGINAS, and that is the most important contribution of all. So pay me, motherfuckers," *Judgy Bitch* (blog), October 22, 2012, https://web.archive.org/web/ 20170812095655/http://judgybitch.com/2012/10/22/women-dont-build -invent-or-produce-anything-of-real-economic-social-or-political-value-but-we-shove-humans-out-our-vaginas-and-that-is-the-most-important-contribu tion-of-all-so-pay-me-motherfuc/.

33 Jamie Ballard, "American Women Are More Likely to Identify as Feminist Now Than in 2016," YouGov, August 9, 2018, https://today.yougov.com/topics /lifestyle/articles-reports/2018/08/09/feminism-american-women-2018; and Megan Keller, "Poll: Less Than Half of Female Millennials Identify as Feminists," *The Hill,* August 14, 2018, https://thehill.com/business-a-lobbying/ 401804-poll-less-than-half-of-female-millennials-identify-as-feminists.

34 William J. Scarborough, Ray Sin, and Barbara Risman, "Attitudes and the Stalled Gender Revolution: Egalitarianism, Traditionalism, and Ambivalence from 1977 through 2016," *Gender & Society* 33, no. 2 (April 2019): 173–200.

35 Laura McKeon, *The F Bomb: Dispatches from the War on Feminism* (Dallas: BenBella Books, 2018), 36.

36 Linda R. Hirshman, *Get to Work: A Manifesto for Women of the World* (New York: Viking, 2006), 2.

37 Jennet Kirkpatrick, "Solidarity and Choice in the American Feminist Movement," *Perspectives on Politics* 8, no. 1 (March 2010), 242.

38 Harriet Sinclair, "Generation Trump: Meet the Women Who Think Feminism Is Cancer," *International Business Times,* June 6, 2016, https://www.ibtimes.co.uk/generation-trump-meet-women-who-think-feminism-cancer-1562980.

39 Jeff Sharlet, "Are You Man Enough for the Men's Rights Movement?" *GQ,* February 4, 2014, https://www.gq.com/story/mens-rights-activism-the-red -pill.

40 Betsey Stevenson and Justin Wolfers, "The Paradox of Declining Female Happiness" (working paper, National Bureau of Economic Research, May 2009, https://www.nber.org/papers/w14969.pdf).

41 Phyllis Schlafly, "Why Women Are Unhappy," *Human Events,* June 16, 2009, https://humanevents.com/2009/06/16/why-women-are-unhappy/?utm _referrer=https%3A%2F%2Fwww.google.com%2F.

42 See, for instance, Francis Bacon, "Confirmation Bias," *Novum Organum,* 1620.

43 Matt Forney, "The Myth of Female Intelligence," Matt Forney (website), April 7, 2014, https://archive.is/i8Dgm#selection-627.0-627.82.

44 See, for instance, Red Pill Women (r/RedPillWomen), Reddit, https://www.reddit.com/r/RedPillWomen/.

45 Theodore Beale, "Feminism Is a Loser's Game," *Vox Popoli* (blog), October 10, 2015, https://voxday.blogspot.com/2015/10/feminism-is-losers-game.html.

46 Theodore Beale, "Immigration and Feminism," *Vox Popoli* (blog), May 26, 2014, https://voxday.blogspot.com/2014/05/immigration-and-feminism.html.

4.

1 "October Is White History Month," Open Forums: Opposing View Forums, Stormfront, October 22, 2001, https://www.stormfront.org/forum/t1671-3/.

2 This video, originally accessed on Ayla's YouTube channel, is no longer available (https://www.youtube.com/watch?v=vzM3XGc1YH0&t=326s).

3 James Zumwalt, "Sweden Opened Its Doors to Muslim Immigration, Today It's the Rape Capital of the West. Japan Didn't," Daily Caller, October 23, 2015, https://dailycaller.com/2015/10/23/sweden-opened-its-doors-to-muslim -immigration-today-its-the-rape-capital-of-the-west-japan-didnt/; and Ann Coulter, "When the Third World Attacks!" Ann Coulter (website), November 18, 2015, http://www.anncoulter.com/columns/2015-11-18.html.

4 See, for instance, @blueearth, "Muslims Rape 11 Year Old Swedish Girl," News: Newslinks & Articles, Stormfront, November 3, 2012, https://www.stormfront.org/forum/t922781/.

5   "New Crime Study: Rise in Sweden's Rape Stats Can't Be Tied to Refugee Influx," *Local* (Sweden), May 29, 2019, https://www.thelocal.se/2019 0529/increase-in-swedens-rape-statistics-cant-be-tied-to-refugee-influx-study-suggests.

6   @Pinpoint, "Pro-White Woman on YouTube Gives Her Take on Muslim Migrants," News: Newslinks & Articles, Stormfront, September 14, 2015, https://www.stormfront.org/forum/t1120729/.

7   Lana Lokteff, "Trad Women vs. the Feminist Lifestyle," October 21, 2015, in *Radio 3Fourteen*, produced by Red Ice, podcast, https://redice.tv /radio-3fourteen/trad-women-vs-the-feminist-lifestyle.

8   Because the YouTube version of this video is no longer available, the comments once found on the platform are not either.

9   Abby Ferber, ed., *Home-Grown Hate: Gender and Organized Racism* (New York: Routledge, 2004), 98.

10 Kelly J. Baker, "The Gospel According to the Klan: The Ku Klux Klan's Vision of White Protestant America, 1915–1930" (dissertation, Florida State University, 2008): 99, http://diginole.lib.fsu.edu/islandora/object/fsu :183606/datastream/PDF/view.

11 Kathleen Belew, *Bring the War Home: The White Power Movement and Paramilitary America* (Cambridge, MA: Harvard University Press, 2018), 165.

12 Ibid, 167.

13 Ferber, *Home-Grown Hate,* 53.

14 Kathleen Blee, *Inside Organized Racism: Women in the Hate Movement* (New York: New York University Press, 1998), image pages.

15 *Homefront,* no. 1 (2017): 6, http://www.wau14.com/wp-content/uploads/ HomeFrontIssueNumberOne2017.pdf.

16 Victoria Garland, "What Role for Women in the Movement?" American Renaissance (website), October 17, 2017, https://www.amren.com /commentary/2017/10/role-women-movement/.

17 Chris Rossetti, "Lost Daughters," National Vanguard (website), June 16, 2019, https://nationalvanguard.org/2019/06/lost-daughters/.

18 Blee, *Inside Organized Racism,* 132–35, 140.

19 Rachel Pendergraft, *Opinions by Rachel Pendergraft* (blog), last updated in 2012, http://rachelpendergraft.blogspot.com/.

20 Claudia Koonz, *Mothers in the Fatherland: Women, the Family, and Nazi Politics* (New York: St. Martin's Press, 1987), 185–86.

21 Ibid, photo pages.

22 Gertrud Scholtz-Klink, "To Be German Is to Be Strong" (speech, 1936, Calvin University, German Propaganda Archive, https://research.calvin.edu/ german-propaganda-archive/scholtz-klink2.htm).

23 Koonz, *Mothers in the Fatherland,* 5, 17.

24 McRae, 1, 4, 116, 173.

25 Ibid, 189; also "Mothers' League of Central High School Flyer," Encyclopedia of Arkansas, https://encyclopediaofarkansas.net/media/mothers-league-of-central-high-school-flyer-6625/.

26 Elizabeth Gillespie McRae, *Mothers of Massive Resistance: White Women and the Politics of White Supremacy* (Oxford: Oxford University Press, 2018), 225.

27 Ibid, 148.

28 Glen Jeansonne, *Women of the Far Right: The Mothers' Movement and World War II* (Chicago: University of Chicago Press, 1996), 26.

29 Ibid, chap. 4, footnote 45.

30 Ibid, 1, 3.

31 "Racist Skinheads: Understanding the Threat," Southern Poverty Law Center, June 25, 2012, https://www.splcenter.org/20120625/racist-skinheads-understanding-threat.

32 Blee, *Inside Organized Racism,* 133.

5.

1 Philip Bump, "The Paris Attacks Have Only Made Trump Stronger," *Washington Post,* November 22, 2015, https://www.washingtonpost.com/news/the-fix/wp/2015/11/22/the-paris-attacks-appear-to-have-vaulted-donald-trump-higher-in-the-polls/.

2 "Freed from Prison, David Duke Mounts a Comeback," *Intelligence Report,* Southern Poverty Law Center, Summer 2004, https://web.archive.org/web/20070927194814/http://www.splcenter.org/intel/intelreport/article.jsp?aid=477.

3 "Extremist Files: David Duke," Southern Poverty Law Center, https://www.splcenter.org/fighting-hate/extremist-files/individual/david-duke.

4 See, for instance, Sarah Dye (Volkishaucity), "Volkmom Episode 1: Yarrow," YouTube, March 10, 2018, https://www.youtube.com/watch?v=sjWBx4Y7f_o.

5 The Truly Vintage Housewife, "WWI posters such as this stressed the need of less waste in the home and with meals," Facebook, March 7, 2019, https://www.facebook.com/TheTrulyVintageHousewife/photos/a.520622618361630/615538168870074/?type=3&theater.

6 Lacey Lynn (@laceylaurenlynn), Instagram photo, December 17, 2019, https://www.instagram.com/p/B6LqpYkgu8W/.

7 @stepfordintexas, Instagram photo, March 29, 2018, https://www.instagram.com/p/Bg6SqUNji1V/?igshid=nk4gqzdic3i1.

8 Rob Bailey-Millado, "Woman Quits Job to 'Spoil Husband' Like a 1950s Housewife," *New York Post,* September 30, 2019, https://nypost.com/2019/09/30/woman-quits-job-to-spoil-husband-like-a-1950s-housewife/.

9 Annie Kelly, "The Housewives of White Supremacy," *New York Times,* June 1, 2018, https://www.nytimes.com/2018/06/01/opinion/sunday/tradwives-women-alt-right.html.

10 Nikole Hannah-Jones, "Our Democracy's Founding Ideals Were False When They Were Written," The 1619 Project, *New York Times Magazine,* August 14, 2019, https://www.nytimes.com/interactive/2019/08/14/magazine/black-history-american-democracy.html?mtrref=t.co&assetType=REGIWALL.

11 Mary Grey (pseudonym), *Walls and Fences* (CreateSpace Independent Publishing Platform, 2017); and Mary Grey (pseudonym), email messages with author, March 2017.

12 "Extremist Files: Christopher Cantwell," Southern Poverty Law Center, https://www.splcenter.org/fighting-hate/extremist-files/individual/christopher-cantwell.

13 These videos, originally accessed on Ayla's YouTube channel, are no longer available (https://www.youtube.com/watch?v=gF4kJ9fSuM4; https://www.youtube.com/watch?v=YygQCMRMJxg).

14 This video, originally accessed on Ayla's YouTube channel, is no longer available (https://www.youtube.com/watch?v=uDDPfKOXS30).

15 Michael Edison Hayden, "U.S. State Department Official Involved in White Nationalist Movement, Hatewatch Determines," *Hatewatch* (blog), Southern Poverty Law Center, August 7, 2019, https://www.splcenter.org/gebert.

16 Cecilia Davenport and Wolfie James, "Alt Right Advice," *The Right Stuff* (blog), 2016–2017, https://therightstuff.biz/cecilia; the column is no longer available on the blog.

17 Kathryn Joyce, *Quiverfull: Inside the Christian Patriarchy Movement* (Boston: Beacon Press, 2010), 12.

18 Emily Johnson, "How Prominent Women Built and Sustained the Religious Right," *Religion & Politics,* April 16, 2019, https://religionandpolitics.org/2019/04/16/how-prominent-women-built-and-sustained-the-religious-right/.

19 Chris A. Smith, "Coded and Loaded: How Politicians Talk About Race and Gender Without Really Talking About Race and Gender," *California Magazine,* Fall 2016, https://alumni.berkeley.edu/california-magazine/fall-2016-greatest-show-earth/coded-and-loaded-how-politicians-talk-about-race.

20 Ann Burlein, *Lift High the Cross: Where White Supremacy and the Christian Right Converge* (Durham, NC: Duke University Press, 2002), 33–118.

21 "Jury Told of Plan to Kill Radio Host," *New York Times,* November 8, 1987, https://www.nytimes.com/1987/11/08/us/jury-told-of-plan-to-kill-radio

-host.html; and Kevin Flynn and Gary Gerhardt, *The Silent Brotherhood: The Chilling Inside Story of America's Violent Anti-Government Militia Movement* (New York: Signet, 1990), 210–13.

22 Pete Peters, "The Bible: Handbook for Survivalists, Racists, Tax Protesters, Militants, and Right-Wing Extremists," Christian Identity Forum (website), https://web.archive.org/web/20170703125037/http://www.thechristian identityforum.net/downloads/Bible-Extremists.pdf.

23 Leonard Zeskind, *Blood and Politics: The History of the White Nationalist Movement from the Margins to the Mainstream* (New York: Farrar, Straus and Giroux, 2009), 174.

24 Kathleen Blee, *Inside Organized Racism: Women in the Hate Movement* (New York: New York University Press, 1998), 57.

25 Christian Israel Archive, "Woman Take Courage (Cheri Peters)," YouTube, April 15, 2016, https://www.youtube.com/watch?v=Ath-tgzIcoA.

26 Kathleen Belew, *Bring the War Home: The White Power Movement and Paramilitary America* (Cambridge, MA: Harvard University Press, 2018), 183.

27 Christian Israel Archive, "Woman Take Courage."

28 Michael D'Antonio, "The Identity Movement and Its 'Real Jew' Claim," The Alicia Patterson Foundation, 1988, https://aliciapatterson.org/stories/identity-movement-and-its-real-jew-claim.

29 Belew, *Bring the War Home,* 184.

30 Burlein, *Lift High the Cross,* 237.

31 Cheri Peters, "The Spirit of Jezebel," *Scriptures for America Worldwide Ministry* (newsletter) 2 (2012): 17–18, https://docplayer.net/120993792-Scriptures-for-america-worldwide-ministry.html.

6.

1 Ian Shapira, "Inside Jason Kessler's Hate-Fueled Rise," *Washington Post,* August 11, 2018, https://www.washingtonpost.com/local/inside-jason-kesslers-hate-fueled-rise/2018/08/11/335eaf42-999e-11e8-b60b-1c897f17e185_story.html.

2 "#IdentifyEvropa: Meet Erica Joy Alduino, Neo-Nazi Organizer," Asheville Anti Racism, March 8, 2019, https://avlantiracism.blackblogs.org/2019/03/08/identifyevropa-meet-erica-joy-alduino-neo-nazi-organizer/.

3 "Charlottesville 2.0," Discord Leaks, Unicorn Riot, https://discordleaks.unicornriot.ninja/discord/server/4.

4 Ibid.

5 "Vanguard America," Anti-Defamation League, https://www.adl.org/resources/backgrounders/vanguard-america.

6   "Heather Heyer Autopsy Report," *News & Advance* (Lynchburg, VA), December 5, 2018, https://www.newsadvance.com/news/state/heather-heyer-autopsy-report/pdf_66cc07e2-a216-54a0-ae0b-ebe652e25ad2.html.

LANA

1.

1   This section draws extensively on interviews and correspondence between Lana and the author that took place between 2017 and 2020. It also pulls material directly from an article previously published by the author: "The Rise of the Valkyries," *Harper's Magazine,* September 2017, https://harpers.org/archive/2017/09/the-rise-of-the-valkyries/.

2   "People Practicing Open Defecation (% of Population)," World Bank Group, https://data.worldbank.org/indicator/SH.STA.ODFC.ZS?most_recent_value_desc=true.

3   This section references dozens of Red Ice videos. As of this writing, the videos are all available on Red Ice's main website (redice.tv).

4   db, "Full Text of Charleston Suspect Dylann Roof's Apparent Manifesto," Talking Points Memo, June 20, 2015, https://talkingpointsmemo.com/muckraker/dylann-roof-manifesto-full-text.

5   "2014 Crime in the United States: Expanded Homicide Data Table 6," Federal Bureau of Investigation: Uniform Crime Reporting, https://ucr.fbi.gov/crime-in-the-u.s/2015/crime-in-the-u.s.-2015/tables/expanded_homicide_data_table_6_murder_race_and_sex_of_vicitm_by_race_and_sex_of_offender_2015.xls, https://ucr.fbi.gov/crime-in-the-u.s/2014/crime-in-the-u.s.-2014/tables/expanded-homicide-data/expanded_homicide_data_table_6_murder_race_and_sex_of_vicitm_by_race_and_sex_of_offender_2014.xls.

6   "2017 Hate Crime Statistics: Victims," Federal Bureau of Investigation: Uniform Crime Reporting, https://ucr.fbi.gov/hate-crime/2017/topic-pages/victims.

7   Conor Friedersdorf, "The Alt-Right's Tactical Cruelty," *The Atlantic,* July 2, 2019, https://www.theatlantic.com/ideas/archive/2019/07/alt-right-tactics/593035/.

8   Emma Grey Ellis, "The Year the Alt-Right Went Underground," *Wired,* January 2, 2019, https://www.wired.com/story/alt-right-went-underground/.

9   Peter Nicholas, "'It Makes Us Want to Support Him More,'" *The Atlantic,* July 18, 2019, https://www.theatlantic.com/politics/archive/2019/07/send-her-back-trump-supporters-his-nc-rally/594268/.

10   "Is Lana Lokteff /ourgal/?" /pol/, 4chan, May 6, 2017, https://archive.4plebs.org/pol/thread/124330967/.

2.

1   Vera Lokteff (@veralokteff), "Vera Lokteff. About," *Vera Lokteff* (blog), July 3, 2018, https://veralokteff.com/2018/07/03/vera-lokteff-about/; and Vera Lokteff (@veralokteff), "Hope Is a Lifeline," *Vera Lokteff* (blog), July 3, 2018, https://veralokteff.com/2018/07/03/hope-is-a-lifeline/.

2   "The Solar Storm w/ Kyle 7-13-14: Alternative Solutions for European Problems," Renegade Broadcasting, July 13, 2014, http://www.renegade-broadcasting.com/the-solar-storm-w-kyle-7-13-14/.

3   Vera Lokteff (@veralok), "The Next Blood Moon," *In Body Experience* (blog), April 7, 2014, https://web.archive.org/web/20170112185357/http://inbodyexperience.com/blog/.

4   Paul Arras, *The Lonely Nineties: Visions of Community in Contemporary U.S. Television* (New York: Palgrave Macmillan, 2018), 137, 139.

5   "Dr. William Pierce—The Turner Diaries," *Coast to Coast AM with Art Bell*, Spotify, May 23, 1996, https://open.spotify.com/episode/5B6cmSPeIAAV TwejKVDvig.

6   "Lana Lokteff: Bio," Lana Lokteff (website), https://web.archive.org/web/20120605232530/http://www.lanalokteff.com/about.php.

7   Brian McElhiney, "Bend Musicians Ramble On," *Bulletin* (Bend, OR), November 25, 2018, https://www.bendbulletin.com/localstate/bend-musicians-ramble-on/article_6d253fb8-2a83-5337-a41e-3be8d3004beb.html.

8   "Piggyback Records: Bio," Piggyback Records (website), https://web.archive.org/web/20040806010412/http://www.piggybackrecords.com/bio.html.

9   Anonymous source, email message to author, December 2, 2019.

10 Red Ice (archived website), https://web.archive.org/web/20051001054819/http://red-ice.net/.

11 Red Ice TV, "Red Ice TV—Episode 2—Pt 1/4—COP15 (UN Climate Change Conference in Copenhagen 2009)," AltCensored (website), January 5, 2010, https://altcensored.com/watch?v=5AqK2kVS6sI; and "Climatologists Under Pressure," *Nature* 462, no. 545 (December 2, 2009), https://www.nature.com/articles/462545a.

12 henrikHenrik (archived website), https://web.archive.org/web/2007101 4071056/http://henrikHenrik.com/journal.

13 "The Solar Storm w/ Kyle 7-13-14: Alternative Solutions for European Problems."

14 Stephen Sloman and Philip Fernbach, *The Knowledge Illusion: Why We Never Think We're Alone* (New York: Riverhead Books, 2017), 173.

15 Daniel T. Gilber, Romin W. Tafarodi, and Patrick S. Malone, "You Can't

Not Believe Everything You Read," *Journal of Personality and Social Psychology* 65, no. 2 (August 1993): 221–33.

16 Lisa K. Fazio, Nadia M. Brashier, B. Keith Payne, and Elizabeth J. Marsh, "Knowledge Does Not Protect Against Illusory Truth," *Journal of Experimental Psychology* 144, no. 5 (August 2015): 996, https://www.apa.org/pubs/journals/features/xge-0000098.pdf.

17 Alice Fahs and Joan Waugh, eds., *The Memory of the Civil War in American Culture* (Chapel Hill: University of North Carolina Press, 2004), 72.

18 Amy L. Heyse, "Teachers of the Lost Cause: The United Daughters of the Confederacy and the Rhetoric of Their Catechisms" (dissertation, University of Maryland, 2006): 177, https://drum.lib.umd.edu/bitstream/handle/1903/4060/umi-umd-3800.pdf?sequence=1&isAllowed=y.

19 Charles G. Lord, Lee Ross, and Mark R. Lepper, "Biased Assimilation and Attitude Polarization: The Effects of Prior Theories on Subsequently Considered Evidence," *Journal of Personality and Social Psychology* 37, no. 11 (November 1979): 2098–109.

20 David W. Blight, *Race and Reunion: The Civil War in American Memory* (Cambridge, MA: Belknap Press of Harvard University Press, 2001), 255–99.

21 "U.S. Education on American Slavery Sorely Lacking," Southern Poverty Law Center, January 31, 2018, https://www.splcenter.org/news/2018/01/31/splc-report-us-education-american-slavery-sorely-lacking.

22 Brendan Nyhan and Jason Reifler, "When Corrections Fail: The Persistence of Political Misperceptions," *Political Behavior* 32, no. 2 (June 2010), 303–30.

23 John McElroy, *Andersonville: A Story of Rebel Military Prisons, 1879,* The Avalon Project, Yale Law School, https://avalon.law.yale.edu/19th_century/ander.asp.

24 Richard Hofstadter, "The Paranoid Style in American Politics," *Harper's Magazine,* November 1964, https://harpers.org/archive/1964/11/the-paranoid-style-in-american-politics/.

25 Brendan Nyhan, "Political Knowledge Does Not Guard Against Belief in Conspiracy Theories," YouGov, November 5, 2012, https://today.yougov.com/topics/politics/articles-reports/2012/11/05/political-knowledge-does-not-guard-against-belief-.

26 Joseph E. Uscinski and Joseph M. Parent, *American Conspiracy Theories* (Oxford: Oxford University Press, 2014), 1–22.

27 Talia Lavin, "The Boundaries of Whiteness Are Protected with Blood and Bullets," *The Nation,* August 5, 2019, https://www.thenation.com/article/replacement-theory-racism-white-supremacy/.

28 Michael Shermer, "Why Do People Believe in Conspiracy Theories?" *Scientific American,* December 1, 2014, https://www.scientificamerican.com/article/why-do-people-believe-in-conspiracy-theories/.

29 "Anti-Government, Identity Based, and Fringe Political Conspiracy Theories Very Likely Motivate Some Domestic Extremists to Commit Criminal, Sometimes Violent Activity," Federal Bureau of Investigation: Intelligence Bulletin, May 30, 2019, https://www.scribd.com/document/420379775/FBI-Conspiracy-Theory-Redacted#fullscreen&from_embed.

3.

1 Twitter Inc. (@Twitter), "Twitter Turns Six," Twitter, March 21, 2012, https://blog.twitter.com/official/en_us/a/2012/twitter-turns-six.html.

2 Alexei Oreskovic, "Exclusive: YouTube Hits 4 Billion Daily Video Views," Reuters, January 23, 2012, https://www.reuters.com/article/us-google-youtube/exclusive-youtube-hits-4-billion-daily-video-views-idUSTRE80M0TS20120123.

3 Andrew Marantz, *Antisocial: Online Extremists, Techno-Utopians, and the Hijacking of the American Conversation* (New York: Viking, 2019), 3.

4 Jason Colavito, "Red Ice Radio's Summer of Anti-Semitic White Pride," *Jason Colavito* (blog), August 28, 2014, http://www.jasoncolavito.com/blog/red-ice-radios-summer-of-anti-semitic-white-pride.

5 Kathleen Blee, *Women of the Klan: Racism and Gender in the 1920s* (Berkeley: University of California Press, 1991), 20.

6 Ibid, 22.

7 "Says Women Here Flock to Join Klan," *New York Times,* September 13, 1921, https://timesmachine.nytimes.com/timesmachine/1921/09/13/98732028.html?pageNumber=5.

8 "Assails Negress-Whippers," *New York Times,* September 13, 1921, https://timesmachine.nytimes.com/timesmachine/1921/09/13/98732028.html?pageNumber=5.

4.

1 Zeynep Tufekci, "YouTube, the Great Radicalizer," *New York Times,* March 10, 2018, https://www.nytimes.com/2018/03/10/opinion/sunday/youtube-politics-radical.html.

2 Jack Nicas, "How YouTube Drives People to the Internet's Darkest Corners," *Wall Street Journal,* February 7, 2018, https://www.wsj.com/articles/how-youtube-drives-viewers-to-the-internets-darkest-corners-1518020478.

3 Kevin Munger and Joseph Phillips, "A Supply and Demand Framework for YouTube Politics," Penn State Political Science, October 1, 2019, https://osf.io/73jys/.

4   Euan McKirdy, "Whole Foods Anti-Gay Lawsuit Dropped After Apology," CNN, May 17, 2016, https://www.cnn.com/2016/05/17/us/whole-foods-offensive-cake-pastor-apology/index.html.

5   Claudia Koonz, *Mothers in the Fatherland: Women, the Family, and Nazi Politics* (New York: St. Martin's Press, 1987), xxv.

6   All of Nelson's blog quotes are from her Goodreads page: Bre Faucheaux, *Bre Faucheaux* (blog), Goodreads, https://www.goodreads.com/author/show/7258303.Bre_Faucheux/blog.

7   All of Nelson's Twitter quotes are from this account: Brittany Nelson (@Tribal_Faerie), Twitter, https://twitter.com/tribal_faerie.

8   Bre Faucheux, *The Elder Origins (Volume 1)* (CreateSpace Independent Publishing Platform, 2013), https://www.amazon.com/gp/product/1494785749/ref=dbs_a_def_rwt_hsch_vapi_taft_p1_i2.

9   Bre Faucheux, "The Problem with Diversity in Books—Rant," YouTube, September 2, 2016, https://www.youtube.com/watch?v=MNroxGwsiWw; this video is no longer available.

10 All of Hargraves's videos quoted here are from her YouTube channel: Blonde in the Belly of the Beast, YouTube, https://www.youtube.com/channel/UCpbyOgUSjTSPpvVUAT2OyHw.

11 Neil Irwin and Josh Katz, "The Geography of Trumpism," *New York Times,* March 12, 2016, https://www.nytimes.com/2016/03/13/upshot/the-geography-of-trumpism.html#commentsContainer.

12 Philip Bump, "The Most Diverse Counties That Supported Trump in 2016," *Washington Post,* August 7, 2019, https://www.washingtonpost.com/politics/2019/08/07/most-diverse-counties-that-supported-trump/; and Richard Florida, "How America's Metro Areas Voted," CityLab, November 29, 2016, https://www.citylab.com/equity/2016/11/how-americas-metro-areas-voted/508355/.

13 Jared Holt, "White Nationalist Radio Host: Interracial Relationships Are 'More Devious Than Blatant In-Your-Face Mass Murdering,'" Right Wing Watch, June 11, 2018, https://www.rightwingwatch.org/post/white-nationalist-radio-host-interracial-relationships-are-more-devious-than-blatant-in-your-face-mass-murdering/.

14 Elizabeth Gillespie McRae, *Mothers of Massive Resistance: White Women and the Politics of White Supremacy* (Oxford: Oxford University Press, 2018), 31, 33–34, 37.

5.

1   @RichardA, "Saint George and the 'White Whore,'" General: Lounge, Stormfront, November 9, 2014, https://www.stormfront.org/forum/t1073035/.

2   Margaret Atwood, *The Handmaid's Tale* (Toronto: McClelland & Stewart, 1985), 56.

3   See, for instance, Amit Varshizky, "Alfred Rosenberg: The Nazi Weltanschauung as Modern Gnosis," *Politics, Religion, & Ideology* 13, no. 3 (September 2019): 311–31.

4   Mattias Gardell, *Gods of the Blood: The Pagan Revival and White Separatism* (Durham, NC: Duke University Press, 2003), 210.

5   Ibid, 173–75.

6   *The Odinist,* 1, no. 1 (August 1971): 1, https://www.amazon.com/ ODINIST-AUGUST-CHRISTENSEN-ODINISM-ASATRU/dp/B00BB PIH58.

7   James R. Lewis, ed. *Controversial New Religions* (Oxford: Oxford University Press, 2004), 390.

8   Gardell, *Gods of the Blood,* 204–05.

9   Lewis, *Controversial New Religions,* 394.

10 Gardell, *Gods of the Blood,* 1.

11 Emmett Gienapp, "White Supremacists May Be Eyeing Meigs County," *Chattanooga (TN) Times Free Press,* February 11, 2018, https://www.timesfreepress.com/ news/local/story/2018/feb/11/white-surpremacists-next-door-wotans-natiplan /463443/.

12 Jesse Singal, "Undercover with the Alt-Right," *New York Times,* September 19, 2017, https://www.nytimes.com/2017/09/19/opinion/alt-right-white -supremacy-undercover.html?module=inline.

13 Will Rahm, "Inside the White Supremacists' Halloween Bash," Daily Beast, November 2, 2015, https://www.thedailybeast.com/inside-the -white-supremacists-halloween-bash.

14 Ben Child, "White Supremacists Urge Thor Boycott Over Casting of Black Actor as Norse God," *Guardian* (US edition), December 17, 2010, https://www.theguardian.com/film/2010/dec/17/white-supremacists-boycott -thor.

15 @ReportDenial, Twitter, October 21, 2017, https://twitter.com/ ReportDenial/status/921641573900865536;   CarolynEmerick (@CarolynEmerick), Twitter, December 22, 2017, http://archive.is/ CWWba; Völkisch Folklorist (@CarolynEMerick), Gab, this content is no longer available.

16 Red Ice TV, "Lana Lokteff—How the Left Is Betraying Women— Identitarian Ideas IX," Internet Archive, February 27, 2017, https://archive .org/details/youtube-BjnH99slHmE.

17 "When Women Are the Enemy: The Intersection of Misogyny and White Supremacy," Anti-Defamation League, July 2018, https://www.adl

.org/resources/reports/when-women-are-the-enemy-the-intersection-of-misogyny-and-white-supremacy.

18   Lyz Lenz, "You Should Care That Richard Spencer's Wife Says He Abused Her," HuffPost, January 13, 2019, https://www.huffpost.com/entry/richard-spencer-nina-kouprianova-divorce-abuse_n_5c2fc90ee4b0d75a9830ab69.

19   Kathleen Blee, *Women of the Klan: Racism and Gender in the 1920s* (Berkeley: University of California Press, 1991), 22.

20   Geraldine Theresa Horan, *Mothers, Warriors, Guardians of the Soul: The Female Discourse in National Socialism* (Berlin: Walter de Gruyter GmbH & Co. KG, 2003), 135.

21   Jon Krakauer, *Under the Banner of Heaven: A Story of Violent Faith* (New York: Anchor, 2004), xxii.

6.

1   Jared Holt, "Rep. Steve King Quotes a White Supremacist While Comparing 'Leftists' to Nazis," Right Wing Watch, September 12, 2018, https://www.rightwingwatch.org/post/rep-steve-king-quotes-a-white-supremacist-while-chiding-calling-people-nazi/.

2   Abby Ferber, ed., *Home-Grown Hate: Gender and Organized Racism* (New York: Routledge, 2004), 45.

3   Camila Domonoske, "A Message of Tolerance and Welcome, Spreading from Yard to Yard," NPR, December 9, 2016, https://www.npr.org/sections/thetwo-way/2016/12/09/504969049/a-message-of-tolerance-and-welcome-spreading-from-yard-to-yard.

4   Elizabeth T. Harwood, "Terrorism and the Digital Right-Wing," *Contexts* 18, no. 3 (July 29, 2019): 60–62.

CONCLUSION

1   @Morgoth, "Feminist Journalists Are Horrified by Alt-Right Valkyries," *Morgoth's Review* (blog), August 25, 2017, http://nwioqeqkdf.blogspot.com/2017/08/feminist-journalists-are-horrified-by.html.

2   Luke Ford, "Harpers: 'The Rise of the Valkyries: In the Alt-Right, Women Are the Future, and the Problem,'" Luke Ford: Stay in Your Lane, August 11, 2017, https://lukeford.net/blog/?p=116424.

3   "Rise of the Valkyries," /pol/, 4chan, August 30, 2017, https://archive.4plebs.org/pol/thread/139576623/.

4   Peter Vernon, "A Climate of Hate Toward the Press at Trump Rallies," *Co-

lumbia Journalism Review, August 2, 2018, https://www.cjr.org/the_media_to-day/trump-acosta-rally.php.

5   Pete Simi and Robert Futrell, *American Swastika: Inside the White Power Move-ment's Hidden Spaces of Hate* (Lanham, MD: Rowman & Littlefield Publishers, 2010), 9.

INDEX

ABOUT THE AUTHOR

SEYWARD DARBY is the editor in chief of the *Atavist Magazine*. She previously served as the deputy editor of *Foreign Policy* and the online editor and assistant managing editor of the *New Republic*. She has written for *Harper's Magazine,* the *Washington Post, Topic, New York* (*The Cut*), and *Elle,* among other publications. In 2019, she was named one of *Folio's* Top Women in Media. Originally from eastern North Carolina, she now lives in Brooklyn with her husband, who writes fiction, and their two rescue pets. Read more of her work at seywarddarby.com.